RESEARCH IN MARKETING

Supplement 6 • 1994

EXPLORATIONS IN THE HISTORY OF MARKETING

RESEARCH IN MARKETING

EXPLORATIONS IN THE HISTORY OF MARKETING

Series Editor: **JAGDISH N. SHETH**
Emory Business School
Emory University

Editor: **RONALD A. FULLERTON**
Associate Professor of Marketing
University of Hartford

SUPPLEMENT 6 • 1994

 **JAI PRESS INC.**

Greenwich, Connecticut   *London, England*

CONTENTS

LIST OF CONTRIBUTORS   ix

PREFACE   xi

PART I.   MARKETING IN ACIENT, MEDIEVAL, AND EARLY MODERN TIMES

THE ORIGINS OF MARKETING: EVIDENCE FROM
CLASSICAL AND EARLY HELLENISTIC GREECE
(500-300 B.C.)
    Terence R. Nevett and Lisa Nevett   1

A DAY'S SHOPPING IN THIRTEENTH-CENTURY PARIS
    Donald F. Dixon   13

SCHOLASTIC MARKETING THOUGHT IN SPAIN:
THE SCHOOL OF SALAMANCA
    Sigfredo A. Hernandez   25

PART II.   MODERN MARKETING THOUGHT

THE UTILITY OF THE FOUR UTILITIES CONCEPT
    Eric H. Shaw   47

BIOGRAPHY AND THE HISTORY OF MARKETING
THOUGHT: HENRY CHARLES TAYLOR AND
EDWARD DAVID JONES
    D.G. Brian Jones   67

THE ADOPTION OF STATISTICAL METHODS IN
MARKET RESEARCH: THE EARLY TWENTIETH
CENTURY
    Richard Germain   87

THE DEVELOPMENT OF SPATIAL THEORY IN RETAILING
AND ITS CONTRIBUTION TO MARKETING THOUGHT
AND MARKETING SCIENCE
Barry J. Babin, James S. Boles, and Laurie A. Babin   103

REILLY'S LAW OF RETAIL GRAVITATION:
WHAT GOES AROUND, COMES AROUND
Stephen Brown   117

PART III.   MARKETING PRACTICE AND CONSUMER BEHAVIOR

GAMES, CONTESTS, SWEEPSTAKES, AND LOTTERIES:
PRIZE PROMOTION AND PUBLIC POLICY
Steven W. Kopp and Charles R. Taylor   151

DATA SOURCES FOR AMERICAN CONSUMPTION
HISTORY: AN INTRODUCTION, ANALYSIS, AND
APPLICATION
Terrence H. Witkowski   167

JOCKEY INTERNATIONAL: A BRIEF HISTORY OF
MARKETING INNOVATION
Richard H. Keehn   183

PART IV.   HISTORICAL APPROACHES
TO MACROMARKETING ISSUES

TOBACCO ADVERTISING ON TRIAL: AN ASSESSMENT
OF RECENT ATTEMPTS TO RECONSTRUCT THE PAST
AND AN AGENDA TO IMPROVE THE QUALITY OF
EVIDENCE PRESENTED
Timothy P. Meyer   205

THANK THE EDITORS FOR THE BUY-OLOGICAL URGE!
AMERICAN MAGAZINES, ADVERTISING, AND THE
PROMOTION OF THE CONSUMER CULTURE, 1920-1980
Richard W. Pollay   221

MARKETING ACTION AND THE TRANSFORMATION
OF WESTERN CONSCIOUSNESS: THE EXAMPLES OF
PULP LITERATURE AND DEPARTMENT STORES
   Ronald A. Fullerton   237

LIST OF CONTRIBUTORS

Barry J. Babin

Department of Marketing
University of Southern Mississippi

Laurie A. Babin

Department of Marketing
University of Southern Mississippi

James S. Boles

Department of Marketing
College of Business
Georgia State University

Stephen Brown

Department of Banking and
   Commerce
University of Ulster

Donald F. Dixon

Penn State University, Great Valley

Ronald A. Fullerton

Barney School of Business
University of Hartford

Richard Germain

College of Business Administration
Oklahoma State University

Sigfredo A. Hernandez

Department of Marketing
Rider University

D.G. Brian Jones

School of Business Administration
University of Prince Edward Island

Richard H. Keehn

Department of Economics
University of Wisconsin, Parkside

Steven W. Kopp

Department of Marketing and
   Transportation
University of Arkansas

Timothy P. Meyer

Department of Information &
    Computing Sciences
Communication
University of Wisconsin, Green Bay

Lisa Nevett

British Academy Postdoctoral
    Research Fellow
University of Durham

Terrence R. Nevett

Department of Marketing
Central Michigan University

Richard W. Pollay

Faculty of Commerce
University of British Columbia

Eric H. Shaw

Department of Marketing
Florida Atlantic University

Charles R. Taylor

Department of Marketing
College of Commerce and Finance
Villanova University

Terrence H. Witkowski

Department of Marketing
California State University,
    Long Beach

PREFACE

A volume such as this could not have been done fifteen or even ten years ago. For then, only a handful of researchers were exploring marketing's past—scholars such as Donald Dixon, Stanley Hollander, Stanley Shapiro, and Richard Pollay worked almost alone. Now, as marketing thought has matured and broadened, more and more marketing scholars have developed significant interests in marketing's past. Interest in marketing history has been fostered by the biennial Marketing History Conferences held since 1983, by special conferences such as that on Historical Perspectives in Consumer Behavior held in Singapore in 1985, and by the increased receptiveness of journal editors and reviewers to historical topics.

All of the contributors here are social scientists; most teach marketing. They include pioneers like Pollay and Dixon, as well as their former students: Hernandez and Shaw studied under Donald Dixon; Germain, Kopp, and Taylor under Stanley Hollander. Some of the most sophisticated work is provided by scholars whose doctoral training was exclusively in marketing, striking testimony to the ability of marketers to extend their research horizons.

The work of the contributors represents some of the best of the work being done on the history of marketing. It exemplifies the mastery of research techniques necessary for serious historical analysis, for example the discovery and evaluation of archival and other raw historical material (see the essays by Jones, Keehn, and Witkowski); or the rich interpretation of writings that emerged in very different past environments, and which are often written in archaic versions of non-English languages (see the essays by Dixon, Hernandez, and Nevett and Nevett). Several of the authors have been able to trace major currents and techniques in marketing back along the sometimes convoluted paths along which they developed, a task that requires skill and patience (see the essays by Shaw, Germain, and Babin, Boles, and Babin).

Four major topic areas are explored here, reflecting the depth and diversity of current historical research in marketing. The first three essays go far back in time and place. Nevett and Nevett show how ancient Greek producers and traders discovered and catered to buyer needs at home and in export markets. These efforts, they argue, are the earliest historically indisputable evidence of what we recognize as marketing. Dixon provides a charming portrayal of shopping in thirteenth-century Paris. The amazingly extensive body of thought on marketing themes developed at the University of Salamanca in Spain in the early modern period is skillfully explicated by Hernandez.

Modern marketing thought is the theme of our second section. In an impressive piece of scholarship, Show traces the familiar four utilities concept back to the Physiocrat school of eighteenth-century French economists, then shows how the idea has developed. Jones weaves together research findings from major archival collections to reconstruct the careers of two of the earliest U.S. marketing professors. Using an adoption of innovation framework, Germain analyzes the statistical methods covered in U.S. marketing research texts into the mid-1930s. Babin, Boles, and Babin evaluate the work of William Reilly and others who developed spatial theory in retailing. Brown adds to our knowledge of retail evolution.

Consumer behavior and marketing practice at the firm and industry level are the themes of the third section. Keehn's finely crafted firm history relates the marketing practice of the Jockey Company since the nineteenth century. Kopp and Taylor provide a fascinating review of retailers "and manufacturers" use of prize promotions over time. In an essay grounded in work that remains neglected by most historians, Witkowski explains how past consumer's behavior can be better understood by studying the material artifacts, or probate records of these, which are still extant today.

The fourth and final section of this collection deals with macromarketing issues. Meyer offers a searching and helpful discussion of efforts to reconstruct the historical environments in which people began to smoke, an issue of enormous importance in the ongoing legal battles over the liability of tobacco companies. Contributing to the growing literature on the historical development of our consumer culture, Pollay demonstrates how U.S. magazines have aggressively cultivated advertisers throughout the twentieth century, portraying themselves as masters of stimulating "buy-urges" for advertisers' products among their readers. Fullerton argues that the aggressive marketing efforts typical of modern marketing have had enormous, though not always intentional, impacts on the consciousness of Western Europeans and North Americans; pulp literature and department stores are developed as case examples.

Ronald A. Fullerton
Editor

PART I

MARKETING IN ANCIENT, MEDIEVAL, AND EARLY MODERN TIMES

THE ORIGINS OF MARKETING:
EVIDENCE FROM CLASSICAL AND EARLY HELLENISTIC GREECE (500-30 B.C.)

Terence R. Nevett and Lisa Nevett

ABSTRACT

The Classical and Early Hellenistic periods appear to offer the earliest point in history at which it is possible to make a reasonable assessment as to whether marketing was being practiced. Applying Houston's (1986) criterion of "customer focus," the authors believe that there is sufficient evidence available, particularly from archaeology, to indicate that traders were indeed involved in marketing practices. Their offerings were adapted to take into account differences in taste between markets, modified to meet changes in demand over time, and presented in ways that enabled their origin to be identified by the purchaser.

I. INTRODUCTION[1]

Scholars of marketing history no longer see the advent of marketing as the Renaissance that followed the Dark Ages of the supposed production and sales

Research in Marketing, Supplement 6, pages 3-12.
Copyright © 1994 by JAI Press Inc.
All rights of reproduction in any form reserved.
ISBN: 1-55938-187-6

eras, or accept the case argued by Bartels (1988, 1976) that marketing thought can be dated from the early twentieth century. As Houston (1986, p. 86) has pointed out, "The marketing concept has been an expression of the marketer's recognition of the importance of the consumer in the buying process. This understanding did not begin with the introduction of the term *marketing concept;* the customer focus clearly existed when the king ordered boots from the bootmaker."

The question then arises whether it is possible to identify any particular era or point in history as marking the beginning of marketing, as manifested by the emergence of this "customer focus" to which Houston refers. In this paper the authors assume such a focus must have been present if it can be demonstrated that traders were designing and modifying their offerings to take into account variations in consumer demand. We believe this was likely to have been the case even in early forms of exchange, since traders would have wished to obtain the greatest value from a transaction, and in order for this to be possible, "It is necessary to understand exactly what the potential exchange partner needs or wants, and to know exactly what the exchange partner would be willing to offer to consummate that exchange." (Houston 1986, p. 83).

Although there are some tantalizing glimpses from earlier periods, particularly the Minoan (3000-1100 B.C.), early Classical Greece appears to be the first to offer sufficient evidence of trading practices for any realistic conclusion to be drawn regarding the existence of a "customer focus." By this time, that is about 500 B.C., trade was beginning to fall into recognizable patterns, stimulated by the growth in population, the rise of the polis (i.e., city state), the setting up of colonies and the emergence of coinage in the sixth and seventh centuries. For the first time, too, there are sources from which reasonable inferences can be drawn. Finds of amphorae, those two-handled vessels characteristic of ancient Greece, provide ample evidence regarding the trade in food and wine, while written sources provide a more rounded picture of what was happening in the area of commerce generally (Finlay 1982).

II.   THE STRUCTURE OF TRADE

By the fifth century finance was being provided on an organized basis for trading expeditions. Richer Greeks made loans available to merchants (*emporoi*) of more modest means who were generally noncitizens. There is some dispute among scholars as to whether this was done as an investment for profit, or through some altruistic motive such as a sense of loyalty to friends or acquaintances, or as a moral obligation to help those in distress. However, the profit motive would seem to have had some influence, if only indirect, since as the polis was run on a cooperative basis and the citizens had a direct say in government, they could vote to distribute any surplus among themselves (Hasebroek 1965).

Loans were advanced for the purchase of ships and cargoes, which were generally used as security. When the trader returned, the loan was repaid with interest. Cities were coming to rely on traders for revenue, for grain that they could not grow in sufficient quantity, and for those raw materials and metals that they could not produce themselves. In addition to this more formalized type of trading, there is also evidence to suggest casual maritime traffic in the Eastern Mediterranean and Aegean, with traders—particularly Phoenicians—sailing from port to port wherever they could find cargoes. They operated, in fact, in much the same way as have the tramp steamers of more modern times.

The cargoes carried by these ships were often bought from artisans in the home market. Manufacture was originally done with local consumption in view, but as far back as archaeological evidence exists, it appears that excess production was being exported, especially to less civilized areas. Some historians consider this still to have been the case in the Early Classical period, and argue that trade represented little more than a disposal of surpluses that were bought up and carried around until a purchaser was found. According to this view, the trader might well have some idea of what he wanted to bring back, but paid little attention to what was needed to obtain it. The weight of the evidence, however, suggests that decisions were being made with particular foreign markets in mind. As will be seen later, goods were sometimes clearly produced for somewhere other than the home market, for example in more gaudy designs or in lower quality versions aimed at less discriminating consumers. Shipowners would buy loads of textiles, pottery, and so on, for sale in foreign markets, or would carry merchants and their goods in return for some kind of payment, perhaps a share of the profits of the trip. Whatever the arrangement, logic suggests that they must have been influenced by what they believed could be bartered most effectively at the port of destination. It seems most improbable that a trader would undertake the risks of a long and hazardous journey, only to arrive with a cargo in which nobody was interested. This view can claim support from Plato, who argues in the *Republic* that the agent of the ideal state must make desirable goods to obtain what the state needs in return. The demands of foreign markets appear therefore to have been an important factor in determining the shape of home production (Cartledge 1983; Austin and Vidal-Naquet 1977).

When shipments were bartered at the port of destination, the trader would try to obtain a profitable return cargo. This might be raw materials, slaves, or manufactured items from the East. Whatever its form, the trader would inevitably be influenced by his ideas of what could be disposed of most advantageously. In other words, in terms of imports too, market demand was having an influence on what was being made available.

III. WHAT WAS TRADED

A. Wine

Wine was traded throughout the Greek world. Although there is insufficient evidence to support a picture of wine being traded on a continuous basis between particular areas, the amount of inferential evidence, particularly in the form of amphorae, suggests something rather more considerable than the occasional shipment to compensate for a bad grape harvest. We know from written sources that the poet Sappho's brother was a merchant selling wine to Egypt, which again seems to indicate the existence of trade on a regular basis. The most acceptable interpretation is surely that wine was regarded as a luxury product, which we know from Pliny to have been the case in Roman times. It also seems likely that—as in our own day—the imported variety had a certain cachet and was probably regarded as being of better quality than the home product.

Salviat (1986) has attempted to estimate the price levels at which wine from various regions was sold. He believes that Thasian wine commanded a premium price of 20 drachmas for 20 liters, and that Chiot wine sold for about 18 drachmas, compared with an average price for other types around 5 or 6 drachmas. There is some support for the view of Thasian wine selling at a luxury price, not only because of its status as a *grand cru*, but also because of references to it in the works of the dramatist Aristophanes (444-385). The sources from which Salviat draws, however, span several centuries, and it must be open to question whether prices would have remained stable for so long a period.

B. Raw Materials

These were required by the Greeks for various industries, for construction, and for the arts. Most areas of Greece had pot clay and stone, though the Athenians and Siphnians were importing marble before 500 B.C. There were also supplies of iron, silver, and copper, though as these were not evenly distributed they must have been traded and imported. Gold was found only in Siphnos and Thasos.

To supplement these resources the Greeks imported timber from Macedonia to be used in construction, shipbuilding, agricultural implements, and as fuel for cooking. Tin, of which they had none, was shipped in from Britain. Iron was brought in from Eastern Asia Minor and Etruria (Italy), and copper probably from Cyprus (Starr 1977, pp. 66-70).

C. Slaves

Originally slaves constituted a luxury item. The Greeks seem to have had a lucrative market in the Near East for young females and eunuchs, whom they obtained especially from Sicily. By the sixth century slaves appear to have become a "mass consumption" item, widely employed in the workshops in Greek colonial centers. It has been suggested recently that the Trojan Wars were fought not over a princess called Helen of Troy but over female slaves, since the seizure of slaves could deprive a region's industry of its means of production (Wood 1985).

It is likely that slaves were an important factor in the growth of the wine trade. Extensive viticulture would have been impossible without a large labor force, and such a force, given the values and conditions of the time, must have required the use of a considerable number of slaves. In the case of Chios, the growth of the wine industry seems to correspond with the importation of slaves on a large scale.

D. Pottery

Many of the finds of Greek pottery from this period are of a casual nature, so that it is impossible to determine their significance. While they suggest trade between Greece and various centers of the ancient world, there is no way of knowing whether this was on a regular basis, whether they represent single consignments carried by itinerant traders, or whether individual items may simply have been picked up by travelers as curios, souvenirs, or presents.

There are sufficient finds, however, to suggest a steady trade between the home market and the Greek colonies, where there may not have been kilns, or where consumers were not satisfied with the local standard of workmanship. A good deal of more functional pottery also certainly made its way to foreign markets as containers for oil, wine, and other products; there can be no other explanation for the widespread discovery of plain, stout vases. With more highly decorated objets d'art such as small perfume flasks, it is impossible to explain their wide distribution, though we can conjecture that articles from the Greek mainland, which was the leading fashion center of the day, must have been in high demand, and were therefore imported by astute traders knowing that they would find a ready market (Boardman 1983, pp. 16-18).

IV. EVIDENCE FOR THE
EXERCISE OF CONSUMER TASTE

A. Colonial Art

The early Greek settlements in the West had to be self-sufficient, so their potters tended to make vases in styles they knew, and art and architecture copied forms they remembered or which artists had brought with them. Their taste tended to be uncompromising in the sense that Greek form was not adapted to native usage except in terms of available materials. Over time these colonies gradually developed their own styles and tastes, though emigrating artists and imports kept them in touch with mainland Greece and its fashions. Since there was usually no native art of a standard to invite imitation, the cultural reference point remained the mainland Greek tradition (Boardman 1983, pp. 192-193).

From the marketing historian's perspective, the significance of the colonies is that the emigrating Greeks did not buy what was available locally. The local native production was of no interest or relevance to them. Their needs and desires were totally different, and could only be supplied by production in a different cultural idiom, either local or imported from the mainland. The production era, in other words, was a myth even in antiquity.

B.   Amphorae

These vessels were used for the storage and transport of a wide range of comestibles including olive oil, grain, dried fish, olives, and also wine. Consumer identification was clearly extremely important, from which it may be assumed that this was a key factor in consumer choice. There were two ways in which amphorae from different places could be identified. First, they were made in different shapes, which would have been particularly important in view of the high proportion of purchasers who were illiterate, particularly slaves making the purchases for a household. Second, many—though not all—amphorae were stamped with an impression while the clay was still wet, often on one or both handles. For example, in the case of Thasian amphorae one side would be stamped with the name of the maker, together with a symbol such as a tortoise, a dolphin, or Hermes, while the name of the local magistrate would appear on the other. There is too much disagreement between scholars as to the significance of these stamps to enable them to be linked beyond doubt with some kind of marketing practice. The magistrate's mark, for instance, could have been used to signify that the capacity of the amphora met certain requirements. (There are what appears to be liquid measures in the museum at Thasos.) It might also be a date mark, since the magistrates changed every year. It has been pointed out, too, that the marks are not always positioned conspicuously, not always being on the handle, and are sometimes almost obliterated by the glaze. There is, however, a school of thought that believes the stamps, like the shapes, were indications of origin for the consumer though it must be said that this position appears to have been reached after rejecting the stamp as an indication of capacity and failing to find anything else to which it can be attributed (Garlan 1982, 1983).

In the wine trade in particular, an indication of origin on the amphorae was apparently of considerable significance. One of the most famous wines was that of Chios, a major exporting area. Chios used an unusually shaped amphora with a swelling in the neck, a feature considered so important that it was depicted on the coinage. In the third quarter of the fifth century the feature was dropped but the new amphorae carried a coin stamp with a sphinx and an amphora in the old shape, apparently as an aid to recognition. Thasos was also noted for its fine wine. The wine was shipped in amphorae made of distinctive reddish clay and stamped with the word *Thasion*, either in full or abbreviated. The amphorae of Lesbos were a distinctive dark grey as the result of a special firing, and carried a unique "earmark," a small tail of clay below the handle. The wine produced in Kos was of lower quality. Its amphorae stamps usually included the letters "KO" together with Koan names and coin symbols, and the amphorae themselves had a distinctive handle shape. The importance of this "branding" was to be reemphasized several centuries later when the Italians began producing imitation Koan wine (a recipe for which appears in Cato's *De Agricultura*] and selling it in imitation Koan amphorae, examples of which have been found at Pompeii (Grace 1961).

The wine trade also provides clear evidence of consumer taste changing over time. During the second half of the fifth century, Thasian wine is mentioned by contemporary writers as a *grand cru*. By the fourth century its preeminent position appears to have been shared by the wines of Chios, as the number of wine producing areas increased. There is little documentary evidence for the third century, though enough to show the Thasian wine was holding its market position. The second century, however, sees a marked drop in the number of references to Thasian wine, and the amphorae stamps disappear. After that, although the wines of Chios and Lesbos are still mentioned, consumer taste had shifted toward salted wines, and those of Southern Italy.

There is also evidence to suggest an export trade in amphorae themselves. Among the discoveries on Thasos has been a Lesbian amphora-type that had buckled in firing and been discarded, presumably at the point of manufacture. Since Thasos as the preeminent vintage would scarcely have needed to present its wine as being from Lesbos, it must be assumed that the island was exporting amphorae for use by vintners and traders on Lesbos (Clinkenbeard 1986).

C. Fineware

This area provides some unmistakable instances of products being modified or altered to take into account differences in taste or demand. Originally it was the Corinthians who were successful in selling vases to the Etruscan market. By the middle of the sixth century however, they seem to have been pushed out by the Athenians, who were producing a style known as Tyrrhenian. This was cheap and gaudy, quite unlike what was being produced for the home market, and often carried mock inscriptions, presumably to impress the Etruscans who would not have been able to read Greek. Later the Athenians had to face local competition in Italy, it is thought from refugee or emigrant potters. Subsequently, they managed to retain a share of the Etruscan market by copying Etruscan vase shapes and decorating them in Athenian style, as was done by Nikosthenes who was operating between 535 and 485. As Starr (1977) points out, this cannot have come about through chance or random occurrence, but must have been the result of a commission by a shipper familiar with the Etruscan market.

The Scythians, a people of central Asian origin who had settled around the southeastern part of the Black Sea, were not impressed by Greek vases until the fifth and more especially the fourth centuries, when Athenian potters began producing lines especially for the Black Sea market. In fact, the Athenians developed a unique Graeco-Scythian style, which is to be found not only in pottery but also in relief goldwork (Amiet 1981, p. 443). The Kelermes tomb finds, for example, include a gilt mirror, the back decorated with animals in the Greek manner, but including a Scythian stylized bear, and two hairy men, thought to be Arimasps whom the Greeks believed inhabited the frozen north, and who would therefore have been a quite suitable decoration—in Greek eyes—for an article destined for the Scythian market. Comparable finds have been made at other Scythian burial sites of a similar period (Boardman 1983, pp. 259-262).

The Scythian market seems to have been opened up originally by the Ionians. This must have represented a considerable achievement because it was a market accustomed to high quality works of decorative art from the Near East. In order to enter the market, the Greeks used objects and styles designed specially to appeal to Scythian tastes, rather than attempting to sell their surplus home market production. While the products may have been basically Ionian, such as bronze mirrors with volute handles, and decorative bronze vases, they were produced in a style that clearly had the Scythian market very much in mind. Starr, in fact, believes that this principle may have been quite widely applied, using for example particular mythical scenes to appeal to particular markets.

As with the developed world today, the Greeks appear to have faced problems from cheaper foreign competition. At the end of the seventh century Naucratis (Egypt) had mass production pottery factories that were apparently selling to Greek traders. They were manufacturing seals with scarab, human, or ram's head backs, seemingly for use as some kind of good luck charm, together with cheap statuettes and little hedgehog vases. Though poorly executed, these articles were obviously widely distributed, judging by where they have been discovered. Since they were so obviously lacking in quality, it is assumed that they must have succeeded by some other form of marketing effort. It may well be that their producers could undercut their Greek competitors by a significant amount, selling perhaps to a new segment in various foreign markets that could not afford the more expensive Greek imports, or that perhaps was so unused to dealing with such articles that its members were unable to distinguish between the different levels of quality. It should be remembered, too, that Naucratis was an important entrepot port, so that its traders may well have had a distributive edge over the Greeks in the Southern Mediterranean.

V. THE MISSING EVIDENCE

Most of what we know about patterns of trade in this period comes from the discoveries of archaeologists, and these inevitably are limited to objects that have been able to withstand the ravages of two and a half millennia—pots, ornaments, and the like. Yet as Starr (1977) points out, this gives us a very incomplete picture of what was actually happening. Taking the analogy of Europe in the Middle Ages, the main item of trade then was textiles. Although few traces of the cloth itself remain, there is ample evidence of its importance in customs records, state documents, literary references, and so on. In the case of the ancient world we have only the occasional glimpse, but it is sufficient to suggest that textiles must have formed an important part of trade at that time also. Sappho and other writers, for example, mention ornate attire dyed in purple, and we know from statues and vase paintings that aristocratic ladies wore elaborate robes. This would suggest the existence of a sense of taste and style in dress, at least among the aristocracy, and since through history the upper classes have generally tended to like imports that often provided the key to fashion leadership and exclusivity, it seems reasonable to assume that the Greeks were no exception.

Specialized textile centers certainly existed, such as Miletus for woolens, and Amorgus for garments made from Egyptian linen. The existence of a major textile export trade could also explain how Greek states trading with the Near East were able to obtain silver from Thrace and Macedonia to cover part of the cost of their Levantine purchases, though equally this could be some other form of trade of which no trace now remains, such as foodstuffs or slaves.

VI. CONCLUSION

We believe that the evidence presented in this paper, while in part inferential, indicates that during the period under consideration, there were variations in demand between regional markets and also over time, and that traders responded to them. Products were designed to cater to local tastes, they were modified as those tastes changed, and they were presented in a way that made them easily identifiable. This is surely sufficient to demonstrate the existence of a rudimentary marketing orientation among traders of the time, and to show that the practice of marketing had begun the long process of evolution.

NOTE

1. Dates other than references are B.C. unless otherwise designated.

REFERENCES

Amiet, Pierre, et al. (1981). *Art in the Ancient World*. London: Faber and Faber.
Austin, M.M. and P. Vidal-Naquet. (1977). *Economic and Social History of Ancient Greece*. London: B.T. Batsford.
Bartels, R. (1976). *The History of Marketing Thought*. Columbus, OH: Grid Inc.
Bartels, R. (1988). *The History of Marketing Thought*. Columbus, OH: Publishing Horizons Inc.
Boardman, J. (1983). *The Greeks Overseas*. London: Thames and Hudson.
Cartledge, P. (1983). "Trade and Politics Revisited. Archaic Greece." In *Trade in the Ancient Economy,* edited by Peter Garnsey, Keith Hopkins and C.R. Whittaker. London: Chatto and Windus/Hogarth Press.
Clinkenbeard, B. (1986). "Lesbian and Thasian Wine Amphoras." *Bulletin de Correspondance Hellenique,* Supp. XIII; pp. 353-362.
Finley, M.I. (1982). *Ancient History. Evidence and Models.* London: Chatto and Windus.
Garlan, Y. (1982). "Les Timbres Amphoriques Thasiens." *Annales*; pp. 837-845.
Garlan, Y. (1983). "Greek Amphorae and Trade." In *Trade in the Ancient Economy,* edited by Peter Garnsey, Keith Hopkins, and C.R. Whittaker. London: Chatto and Windus/Hogarth Press.
Grace, V. R. (1961). *Amphoras and the Ancient Wine Trade*. Princeton N.J.: American School of Classical Studies at Athens.
Hasebroek, J. (1965). *Trade and Politics in Ancient Greece*. New York: Biblo and Tanner.
Houston, F. S. (1986). "The Marketing Concept: What it is and What it is Not." *Journal of Marketing,* 50 (April); pp. 81-87.
Plato. (1956 [ca. 400 B.C.]). *The Republic.* Translated by H.D.P. Lee. Isleworth: Penguin.
Salviat, F. (1986). " Le Vin de Thasos: Amphores, Vin et Sources Ecrites." *Bulletin de Correspondance Hellenique,* Supp. XIII; pp. 145-195.
Starr, C. G. (1977). *The Economic and Social Growth of Early Greece*. New York: Oxford University Press.
Wood, M. (1985). *In Search of the Trojan Wars*. London: BBC.

A DAY'S SHOPPING IN THIRTEENTH-CENTURY PARIS

Donald F. Dixon

ABSTRACT

A description of the activities of the street vendors of thirteenth-century Paris is taken from contemporary documents, including a poem about a consumer-buyer and one about a retailer. The cries of the vendors describe the goods offered, extol their virtues, and announce the terms of sale. Both new and used goods are sold, and various repair services are offered. Neither buyer nor seller is satisfied with his fate.

Paris became an important commercial, administrative, and educational center in the thirteenth century. With a population of roughly 60,000, Paris was one of the largest cities in the Christian world, rivaling the Northern Italian cities of Florence, Genoa, and Venice, and the Flemish cities of Bruges and Ghent. The city had been founded by the Romans at a point in the Seine where the river divides to form an island. This island became the "Ile de la Cité," that remained the core of the growing urban area. It was here that the royal palace and court of the Capetian kings, and the great Notre Dame cathedral were built.

Research in Marketing, Supplement 6, pages 13-23.
Copyright © 1994 by JAI Press Inc.
All rights of reproduction in any form reserved.
ISBN: 1-55938-187-6

The expansion of trade in the twelfth century stimulated the growth of Paris because northern France was the crossroads of a communications network connecting Flanders, the greatest industrial area in northern Europe, with northern Italy, the Mediterranean's commercial center. The city's location on the Seine became especially important with the establishment of the Champaign fairs. In the thirteenth century the annual fairs at Troyes, Lagny, Provins, Brie, and Bar-sur-Aube were Europe's largest. Paris also was located on the land route, linking Flanders with the Rhone and Loire valleys, that provided a means of reaching the Mediterranean. The city's academic prominence arose from the ecclesiastical education centers founded to provide the jurists, notaries, and scribes needed for the administration of public and private business.

Thirteenth-century Paris was a walled city, forming a circle encompassing both banks of the Seine, with the Cité at its center. The major streets branched out from the Cité toward the city gates like spokes of a wheel. The wall was constructed as a means of defense against the English, but it also performed the everyday function of controlling access to the city. The gates were guarded during the day, and closed at night. Travelers were intercepted at the gates so that the taxes that provided a significant part of the city's income could be levied on goods carried by merchants. Markets arose immediately inside the gates where sellers arriving from outside the city could bring their goods most conveniently.

Paris was divided into three areas, the town, the Cité, and the university, each specializing in one of the city's functions. The university section was located on the left bank; The University of Paris and the Sorbonne were both founded in the thirteenth century. The left bank was connected to the Cité by the Petit Pont. The town was the commercial center, on the right bank, connected to the Cité by the Grand Pont, that led to the Rue Saint Denis, the main north-south artery.

One hundred and one trade guilds were registered in Paris. In mid century Etienne Boileau, the "provost of merchants" under Louis IX, compiled an official *Book of Trades*, recording the customs and regulations of the city's trade guilds (Boileau 13th c.). (These guilds are listed in the Appendix.) This paper lets us imagine the city as seen by a thirteenth-century shopper. The division of labor is extensive; hat makers, for example, form six different guilds, distinguished by the material used in manufacture. However, the assortments sold by some guilds are very wide. The saddle makers sell plain and decorated saddles, riding clothes, pillows, and currycombs. Buckle makers also sell blinders, bits, reins and bridles for horses.

Goods are sold in shops, by street vendors, and in specialized markets. The meat market is near the Grand Châtelet, the fortified tower guarding the northern approach to the Grand Pont. The bread market is in the Place Maubert, on the left bank. Flowers and eggs are sold near the Petit Pont. The herb market is on the Ile de la Cité. On Saturdays, when most of the shops are closed, goods are sold at the great Halles market on the northern edge of the right bank. In the Halles each trade has its own area, as do merchants from the surrounding provincial towns.

The typical shop, as described by Viollet Le Duc (1867), is a room on the ground floor of the shopkeeper's house. The side of the room facing the street is enclosed by two horizontal shutters, spanning the entire width of the room, and opening outward. The upper shutter, hinged at the top, opens to form an awning. The lower shutter is hinged so that when lowered it forms a shelf for displaying goods. When the shop is open the craftsman works in full view of passers-by. Some guild regulations specify this arrangement as a means of assuring that the craftsmen does honest work.

Customers do not enter the shop, but remain standing in the street, while the shopkeeper remains inside. The streets are narrow, approximately five meters wide near the wall, and three meters wide in the Cité. Since adjacent shops sell similar goods in such a congested space, it is not surprising that guild regulations forbid shopkeepers to attempt to entice customers from other shops. Moreover, the shopkeeper is limited in his use of criers; if he keeps a crier he can have only one; some trades require that the crier be the master himself, or his wife.

Shops selling similar goods are grouped together, in different parts of the city. Booksellers, illuminators, and scribes are located on the left bank in the university area. The apothecaries, who sell confections as well as medicines, are found in the Cité, near the cathedral of Notre Dame. Money changers and goldsmiths are found on the Grand Pont, which is the most secure part of the city because it is protected by the Grand Châtelet. Contemporary illustrations of these, and other shops, are found in the illuminated manuscript of *The Life of St. Denis* (Egbert 1974). The leather sellers also are found on the Grand Pont. Butchers and fish sellers have their shops close to the Seine, on the right bank near the Grand Châtelet. The drapers also are located near the Grand Châtelet on a street parallel to the Seine. Mercers, saddlers, and stirrup makers are near the Rue Saint Denis. Dealers in old clothes and furniture are further from the river, near the Saint Martin gate. The weavers are near the Temple gate. The bow makers, who also sell arrows, spears and slings, are located near the Saint-Dennis gate. Coopers, curriers, and potters are found on streets surrounding the Halles (Halphen 1909).

The streets of thirteenth century Paris are busy and noisy. Shopkeepers cry their wares, not depending on their signs to attract customers. Crying is the only means available for the street vendors to attract customers. A vendor's cry, somewhere between speech and song, typically remains unchanged for many years, and is passed on from one generation to the next. The cry becomes a mark of distinction analogous to a shop's sign. But a cry may contain more information than a sign; it can describe the assortment offered, special characteristics of particular goods or services, and the terms of sale.

This paper focuses on the Parisian street vendors and their cries; illustrations of some of these criers are also found in *The Life of St. Denis* (Egbert 1974). The framework of the paper is suggested by a thirteenth-century poem written "because poverty commands it" (Villeneuve 13th c.). The poet, Guillaume, complains that he is penniless because the criers have enticed him to spend all his money. The poem describes these vendors and their cries:

> For I will tell you in what guise
> And in what fashion go those
> Who have wares to sell,
> And who think of making their profit,
> Who certainly will not cease to cry,
> In the streets until night.

Some additional information is derived from the *Dictionarius* of John de Garlande (13th c.) who taught at the Universities of Paris and Toulouse early in the thirteenth century. This work, designed to help students learn their Latin vocabulary, describes the sights that one sees in the streets of Paris, including the shopkeepers and street vendors crying their wares, and the goods and services offered. A detailed description of the offerings of one type of street vendor, the mercer, or seller of "small wares," is drawn from a poem describing the mercer's stock and cries (Le Mercier 13th c.).

Our guide, Guillaume, begins his poem with the opening of the public baths early in the morning:

> Hear them cry at the break of day,
> Sirs, go then to bathe,
> And stew without delay:
> the baths are warm, its no lie.

Immediately afterward, Guillaume's attention turns to food. The cries resound:

> Of those who sell fresh herring.
> While others cry live eels.
> Herring sour and white, freshly salted,
> Take our herring that we wish to sell.

Sardines, "fish from the ponds of Bondy," and "good whiting, fresh and salted" are also offered.

Pie makers sell meat pies made of pork, chicken, and eels, with pepper added, and tarts stuffed with soft cheese and eggs. Butchers sell ox meat, horse meat, and pork, to the naive provisioners of student lodgings. Apparently student fare is meager. However, the pork butchers are held in high esteem by the students; sausage and tripe are enjoyed by this "robed rabble." Cookshops purchase fresh meat from butchers and sell roast and broiled meats. They also offer geese, doves, and other fowl roasted on hazelwood spits:

> Birds, pigeons and salted meat,
> Fresh meat very well dressed
> And garlic sauce in great quantity.
> Then honey, God give you good health.

On fasting days cookshops offer fish and vegetables. One shop offers vegetable and pea soup; next door, hot beans may be purchased.

Guillaume also finds pastries and hot cakes, as well as:

> Hot pancakes, scalding hot,
> Rissoles—the very foodstuffs to throw dice for.

Sellers of butter, cheese, and milk are found in the Pierre-au-Lait, crying:

> I have good Champagne cheese,
> There is also cheese from Brie,
> Don't forget my fresh butter,
> Or milk, her neighbor.

Grocers sell both hard and soft cheeses, displayed near sulfur burning candles so that they will ripen better. There are many sellers of household provisions:

> I have prime red apples,
> Like rubies as I hear it.
> I have chestnuts from Lombardy,
> Figs from Malta in abundance,
> I have raisins from Damascus, raisins.
> I have leeks, and I have turnips,
> I have peas in the pod, all new.
> Others cry new beans;
> And measure them out in bowls.
> I have ginger, I have garingaut,
> To strengthen and clear the voice.
> Garlic and onions of lasting odor.

And of course, there is wine. A guild of official wine "crieurs" is employed by the royal provost to verify the opening of kegs and the payment of taxes. Some of the guild regulations are unique. A crier may choose to cry for any tavern that does not already employ a crier, whether or not the tavern owner wishes. Criers visit the taverns each morning to learn what wine is available, and walk through the streets carrying a wooden pot of wine for tasting. This procedure is repeated a second time each day, except on Fridays, Sundays, during lent, and the eight days of Christmas. On these days wine is cried only once.

The wine criers attract attention both by crying and by beating on their pots with sticks. The prices of various measures in which wine is sold also are announced:

Shall we cry the wine of King Louis?
Let us cry it in several places.
Good strong wine at thirty-two
And at sixteen, at twelve, at eight.

Terms of sale are sometimes included as part of the street vendor's cry. Coal, for example, is one sou per sack, and tanning bark is two oboles per bundle. Sometimes vendors consider their wares to be expensive:

Now here are more expensive goods.
Hymn books, with many great songs.
I have whole pomegranates,
But they seem to me very dear,
Nevertheless I can easily sell them,
Receiving either money or its worth.

Payment is not always in money. The mercer sells belts, for which he asks three sous or an egg. Other cries suggest additional means of payment:

Come forth, dame, come,
Come forth, pay
With egg, or with iron, or with money
I will exchange needles for old iron,
For I will sell that very cheap.

There is a ready market among the vendors for used items taken in exchange for their goods. For example, worn or damaged items made of metal, such as kitchen pots and pans, can be melted down and reused:

Who has old iron to sell, bring it here,
Others have other news to tell
Who sells old pots and frying pans?

Many other sellers compete for Guillaume's attention. One, carrying a sack on a stick to hold his goods, is wearing tippets attached to his hood, bows and buckles, leggings and knee socks, along with jingling bells.

If one is searching for household items, there are various offerings:

There are mats and little mats
Candle with wick of cotton, candle
Which lights more than any star!
I have needles for sewing;
I have thimbles for seamstresses

Toilet articles also are available: fine soap from Paris, and boxes in which to put it, combs, rose water, and for the women, cotton for putting on rouge, and powder. The many medicinal products include sulfur for restoring hair to bald heads, and ointments to cure the gout.

Household items can be obtained from the mercer, who also offers clothing and jewelry. Certainly he is very anxious to make a sale:

> I am a mercer, and carry mercery,
> Which I would sell willingly,
> For I am in want of money.
> Now, if it please you to listen,
> I can easily describe the mercery that I carry;
> But I find them very heavy.

The mercer's assortment is very broad:

> I have fine gloves for little damsels;
> I have leather purses with buttons,
> I have all sorts of purses,
> Both of silk and leather,
> Which I would very willingly sell;
> And I have some also of linen.
> I have handsome kerchiefs for ladies,
> And fine lace for the hair,
> That I shall sell to the pretty maids
> I have beautiful silver pins,
> As well as brass ones,
> That I sell to the pretty women.
> I have brass clasps and rings,
> And very fine belts and fallois,

Furthermore, if it isn't in stock, you should ask for it:

> I don't know what I should tell you more;
> In the world there is no mercery
> Which men or women can buy,
> That I cannot now find for them.

Some channel conflict seems to exist. There is criticism of men who usurp the sales of items such as napkins, kerchiefs, and shawls, that traditionally were sold by women.

One does not always buy new products; sometimes repairs are required:

> Who has a coat or leather-lined mantel
> Should bring it to me to mend!
> I will mend coats and overcoats
> And I will refasten washtubs;
> I also know how to mend bread boxes and benches
> I do right well what I know how to do.
> I will polish tin pots,
> I will mend your tankards.

Silver wire is used to repair tankards made from maple, and brass wire for those made from inferior wood. Unfortunately, some of those who offer to perform repairs do shoddy work. And there are other questions of business ethics as well. Despite guild regulations, clothiers sometimes sell shoddy garments. Buyers also are cheated when cloth is woven with defective wool and cotton. The eggs in the tarts sold by the pie makers sometimes are spoiled.

University students seem to be special targets of unscrupulous sellers. Grocers sell to students at prices that are higher than they should be. Glovemakers deceive students by selling them gloves made of inferior material. Booksellers also take advantage of students "by buying too cheaply and selling too dearly and thinking up other frauds" that make books too expensive. The Convent of the Friars requires booksellers to swear that "in receiving books to sell, storing, showing, and selling the same in their other functions in connection with the university, they will conduct themselves faithfully and legitimately." Students and teachers are prohibited from dealing with any bookseller who violates university rules (Regulations of Booksellers 1275).

For entertainment, Guillaume can obtain loaded dice:

> I have large and small dice,
> From Paris, Chartres, and Rheims;
> And I have two (I am not joking)
> Which when tossed, fall upon the aces.

There also is a serious side to life. Guillaume often meets beggars asking for alms:

> I tell you, on these streets,
> The throngs of these poor people are great,
> Listen to the crying though these streets:
> Beggars, Ye Gods; Who calls me?
> Come here, empty this bowl.
> These go crying in the morning,
> Bread for the Sachetin Friars, for the Carmelites,
> For the poor prisoners, locked away.

And sometimes there is a funeral:

> When a man or woman is dead,
> You hear cries, pray for his soul,
> By ringing a bell through these streets,
> Then you hear other poor people
> Cry out loud tears of anguish.

At night, after curfew, criers offer pastry cones, wafers, and meat pies for sale from wicker baskets suspended from leather shoulder straps:

In the evening, hear without waiting any longer,
In a loud voice without delay,
Ye Gods, who is calling, the wafer-seller?

It also may be in the evening that sellers and buyers review their daily activities. The mercer is not at all satisfied with his trade:

I never could obtain any property with it,
And never from any thing that I carried
Did I gain enough to eat.
Therefore I will set my pack down,
I will not meddle any more with it.
Thus I return to the bilet, [a game of chance]
Which I know better how to employ.
Pray God that he will give me profit.

And Guillaume is even more unhappy:

Help, God of Majesty!
What a misfortune that I was born.
How I am misdirected!
There are so many goods to buy,
I cannot stop myself from spending.
The little I have, I have spent,
So that poverty has mastered me.
Finally I had to sell my clothes,
Gluttony ruined me:
So that I no longer know what will become of me.

Although the modern marketing structure differs markedly from that of the thirteenth century, it seems that human nature has remained unchanged.

APPENDIX

List of Trade Guilds, Paris, Thirteenth Century

Bakers	Dealers in Fruit and	Locksmiths—brass
Millers	Vegetables	Metal workers
Corn dealers	Workers in precious metals	Bucklemakers—iron
Measurers—corn	Pewterers	Bucklemakers—brass
Criers of wine	Makers of rope	Drawers of wire—iron
Measurers—liquids	Tin workers	Drawers of wire—brass
Tavern keepers (wine	Blacksmiths	Nail makers
sellers)	Makers of knife blades	Chain mail makers
Brewers and sellers of beer	Makers of knife handles	Makers and sellers of bone
Dealers in bread and salt	Locksmiths—iron	rosaries

(continued)

List of Trade Guilds, Paris, Thirteenth Century (Continued)

Makers and sellers of coral rosaries	Weavers—wool	Haberdashers
Makers and sellers of amber rosaries	Oriental tapestry makers	Dealers in old clothes
Crystal and precious stone cutters	Domestic tapestry makers	Purse makers
Beaters of gold and silver filaments	Fullers	Saddle makers
Beaters of gold and silver leaf	Dyers	Carpenters
Beaters of tin	Hosiers	Blazoners
Braid makers	Dress makers	Harness makers
Spinners—large spindles	Linen makers	Makers of nails and small iron objects
Spinners—small spindles	Dealers in hemp and yarn	Leather dressers
Lace makers	Dealers in canvas	Shoemakers
Workers in silk cloth	Pin makers	Shoemakers—sheepskin
Makers of breeches	Statuette and crucifix makers—sculptors	Cobblers
Silk merchants	Statuette and crucifix makers—decorators	Curriers
Metal founders and casters	Dealers in cooking oil	Glove makers
Makers of brass clasps	Dealers in candles	Hay sellers
Makers of buttons and shoe buckles	Makers of jewel cases	Hat makers—flowers
Weavers—silk	Decorators of jewel cases	Hat makers—felt
Lamp makers	Dealers in combs	Hat makers—cotton
Coopers	Dealers in ivory, bone, ebony	Hat makers—peacock feathers
Carpenters	Cooks	Hat makers—fur
Masons	Poultry sellers	Hat makers—embroidery
Makers of wood bowls and plates	Dice makers	Surgeons
	Button makers—brass	Sword furbishers
	Caretaker of public baths	Bow and arrow makers
	Potters	Fishermen
		Sellers of fresh-water fish
		Sellers of salt-water fish

REFERENCES

Boileau, E. (13th c.) "Les Métiers et Corporations de la Ville de Paris" ("The Trades and Corporations of the City of Paris.") *Reglemens sur les arts et Métiers de Paris au XIIIe siècle*. Reprinted in *Collection de documents inédits sur l'historie de France, premier série, histore politique*, 31. Paris: Rene, de Lespinasse et François, 1879.

Egbert, V. (1974). *On the Bridges of Medieval Paris*. Princeton: Princeton University Press.

Garlande, J. de. (13th c.). *"Dictionarius"* ("Dictionary"). In *Volume of Vocabularies*, edited by Thomas Wright. Privately printed, 1882.

Halphen, L. (1909). *Paris sous les Premiers Capétiens [Paris Under the Early Capetians.]* Paris: Ernest Leroux.

Le Mercier (The Mercer). (13th c.). In *Fabilaux inédits tires du Manuscrit de la Bibliotèque du Roy, 1830-1239*, edited by A. C. M. Robert. Paris: Privately printed, 1834.

Regulation of Booksellers. (1275). "Chartularium Universitatis Parisiensis, I, 532-534." In *University Records and Life in the Middle Ages*, edited by Lynn Thorndike. New York: Columbia University Press, 1944.

Villeneuve, G. de la. (13th c.). "Les Cris de Paris (The Cries of Paris). In *Fabliaux et Contes des Poètes François*. Paris: Barbazan, 1808.

Viollet Le Duc, M. (1867). *Dictionnaire raisonné de l'architecture Francais du XIe au XVIe siècle* [*Analytical dictionary of French architecture of the 11th-16th Century*]. Paris: A. Morel.

SCHOLASTIC MARKETING THOUGHT IN SPAIN:

THE SCHOOL OF SALAMANCA

Sigfredo A. Hernandez

ABSTRACT

This paper provides evidence that a high level of marketing thought was achieved in sixteenth-century Spain by the schoolmen of Salamanca. Marketing activities were considered inherently just. The contribution of marketing to social welfare was recognized: First, by acknowledging the role that the history of marketing played in the achievement of society's material goals. Second, by conceptualizing the exchange, physical distribution, and facilitating functions of marketing as transformations of the product, which resulted in time, place, and possession utilities.

I. THE SCHOOL OF SALAMANCA

Scholasticism refers to the set of doctrines and ideas that developed in the medieval universities that began to be organized in twelfth-century Europe.

Research in Marketing, Supplement 6, pages 25-44.
Copyright © 1994 by JAI Press Inc.
All rights of reproduction in any form reserved.
ISBN: 1-55938-187-6

Scholasticism, as opposed to the rest of Europe, did not reach its high point in Spain until the sixteenth-century. This period is known in Europe as second scholasticism or late scholasticism.

The School of Salamanca was queen among Spanish universities during the late scholastic period. The seventy chairs of the university were filled by the best scholars of the age. The members of this group of scholars—the School of Salamanca, as they are generally called, were celebrated mainly for their work in the field of natural law, which they applied, as a secondary but still important matter, to problems of commercial morality.

These late scholastics witnessed a different world than the one experienced by their predecessors in the Middle Ages. They witnessed the increase in commercial activity associated with the discovery of America. The new reality of an increasingly capitalistic world influenced their attitudes toward commercial practices and their own scholastic work that resulted in significant contributions to marketing thought.

Among some of the notable contributions to marketing and economic thought of the Salamanca schoolmen were: (a) the initial outline for a theory of interest; (b) the creation of a theory of value for commodities and money that was a step away from a full fledged theory of supply and demand; (c) the formulation of the quantity theory of money and a theory of foreign exchange based on it; (d) the recognition of the social contribution of marketing; and (e) the development of a theory on the origin and evolution of marketing.

II. MARKETING AND JUSTICE

The members of the School of Salamanca were primarily concerned with the problem of justice in human behavior. The moral aspects of exchange transactions, as a subset of human behavior, were studied under the title of commutative justice.

Commutative justice is rooted on the principles of natural law. Natural law was of greater moral and theoretical value to the schoolmen than civil law since, in contrast to the latter, it was considered universal, unchangeable, and with principles that were innate in all men (Gratian 1975; Aquinas 1975). The natural law is summed up in the golden rule (Gratian 1975; Aquinas 1975) and the love of God, or good in general (Aquinas 1975). Furthermore, the natural law can be identified by acts governed by human reason, the assumption being that man has a rational tendency toward the good (Aquinas 1975). This is the main explanation of why actions governed by passions constitute a sin against justice. Marketing activities presented a good opportunity for human passions to rule behavior and the schoolmen were very much aware of it. They addressed these sins against justice in their teachings and treatises.

Reason and rationality predominates in the schoolmen's work since this is the way to truth and justice according to natural law.

A. On Marketing and the Marketer

Is the occupation of the merchant, marketing, a sinful one? This question was often addressed by the Spanish schoolmen in their teachings and later communicated through moral instruction handbooks to merchants.

It is clear from their writings that marketing activities were open to a great number of temptations. However, no marketing activity, with the exception of money lending, was considered in itself a sinful one. What was considered sinful was the desire for profit and wealth as an object in itself rather than it being a means to an end. The immoderate desire for wealth constituted a sin because it was considered "unnatural." That is, this desire for profit was not moderated by reason and as such constituted a violation of the natural law. This thought is definitely part of the legacy of Aristotle's *Politics* and St. Thomas Aquinas' *Summa Theologica* to the School of Salamanca.

The treatise written by Luis Saravia de la Calle (1544), which enjoyed considerable influence, starts with a lengthy exhortation against merchants desire for riches. Saravia repeatedly quotes St. Paul on this passage that is printed in large sized letters: "THOSE WHO WANT TO BE RICH FALL IN TEMPTATION AND ON THE SIDE OF THE DEVIL" (pp. 4-5). According to Saravia, the unlimited desire for riches is present in all occupations not only in marketing. "Those who want to be it [rich] in any manner, and strive to be, either at the service of the nobility or princes, or selling his skills, or exchanging their states, or dealing in merchandise, or risking his person in the wars..." (p. 4). Marketing is, however, open to many temptations. "I do not condemn negotiations nor merchandise because of sin, for being bad in itself, for being mortal [in itself] but for being dangerous" (p. 12).

Tomas de Mercado's treatise (1571), frequently cited by other writers, is consistent with Saravia's views. In addition, Mercado attributes the bad reputation of marketing as an occupation to the temptations associated with it. "Because of this opportunity the opportunity to sin the merchant's craft always had a bad reputation among learned men, whether they were Gentiles or Catholics..." (Book II, p. 23).

Mercado makes a clear-cut distinction between the occupation and the person in it. It is the person who is at fault regardless of the occupation.

If I lie and swear, vices and sins are mine, not from the craft, that very well could be executed if I did not want to lie nor swear. This advises me and persuades me, not to go away from being a merchant, but to go away from being a liar and a forswearer. If this occupation you ask me to leave, tell me which do you want me to keep busy with? There is no occupation in the republic that the despicable man can not use wrong (Book II, pp. 24-25).

The position of the School of Salamanca concerning the morality of marketing is well represented in the work of Domingo de Soto (1975), one of his founding members:

> Commerce is not in itself good, that is, intrinsically, such as virtue is to charity, nor it is intrinsically bad, such as the untruth, but it is indifferent, such as eating, that can be done well or bad, according to the quality of the end and of the consequences (p. 642).

His second conclusion pertains to the "quality of the end." "If the end of commerce is considered in itself, which is profit, it presupposes some vileness." However, this condition can be corrected if "profit is directed toward another motive" (p. 643), in such a case profit can be procured licitly. The orientation of the profit motive toward other more honorable ends is what Mercado (1571) had in mind in his advise to merchants.

Mercado recommends the merchant that in order to avoid sin in his trade, he must have "righteous intentions." The first one, in order of predominance, is "to provide the republic of the food, clothes and merchandise that it needs" (Book II, p. 25). The second one, even when Mercado admits it is a waste of time to preach it, is to give to the poor from their business profits (Book II, p. 26). The third one, "to sustain with his negotiations and benefits the expenses of his household" (Book II, p. 27). The problem, according to Mercado, is that "They pay more attention to the latter [which is the lowest] than to the first and second [which are] so superior" (Book II, p. 27). The latter intention is righteous and thus natural, but from it the desire to become rich is only a step away.

The only marketing activity that constituted an exception to the rule was money lending. It was not the immoderate desire of profit, but the intention to profit from money lending which constituted in itself a sin against justice.

The title page of Luis de Alcala's (1546) *Treatise of Loans* holds a picture of a merchant picking up a bag of money from the ground with a snake (a symbol of evil) coming out of it. A second man stands behind the merchant with an aureole on his head, presumably his confessor, who indicates with his index finger to the snake and the bag. The confessor seem to be warning the merchant of the dangers that money lending present to his soul.

Alcala's handbook opens with the following analogy:

> The money of the profiteer [money lender - usurer] is similar to the bite of the snake called aspid. Because he who receives her bite as with pleasure he sleeps, and with that sweetness of his sleep he dies due to the poison that had secretly spread to all his limbs.

Alcala is clearly suggesting that profit on a loan may seem a temporary benefit to the merchant but it really becomes the perpetual loss of his soul. The school's condemnation of money lending at interest did not represent in any form a condemnation of marketing. The underlying reason for the usury prohibition was found in the ancient conception of a loan as a gift only to be repaid if possible. The schoolmen's conception of a loan changed gradually, fueled by the expansion of marketing activity that followed from the discovery of America and that resulted in an increase in the use of credit. By the end of the sixteenth century, money lending was considered a legitimate marketing activity.

B. On the Just Price

The theory of the just price, a typical scholastic topic, is studied under the domain of commutative justice that rules over the exchange between individuals. Commutative's justice main principle is the negative form of the golden rule: Do not do to another what you don't want done to you. The observance of this principle is identified with the equality that should be maintained in the exchanges. Molina (1975) explains what this principle is all about in market exchanges: "Commutative justice consists in equality as to value between price and object" (p. 135).

The just price theory was treated as a separate topic from the usury theory in the work of the Spanish schoolmen. The application of just price principles to the loan transaction becomes more common among the late Jesuits. By then, the loan was more commonly viewed as a market transaction; the lender was viewed as a seller, the interest as a price, and money was "the tool of the merchant" that was sold.

The concern of the schoolmen with the problem of morality in market transactions acted as a powerful motive that resulted in substantial contributions to the understanding of marketing at the micro level. "Preoccupation with the ethics of pricing, as the example of the later scholastics [the School of Salamanca] suffices to show, is precisely one of the strongest motives that man can possibly have for analyzing actual market mechanisms" (Schumpeter 1954, p. 60).

It is this close study of market mechanisms by the School of Salamanca that makes possible; (a) the development of a utility theory of value for commodities; (b) the study of fraud, deception, and monopolistic practices in marketing; and (c) the development of a utility theory of value for money.

1. Utility Theory of Value

The just price is generally defined by the Spanish schoolmen as the one resulting from the "common estimation" of men. "The price of the thing must be sought in the common estimation of men" (Vitoria 1957, p. 603). A general consensus also existed concerning the factors that may affect this "common estimation." A typical definition is the one presented by Saravia de la Calle (1544).

> Excluding all deceit and malice, the just price of a thing is the price which commonly fetches at the time and place of the deal, in cash, and bearing in mind the particular circumstances and manner of the sale, the abundance of goods and money, the number of buyers and sellers, the difficulty of procuring the goods, and the benefit to be enjoyed by their use, according to the judgement of an honest man (p. 27).

The principal factors affecting the determination of the just price can be reduced to three.

> So that in order to determine the just price, we need only to consider these three things: Abundance or scarcity of goods, merchants [buyers and sellers], and money - of things which people want to barter and exchange for money. This doctrine is founded on Aristotle's dictum 'precium re: humana indigentia mensurat,' the price of things is measured by human needs (Saravia de la Calle 1544 p. 28).

The comments by Saravia reveal the Spanish schoolmen's advanced knowledge of the market forces that determine price. They recognized the role of the supply mechanism in the "abundance or scarcity of goods" and in the number of sellers. Not only did they recognize that these forces affected price, but they also predicted correctly the direction of price changes from their variation.

The School of Salamanca was one step away from developing a full-fledged theory of supply and demand. Soto (1975) came close to describing a supply and demand schedule. "The abundance of buyers increases the price of goods and their scarcity reduces it; and vice versa, the abundance of sellers reduces the price and their scarcity increases it" (p. 645).

The just price was based, in the tradition of the School of Salamanca, on a utility theory of value. "The value of things is not considered as residing in their entities but in their utilities and advantages" (Molina 1975, p. 149). The price of things is based on human needs.

> The price of goods is not determined by their nature but by the measure in which they serve the needs of mankind.... If no one needed the goods of labour of his fellows, men would cease to exchange their product. We have had to admit then that *want* is the basis of price (Soto 1978, p. 84).

The doctors recognized the distinction between physiological and psychological needs. Soto (1978) clarifying the meaning of want (indigentiam) explains this difference. "When, however, we speak of 'want' we understand also that the Republic has need of adornment. We include not only such things as are necessary for human life, but also such as render it pleasurable and splendid" (p. 84).

Francisco Garcia (1978) explains that utilities are of many kinds. In addition to the identification of physiological needs, Garcia recognizes three types of psychological needs but pinpoints that it is next to impossible to enumerate them all.

> This utility, which causes us to esteem things and hold them dear, is of many kinds. A thing may be used in a way that is necessary for the preservation of life, as in eating, drinking, clothing ourselves, and remedying pain and human ailments. Or, we may use it for our pleasures and human pastimes, such as when we read a book, contemplate the nature of things, or ride a horse. Or, it may serve for the adornment of mankind or to delight our curiosity; and for this use gold and silver, precious stones, silk, brocade, tapestry, and many other such things are particularly appropriate. There are other uses that serve the infinite demands of mankind, which beyond a certain number, cannot be comprehended (p. 104).

The distinction between physiological and psychological needs did have an impact on the determination of the just price. Vitoria (1957) virtually exempts nonnecessary goods, those not directed to the satisfaction of physiological needs, from the "common estimation" principle.

> Thus, if the things not necessary to human uses are sold for much more than what they are worth and the buyer receives them voluntarily and freely, then in this case there is nobody obligated to make restitution because he who wants does not receive injury [volenti non fit injura] (p. 607).

The free will of the buyer, in the absence of ignorance or fraud, makes such transactions lawful.

Garcia discusses three reasons for an object to be of greater utility (value) than another. "Firstly, one thing may have many uses and serve for more purposes than another" (p. 104). That is, the more needs served by the product, the higher the value of the product, all other things being equal. "Secondly, one thing may render a greater service than another" (p. 104). The more important the needs served by the product, the higher the value of the product, all other things being equal. "Thirdly, a service may be better performed by one thing than another" (p. 104). This last reason concerns the relative capacity of the object to meet certain needs.

A just price theory was not only postulated on the basis of human needs but defended from the cost value approach used by John Duns Scotus (1894). the position of the School of Salamanca is first stated by Vitoria (1957) when enumerating the factors that should not be considered in the determination of the just price.

> ...the nature of the thing should not be considered, neither the price at which it was bought, that is, how expensive it was and with how much industry and danger (it was obtained), ex. Peter sells wheat; when it is purchased, no consideration should be given to the expenses incurred by Peter nor his industry, but only to the common estimation - 'at its worth' (p. 604).

Saravia de la Calle (1544) provides the rationale for this position.

> If we had to consider labour and risk in order to assess the just price, no merchant would ever suffer loss, nor would abundance nor scarcity of goods and money enter into the question.... Why should a book written out by hand be worth more than one which is printed, when the latter is better, though it costs less to produce? Finally, why when the type of Tolouse is the best, should it be cheaper than the vile type of Paris? (p. 30).

There are two arguments here. First, the business of the merchant is a risky one, but the burden of such risk should lie entirely on his shoulders, not the buyer. Hopefully, his gains will compensate for his losses. "The art of commerce is largely dependent upon chance, and merchants should learn to bow misfortune and to wait for better times to come..." (Soto 1978, p. 86). Second, the consumer should not pay for the inefficiencies of the merchant.

These arguments are more clearly presented by Molina (1975) who, following Soto (1978), directly attacks Scotus, on the cost pricing issue.

> The price of goods is not to be gauged by the gains of merchants or their losses but from the common appraisal of them in the place where they are sold, in view of all the current circumstances. And this is true whether through *ill-luck* or *lack of skillful dealing*, they gain little or even suffer loss, or with *good luck* and *energetic trading* they make a great gain (p. 151).

So far, the impression given is that cost pricing was rejected in all circumstances by the Spanish schoolmen. This is not the case. The price determined by "common estimation" is the just price only under the presence of a large number of sellers and buyers in the market, (Vitoria, 1975). The just price is then the market price under competitive conditions but not when the number of buyers or sellers is small. "The just price of the thing cannot be taken from the common estimation of men because they are few who buy and sell...(p. 605). How should the just price be determined in such cases? "Before establishing the price according to the common estimation of men, consideration should be given to those conditions, that is, the expenses, the labour, the dangers and the scarcity, that also increases the price of the thing" (p. 605). In these cases, the judgment of honorable men is required for setting a reasonable price.

A special case in which buyers and sellers are small in number is when a product is brought or introduced to a place for the first time. "...there could be some room for this consideration of the expenses, costs and dangers in the place where no price exists for this thing" (Saravia de la Calle 1544, p. 32). And in the words of Molina (1975):

> When a new product is imported in a province the just price must be established and evaluated according to the judgement of prudent men, taking into account the quality, utility, quantity imported, and so the expenses, dangers and difficulties required for bringing

it, and even its novelty which makes it more precious" (p. 696). In this case, even a high profit is justified. "And the price should not be condemned as unjust because of an elevated profit, if the thing, because of its rarity and novelty is considered precious and it has many buyers, no other rule can be established on this matter (p. 696).

Molina (1975) also indicates that cost pricing be used in estimating the just price in the case of a public monopoly. A public monopoly is one granted by the governmental authorities because otherwise the commodity will not be supplied (p. 152).

In sum, the just price is given by the common estimation of men with the noted exceptions. But how is this price set in practice in order to guarantee the equality of the exchanges? The schoolmen recognized this practical difficulty by referring to a range or latitude in the just price and not one permanent price. According to Soto (1978):

> Uncontrolled prices are not indivisible but enjoy a certain latitude within the bounds of justice, of which one extreme is called the 'rigid,' the other the 'merciful,' and the middle the 'moderate' price. If an article may justly be sold for ten ducats, then it may also be sold for eleven or for nine...(p. 86-87).

The just price as the market price is subject to variation from supply and demand conditions. Mercado (1571) after defining the just price, admits that it "is more variable [as taught by experience] than the wind" (p. 46). Alcala (1546) has suggested to merchants a way of dealing with this practical problem. He suggested to take an average of the range if in doubt (p. 4). Although the Spanish schoolmen treated the just price or market price as fluctuating within a price range, there is no evidence in their writings of a natural or long run equilibrium price.

2. Fraud and Deception in Marketing

Monopolistic practices were generally condemned by the Spanish schoolmen as means to increasing prices through fraud and deception. The price set in such cases was considered an unjust one and subject to restitution of the injured party. "...if deceit or fraud exist when establishing the price of the thing [it] is not just. This fraud and deceit can result from 'monipodium' [monopoly] on the part of the buyer or on the part of the seller. Then, the buyer or seller who uses such deceit is obliged to make restitution" (Vitoria, 1975, p. 606).

Monopoly or conspiracy to fix or control prices whether by sellers or buyers was generally condemned by the schoolmen (Soto 1975; Saravia de la Calle 1544; Alcala 1546; Mercado 1571; Albornoz 1573).

At the root of the attack against monopolistic practices was the idea originally advance by Vitoria (1957) that the just price requires the nonexistence of necessity nor violence (p. 607). Vitoria was defending the freedom of choice of each part to a transaction that was indispensable for the equality of the exchange. Monopolistic practices violated this freedom of choice, which according to Albornoz (1573), is the substance of the contract of sale. Albornoz explains that the monopoly (estanco) is "founded in forced force, which prevents, and directly opposes the substance of the contract, because the justice of the price consists in the will of he who pays it..." (p. 67). Albornoz was referring to a monopoly of supply. The buyers' freedom of choice is impaired by the insignificance of his force compared with that of the sellers. The seller is the only real party to the exchange. "...the seller alone represents all the characters of this comedy" (p. 67). Soto (1975) suggests that in such a case the buyers can "justly join in monopoly [monopsony], responding in a certain manner force with force they can use of the contrary wisdom; for example, they can agree among them not to let anybody buy unless it is at a given price" (p. 645).

Monopolistic practices were generally perceived by the doctors as restraints to trade. This idea cannot be more clear than in the work of Albornoz (1573). Albornoz prefers to use the Spanish word "estanco" instead of "monipodio," or "monopolio" when referring to a monopoly. The three words mean the same thing but "estanco" has an additional meaning, "to damn up or to stagnate" which gives a better idea of the real impact of monopolistic practices on the marketing process.

> This monopoly [monipodio] is properly called in [Spanish] *estanco*, which means in [Spanish] to damn up, to stop the thing that flows,...and because the trade of any supply or good consists in passing from one hand to another, and he who takes it all for selling it (and prevents anybody else from having it) impedes the course of the good, and he damns it up, for this reason is called *'estanco'* (p. 67).

Another name given by Albornoz, Mercado, (1571, p. 104) and other schoolmen to these monopolistic practices is "atravesar la mercaderia" which, literally, means to obstruct the good, that is to impede the normal flow of the good. Therefore, monopolistic practices were recognized as restraining the marketing process.

The position of the School regarding the just price principle of "common estimation" ran also against the practice of price discrimination. "But it is not licit to sell more dearly because of a private necessity and utility as is considered by St. Thomas, because only one's necessity would not increase the price of the thing" (Vitoria 1975, p. 91). This by no means represents a strong restriction on price discrimination because of the latitude that existed in the just price.

It is not until the end of the sixteenth century that the School's position toward monopolistic practices is liberalized in the work of Molina (1975). Molina accepts price collusion among sellers as long as they set a just price.

When the merchants agree among them on a price which, regardless of this agreement, would be just but 'rigid' [the highest extreme of the range], they would sin against the charity of their neighbors and would deserve to be fined with a heavy penalty by the public authorities; however, *I do not believe that they sin against justice* and as a consequence, they are not obliged to make restitution, as long as none among them would prohibit, through fraud, violence or fear, others to sell at a lower price (p. 694).

This is an acceptance of the practice in terms of its end result. If the consequence of monopoly as reflected in the price is the same as in the presence of competition, then there is no reason to believe that the former is more or less just than the latter. Monopoly is still a sin against charity because it presupposes a selfish interest in the part of the sellers. However, the outcome of this self interest might be a just one.

A similar view is presented by Molina concerning two other monopolistic practices of merchants: hoarding and speculation.

The men who buying what in time of scarcity they sell with the purpose of selling dearly and profiting, if they buy at the current just price and sell later also at the just price, they are not an obstacle to the members of the republic..., quite the contrary, *they are useful to the republic* (p. 694).

The end result is just. The goods become more abundant in their time of scarcity cushioning in this way the increase in prices. Molina seems to suggest that the speculators provide a beneficial function to society by smoothing out the cycles of excess supply and excess demand in the commodity. This is very progressive thinking for his time.

The exclusion of all fraud and deceit in the determination of the just price also pertains to the promotion and communication of product information between buyer and seller. The schoolmen were prompt to recognize that information imbalances between buyer and seller, concerning the product, often reflected opportunistic behavior exhibited by one of the parties to the transaction. Information imbalances could then disrupt the equality between price and object (value) being exchanged. Typically, but not always, the information imbalance favored the seller.

Saravia de la Calle (1544) points out that the seller would often try to conceal information which would reveal product defects or faults. Saravia identifies three major defects. First, when one thing is sold for another; ex. to misrepresent brass as gold. Second, when misrepresentation occurs in the quantity sold by tricking the customer on the product weight and measures. Third, the attribute of the object is misrepresented; for example when the wild horse is sold by claiming is tame (p. 32).

The seller must compensate the buyer in return if he is aware of any defect in the product's quantity or quality. However, "The seller is not compelled to tell the flaw of the thing with the condition that he decreases the price in proportion to the reduction in the goodness of the thing with results from the flaw" (p. 32). In other words, the seller must make a living out of selling, negative promotion would run contrary to this objective and since the relevant information is contained in the price anyway, the injustice is removed by reducing the price. The equality between value and price is maintained.

The buyer also could have information advantages over the seller. "...if one knowing the value of a pearl buys it for ten cents [a 'real'] from a farmer who does not know that it is worth more, he would sin and would be compelled to provide restitution" (p. 35). The rights of the parties are thus equally protected from information imbalances.

3. Money, Value and Prices

The School of Salamanca's concern with money resulted from the large volume of gold and silver that circulated in the Spanish economy following the discovery of America. They were the first to recognize the relationship between the quantity of money and the price level. This knowledge was also confirmed in their study of particular markets at the micro level. The Spanish schoolmen inherited from Aristotle his conception of money as a medium of exchange and added their own view of money as a commodity.

Aristotle's view of money as a medium of exchange implied that money was sterile. Thus, profits on money changing were unnatural. Azpilcueta (1978) response against the Aristotelian argument is based on the conception of money as a commodity.

> Nor is it true that to use money by changing it at a profit is against nature. Although this is not the first and principal use for which money was intended, it is none the less an important secondary use. To deal in shoes for profit is not the chief use for which they were invented, which is to protect our feet: But this is not to say that to trade in shoes is against nature (p. 91).

Once money is accepted as a commodity the explanation of its value becomes a byproduct of the social utility theory of value.

> ...that all merchandise becomes dearer when it is in great demand and short supply, and that money, in so far as it may be sold, bartered, or exchanged by some other form of contract, is merchandise and therefore also becomes dearer when it is in great demand and short supply (p. 94).

Money as a commodity also becomes subject to the "common estimation" principle of the just price theory. Mercado (1571) on the price of money concludes that: "It follows that the rate (of exchange) can be founded on no other reason (if it is to have a foundation at all) but the *diverse estimation* in which money is held from city to city" (Book IV, p. 21). The subjective value of money is also clear in the writings of Francisco Garcia (1978). "Now, it happens with money as with other goods, that at one time or place they may be more *highly esteemed* and valued than at another, although their quality and nature may not have varied" (p. 106). Thus, the just price of money is based on the diversity of its estimation or utility in different times and places. Therefore, money changing was, considered a socially valuable activity.

III. THE SOCIAL CONTRIBUTION OF MARKETING

The social contribution of marketing was recognized by the School of Salamanca in two major ways: (a) by acknowledging marketing's historical role in the satisfaction of human needs, and (b) by identifying and recognizing the social value of marketing functions.

A. Origin and Evolution of Marketing

The origin and evolution of marketing is tied to the origin and evolution of man in the writings of the Spanish schoolmen.

In the original state, a state of abundance, all property was common or social. "...everything belonged to one, and everything to all. And there was nothing of which everybody could not use and take advantage" (Mercado 1571, p. 18). Marketing does not exist at this stage since needs can be satisfied easily from the free resources of nature. All exchange is purely social. "...there in the state of innocence, no trade nor farming existed since the earth and the elements gave man everything he needed" (Saravia de la Calle 1544, p. 72). Then, the original sin took place and the common wealth was allocated into parts among men, which resulted into the creation of private property. Also, with the "fall" from the original state, human needs increased and became more urgent. Man became more dependent on temporary goods (Mercado 1571, Book II, p. 18).

A division of labor also occurred at this stage that was probably based on the distribution of the common stock of land to each man:

> For the reason that we incurred, because of the sin [the original sin] in this punishment that we will be sustained by the sweat of our face, farming the land: There is no negotiation nor gain so noble and chivalrous that does not depend on the land or has some reason in it. Because of this, in some parts, the majority are farmers and in others shepherds...according to whether the disposition of the land is more favorable to some of these aims and ends (Book II, p. 16).

In other words, the disposition of the land determines whether it is more efficient to specialize on one occupation or another.

Because of specialization, "...since the needs of man are many and he is not enough to satisfy them all, *barter* of things by things was found..."(Saravia de la Calle 1544, p. 72). Barter is the initial stage in the evolution of marketing.

At this juncture, we need to clarify one point. The appearance of barter after the original sin implies no moral judgment from the schoolmen on the nature of marketing. Marketing was always considered by the Spanish schoolmen as a natural and legitimate activity. The before-after connection between the original sin and marketing is purely coincidental. Marketing was a direct effect of the emergence of private property and the division of labor that resulted from it. Vitoria (1957) explains that the reason for the emergence of private property was to be found in the ratio of population to the resources that could be obtained naturally from the land. "Therefore, if the human race would have multiplied in the state of innocence, the appropriation of goods would have taken place, because otherwise, they could have not survived" (p. 602). In such a case, marketing would have begun in the original state and not after the original sin. Consequently, there was no cause-effect relationship between the original sin and barter.

Barter, which was rooted in human needs, proved to be an inconvenient and inefficient method of exchange (Saravia de la Calle 1544, p. 72; Mercado 1571, p. 20). This point marks the origin of buying and selling and of the invention of money (Mercado 1571, p. 20). Azpilcueta (1978) explained the inconvenience of barter that found a solution with the invention of money.

> Exchange, or the barter of things other than money, as the juris consult Paulus elegantly shows, is a much more ancient contract than that of sale and purchase, which began after money was invented. Before the invention of money, anyone who wished to exchange his house for another was obliged to seek out some person who had the house he wanted and who was willing to exchange it; while a man who had wine and wool but no wheat or shoes would try to find another who had wheat and shoes and was prepared to make the exchange...(p. 89).

The essence of buying and selling was pretty well understood by Vitoria (1957). "The contract of purchase and sale was being introduced for the common utility of seller and buyer, since each one needs the thing of the other" (p. 75). Its social importance was recognized by Albornoz (1573). "The contract of purchase and sale is the most important, extended and intricate of the law, because it is the nerve of the human life by which the universe is sustained..." (p. 62).

The last step in the evolution of marketing is the emergence of the marketing specialist or middleman. Mercado (1571) explains that the first specialists came about because of the scarcity of gold and silver that were so useful as a medium of exchange. It can be inferred that in the absence of these two metals, the exchange system would have reversed to one of barter. Consequently, the first middlemen contributed to maintain the efficiency of the marketing system.

...Each one would purchase with this metal, specially after being coined, whatever was convenient for the provision of his family. And realizing that many times it was lacking in the ground, many took upon themselves to bring it from outside at their own cost, and once bought, it was sold to the neighbors with some profit above the cost and expenses incurred. [These men] were initially called merchants by the common people because of their continuous use of buying and selling (Book II, p. 20).

Notice that the appearance of the marketing specialist could have coincided with an increase in the volume of marketing transactions that resulted in the scarcity of the medium of exchange. It is when the volume of transactions is large that the middleman can achieve greater economies for the marketing system by reducing the number of exchange transactions (Alderson 1954). Thus, the social need for the middleman may have been two-fold.

These first merchants received compensation that covered not only expenses, but a profit, which indicates that the community recognized their social contribution. However, the social contribution of the merchant is different from that of the farmer or the shepherd because he does "not seek, nor wait for the substance or quality of his thing ['ropa'] to change..." (Mercado 1571, Book II, p. 20). He does not provide in modern jargon, form utility. The social utilities and the majority of the marketing functions that the merchant provides can be found in the writings of the Spanish scholars.

In conclusion, the knowledge of the Salamanca schoolmen about the origin and evolution of marketing is remarkable for their time and compares favorably with the information found on such topics in contemporary marketing textbooks (i.e., McCarthy and Perrault 1991; Stanton 1990).

B. The Functions of Marketing

The schoolmen of Salamanca recognized the nature and importance of the exchange functions: buying and selling. The possession of product information was considered indispensable to buyer and seller for judging the relationship between price and value. In the schoolmen's framework, product and promotion were tied to the price element of the marketing mix. Other activities were considered inherent in buying and selling.

Albornoz (1573) seems to suggest an information function that is inherent in the contract of purchase and sale and which overcomes a gap between seller and buyer. "... In the absence of this contract, men would not have what others have in excess and they lack, nor what they have in excess will be *known* by those who lack it..." (p. 62).

The negotiation of terms is recognized by Albornoz as an integral part of the exchange contract. He defines the contract as "*Dispute* or argument made between men with the consent of the parties for the true price, in which the buyer *comes to terms*" (p. 57).

The physical distribution functions of transporting and storing were to be found in every sixteenth-century treatise on commutative justice or handbook for the moral instruction of merchants. A consensus existed among the scholars of Salamanca concerning the social importance of these two functions.

Soto (1975) clearly recognized the social necessity for the transporting function of the merchant and the inconvenience that its inexistence would entail. In discussing the social importance of marketing, he states:

> Neither can each individual in need make long trips in order to obtain the small quantities of goods that they need; nor all who have in excess can transport their surplus to another place; therefore, those are necessary who would understand the task of taking commodities from one place to another (p. 643).

Vitoria (1975) also recognizes the social importance of transportation, but in addition, he acknowledges the right of the merchant to receive compensation for it:

> Of these merchants I say that it is licit for them to sell their merchandise more dearly, since a change of place have taken place; because the purchase and sale are not effected in the same place. Also, because it is necessary to the wellbeing and provision of the Republic, because there is no where a city which has all that is necessary for the uses of men. And if those who transport commodities do not gain something, nobody would want to transport them (p. 95).

The schoolmen understood, as these comments indicate, that transporting caused a transformation of place which resulted in utility. This is not an individual utility as modern economic theory would suggest. This is a social utility of place that reflects the role of the marketing system in advancing the material goals of society.

The storing function was alluded to by many of the schoolmen when they referred to the job of the merchant as one involving transformations of time. "The merchant does not seek nor wait for the substance or quality of his thing to change, but *time* and with time the price..." (Mercado 1571, Book II, p. 20).

The social necessity of the storing function was directly recognized by Soto (1975).

> And what we say about place can be applied to time. It normally happens that in a time there is abundance of goods and scarcity in another, but however, not all poor men can conserve their products, for this reason, if it were not for the existence of those who buy them for the end of keeping them for another time, the Republic would not be able to remain unharmed. Furthermore, when the commodities are unloaded in the seaport or in the city, middlemen are necessary to keep its abundance through time, because the individuals cannot provide themselves for the future (p. 643).

Implicit in this statement is the idea that the storing function could be shifted from the merchants to the more wealthy consumers that could afford it. However, the poor were in the majority, so it followed that merchants were needed to provide this function. Other facilitating functions were recognized as well.

The breaking bulk function was generally discussed in conjunction with the physical distribution functions. Vitoria (1975) is the first to discuss it under the name of "method of sale" which is a factor to consider in the determination of the just price.

> I say that, even when buying in large quantities results in a cheaper good, nevertheless it is licit for the merchant to sell later the same good more dearly in smaller quantities ['por menblem']...I say that, even when the price changes, there is no problem when one buys in large quantity, because the method of selling the merchandise increases or decreases the price of the object. And in this way, one can sell 53 measures receiving thirty five cents ['tres reales y medio'] for each one, and not to sell only one but for forty cents ['cuatro reales'] because this is the common price, for reason of the method of sale at wholesale and at retail (p. 79).

Breaking bulk then is understood as another marketing transformation that is socially valuable and must be compensated through payment of a higher price. What would happen if such a function were not compensated? Vitoria answers that "The Republic could not be sustained with comfort, since those who transport the commodities would not like to wait around to sell in smaller quantities ['por menudo']" (p. 97). They obviously preferred to sell at wholesale.

The significant role that financing played as a facilitating function in buying and selling was well comprehended by the Spanish schoolmen. However, this recognition, particularly in the early part of the sixteenth century, was not always explicit and direct because of the usury prohibition. Vitoria's defense of a common evasionary practice used by the merchants in the fairs is indicative of this recognition. Some merchants, in order to borrow money without incurring usury, would buy at retail price large quantities of a product and then they would immediately sell it at the wholesale price which was cheaper. The transaction was a commercial loan in disguise. However, according to Vitoria (1975), there was no usury in it, only a contract of purchase and sale of commodities at different prices (p. 79). A similar attitude is displayed by Vitoria when considering sales on credit. He considered it licit for the seller to set a higher price when selling on credit than when selling for cash, if the price difference was not an excessive one. Vitoria used the latitude of the just price to justify the transaction (p. 93). Molina (1975) considered legitimate a higher price on credit sales than on cash sales in compensation for the risk incurred by the seller.

A more tangible statement on the recognition of the importance of credit in market transactions was given in the contribution of the School of

Salamanca to the development of the usury doctrine. The outcome: virtually all credit for marketing transactions was recognized as licit and legitimate.

Risk taking was also widely recognized as part of the merchants trade but compensation was not generally allowed for it. The assumption being that good times would compensate for not so lucky times. The "common estimation" principle prevailed over risk and the merchant's expenses in the determination of the just price. However, compensation of the middleman's risk was allowed under noncompetitive conditions, and as indicated, on credit sales.

So far, we have seen that whenever a transformation or change occurs in the commodity, the schoolmen allowed for the compensation of some function. But could the merchant receive compensation when no apparent transformation takes place? Vitoria's response is in the affirmative, even when he does not sound so certain about it. "It seems so, because the price of the thing does not consist of something indivisible; that is, if no excess occurs beyond the just price, it seems that it could be sold for more" (p. 97). This thinking is not typical for his time since as he admits, "the judgement of all the doctors is leaning toward the opposite opinion" (p. 97).

Later Juan de Lugo (1642), states that compensation when there is no transformation of the commodity does not depend on the latitude of the just price. Lugo's response came as a result of the opinion of a schoolman of insignificant influence who implied in a case of sale with repurchase agreement that the price could in no way be altered because the nature and substance of the article were unchanged.

This singular opinion is deservedly rejected by everybody, because the value of things is not derived from their nature alone considered in itself but with reference to human uses; and this utility decreases when a buyer receives an article without full power to dispose of it as he wills (p. 149).

Lugo seems to be saying that even when there is no apparent transformation of the commodity, "possession utility" is changed and it should be reflected in the price. This utility comes with the transfer of title inherent in all exchange transactions. As Lugo correctly points out, this utility is tied to the right of using the product.

In summary, the School of Salamanca recognized the most important functions of marketing. The functions were understood as changes that occurred in the commodity or its use which resulted in the creation of social utilities: place, time and possession. The transformation of form was generally identified as an outcome of nonmarketing activities.

The Spanish schoolmen understood very well the contribution of marketing to the goals of society. Even Soto (1975), one of the most conservative members of the School, recognized that "commerce is without any doubt ['simpliciter'] necessary to the Republic" (p. 643)

IV. SUMMARY AND CONCLUSION

The doctors of the School of Salamanca recognized the contribution of marketing to social welfare. Marketing activities were considered just, but not completely free, of social costs. However, the Spanish doctors attributed these social costs not to the activities but to some marketers who were dominated by their excessive passion for riches. The School's condemnation of money lending at interest did not represent in any form a condemnation of marketing.

The doctor's understanding of the social contribution of marketing resulted from their just price theory. The just price theory was, for the Spanish schoolmen, nothing but a theory of social value. Social utility, "common estimation," was at the root of price, which was the market price. Only under monopoly conditions of demand or supply was the market price not considered a good indicator of social utility. Cost pricing following the judgment of a "good" man was then allowed as a proxy to the "common estimation." Therefore, changes in the price of a commodity reflected changes in social utility.

Marketing functions were recognized as valuable to society because their performance increased social utility through different types of transformations. This is the reason why a higher price could be charged, according to the schoolmen, when a marketing function was provided. The latitude of the just price was also used for justifying a higher price for some marketing functions that, at the time, were not completely accepted.

In conclusion, what we know today about the social contribution of marketing does not seem to differ radically from what the members of the School of Salamanca knew more than four hundred years ago.

REFERENCES

Albornoz, B. (1573). *Arte de los Contratos*. Valencia, Spain.

Alcala, L. (1546). *Tractado de los Prestamos que Pasan entre Mercaderes Y Tractantes*. Toledo, Spain

Alderson, W. (1954). "Factors Governing the Development of Marketing Channels." In *Marketing Channels for Manufactured Products*, edited by Richard M. Clement. Homewood, IL; Richard D. Irwin.

Aquinas, St. Thomas (1975). "Summa Theologica." Pp. 294-403 in *El Pensamiento Social y Economico de la Escolastica*, edited by R. S. Bravo. Madrid: Consejo Superior de Investigaciones Cientificas.

Azpilcueta, M., called Navarrus. (1978). "Comentario Resolutorio de Usuras." Pp. 89-95 in *The School of Salamancaedited*, by M. Grice-Hutchinson. Oxford: Clarendon Press.

Duns Scotus. J. (1894). *Quaestiones in Quartum Librum Sententiarium*. Paris: L.V.

Garcia, F. (1978). "Tratado Utilisimo y muy General de Todos los Contractos." Pp.103-108 in *The School of Salamanca*, edited by M. Grice-Hutchinson. Oxford: Clarendon Press.

Gratian. (1975). "Gratian Decretals." Pp. 289-293 in *El Pensamiento Social y Economico de la Escolastica*, edited by R. S. Bravo. Madrid: Consejo Superior de Investigaciones Cientificas.

Lugo, J. (1942). *De Justicia et Jure*. Lyons.

McCarthy, J. E. and W. D. Perrault, Jr. (1991). *Basic Marketing*. Homewood, IL: Richard D. Irwin, Inc.

Mercado, T. (1571). *Suma de Tratos Y Contratos*. Seville, Spain: Hernando Diaz.

Molina, L. (1592). "De Justicia et Jure." Pp. 673-696 in *El Pensamiento Social y Economico de la Escolastica* edited by R. S. Bravo. Madrid: Consejo Superior de Investigaciones Centificas.

Noonan, J. T. (1957). *The scholastic analysis of usury*. Cambridge, MA: Harvard University Press.

Saravia de la Calle, L. (1544). *Instruccion de Mercaderes muy Provechosa*. Spain: Medina Del Campo.

Schumpeter, J. A. (1954). *History of Economic Analysis*. New York: Oxford University Press.

Soto, D. (1975). "Releccion Sobre el Libro Cuarto de las Sentencias Acerca de Domino." Pp. 632-650 in *El Pensamiento Social y Economico de la Escolastica*, edited by R. S. Bravo. Madrid: Consejo de Investigaciones Cientificas.

Soto, D. (1978). "De Justicia Et Jure." Pp. 83-88 in *The School of Salamanca*, edited by Marjorie Grice-Hutchinson. Oxford: Claredon Press.

Stanton, W. J. (1990). *Fundamentals of Marketing*. New York: McGraw-Hill Book Company.

Vitoria, F. (1957). "Comentarios a la Secunda Secundae de Santo Tomas." Pp.72-101 in *Francisco de Vitoria: Una Teoria Social del Valor Economico*, edited by D. Iparrigue. Bilbao, Spain: Editorial del Mensajero Corazon de Jesus.

Vitoria, F. (1975). "Comentarios a la Secunda Secundae de Santo Tomas." Pp. 583-631 in *El Pensamiento Social y Economico de la Escolastica*, edited by R. S. Bravo. Madrid: Consejo Superior de Investigaciones Cientificas.

PART II

MODERN MARKETING THOUGHT

THE UTILITY OF THE
FOUR UTILITIES CONCEPT

Eric H. Shaw

ABSTRACT

The evolution of the four utilities concept is examined. It was conceived by institutional economists to explain that merchants contributed value, like farmers or manufacturers. Marketing pioneers used the concept to describe the nature and scope of market distribution. It was next applied to identify marketing functions. Contemporary scholars have linked the concept to marketing management. The historical perspective provides a basis to evaluate the utility of the four utilities concept for modern marketing thought.

I. INTRODUCTION

One of the oldest and most widely employed concepts in marketing is the four utilities concept. It was developed by economists to resolve a problem with the theory of labor productivity and was carried over into marketing to define the nature and scope of the field. The concept was later employed to identify the functions of middlemen and subsequently extended to all of the marketing

Research in Marketing, Supplement 6, pages 47-66.
Copyright © 1994 by JAI Press Inc.
All rights of reproduction in any form reserved.
ISBN: 1-55938-187-6

functions. Most recently, the four utilities concept has been related to the four P's of marketing management.

Because of its centrality to marketing thought several questions naturally arise. How well does the four utilities concept describe the marketing phenomena to which it has historically been applied? Is the concept robust enough to clarify the phenomena to which it is currently being employed? Does it have the potential for explaining future marketing phenomena to which it may be applied?

The major difficulty in answering these questions is that the four utilities concept is so widely accepted that it is taken for granted. Few writers have examined any aspect of its development. Due largely to neglect, the genesis and evolutionary trail of the four utilities concept are generally considered extinct. Most references to its authorship in the marketing literature are vague attributions to "early economists," leading Ellis and Jacobs (1977, p. 21) to conclude: "The origins of the traditional utilities of form, time, place, and possession are apparently now lost in the annals of antiquity." Yet to comprehend the subtleties of the concept it is necessary to start at the beginning as they emerge.

The purpose of this paper is to search the literature and examine the historical development of the four utilities concept, the areas in which it has been applied, the problems that arise in application, and the extent to which the four utilities concept is relevant for modern marketing thought.

Utility is generally defined as the capacity to satisfy consumer wants. The economic value of market goods to a consumer is explained by the creation of four types of utility. *Form utility* is created by making materials into a product that is wanted and is used to explain the contribution of manufacturing to satisfaction. *Time utility* and *place utility* are created by having a product or service available when and where it is wanted, and *possession utility* is created by transferring ownership to whom it is wanted. These last three types of utility are used to explain the contribution of marketing to satisfaction. Although other types of utility are occasionally mentioned in the literature, these four are generally recognized and traditionally known as "the four utilities concept."

II. THE ECONOMIC PROBLEM

The economic problem to which the four utilities concept offered a solution concerns the issue of productive and unproductive labor. This issue was first raised by the Physiocrats, one of the earliest economic schools of thought founded in eighteenth-century France. The Physiocrats held that only farming—because of the assistance of nature—could produce a net product or surplus. Hence, only farmers provided value and were productive. Other types of labor such as manufacturers, who merely changed the shape of materials, or merchants, who merely changed the location of products, were regarded as "sterile."

Surprisingly, a leading Physiocrat was one of the first to imply the four utilities concept. A.R.J. Turgot (1766, p. 362) noted: "The consumer is interested in obtaining [*possession*] the things [*form*] he needs, when he wishes them [*time*], and where he wishes them [*place*]" (italics added). Although his statement argues against the sterility of any type of labor, Turgot was caught in the web of the Physiocratic framework and did not recognize the significance of his point. It was not until almost a century later that economists realized it was not a surplus that gave labor value making it productive, but rather any labor that produced utility provided value and was therefore productive. But this was such a subtle and difficult chain of reasoning, it even misled two of the greatest thinkers of the time—Benjamin Franklin and Adam Smith.

After dining with some prominent Physiocrats in October 1767, during a brief sojourn in Paris, the American statesman and philosopher, Benjamin Franklin (1767) accepted the Physiocratic doctrine as his own:

[England] is fond of manufactures beyond their real value, for the true source of riches is husbandry. Agriculture is truly productive of new wealth; manufacturers only change forms [and merchants only change places] and, whatever value they give to the materials they work upon, they in the meantime consume an equal value in provisions, etc.

This notion that some labor was more productive than other labor soon became embedded in economics.

Following the Physiocrats, the Father of Classical Economics, Adam Smith (1776, p. 639) noted that "the labour of farmers...is certainly more productive than that of merchants, artificers and manufacturers." Moreover, manufacturers were regarded as more productive than merchants, but even lowly merchants should not be considered "in the same light" as those whose "work consists in services." Because Smith's influence dominated economic thinking, his views on a hierarchy of labor based on the productivity of various types of employment bequeathed to subsequent generations of economists a strawman that provided a continuous source of controversy. Shumpeter (1968, p. 628) calls the labor productivity issue a "dusty museum piece" and regards it as a case study in "futility."

This museum piece, nonetheless, has had significant repercussions for marketing thought because the issue of productive and unproductive labor was ultimately resolved in terms of the four utilities concept. One of the earliest economists to cut through the confusion of the labor productivity issue, J. R. McCullock (1844, p. 177), argued that "labor employed in carrying commodities from where they are produced to where they are to be consumed, and in dividing them into minute portions, so as to suit the wants of consumers, are really as productive as if they were employed in agriculture or manufacture." Thus, McCullock implies some of the utilities in dismissing the whole issue of a hierarchy of labor productivity.

Although more concerned with marginal utility, Carl Menger (1871, p. 238), a founder of the Austrian School, also implied the utilities concept. He observed that product markets link: (1) persons, (2) quantities, (3) places, and (4) time periods (p. 242); thereby suggesting possession, form, place, and time utilities. Menger also realized that "a thing has utility only if all available units of the thing together yield a total utility" (p. 118). This insight was lost until its rediscovery in the mid-twentieth century by Wroe Alderson (1957).

The American Institutionalists were the first to explicitly separate utility into component parts. Although the types were slightly different, the concept appears to have originated with John Bates Clark (1886, p. 25) who writes: "utilities are of four kinds...elementary utility, form utility, place utility, and time utility." Elementary utility referred to the extractive processes, such as, agriculture and mining, in contrast to form utility which was related to manufacturing processes. Clark also regarded the merchant, buying in large quantities and reselling in smaller quantities, as a producer of form utility: "The subdivision of articles purchased in bulk to suit the wants of the consumer is to be regarded as the creation of form utility" (1886, p. 26). The idea that breaking bulk produces utility anticipates Kotler's (1988) notion of "quantity utility" by a century.

Richard T. Ely (1889), distinguished among types of labor based on the various types of utility they produced, which he originally referred to as value:

> It is with the production of [elementary] value that agriculture, mining, and other branches of extractive production are concerned. Form value is due to form and shape given to raw materials... by manufacturers. Time value and place value [result from] goods brought to the place where needed or saved till the time when needed. The merchant produces these kinds of values (1889, p. 179).

In a later work, Ely (1893) used this four-way division as an argument for resolving the hierarchy of labor productivity problem. However, he shifted terms from the four values nomenclature here to the four utilities terminology as follows:

> It has seemed to some, even among economists of an earlier time, that the farmer is more truly a producer than the manufacturer, and the manufacturer more than the merchant; but careful thought discloses the fallacy of such a view. All industrial classes alike produce one or more of the four sorts of utility described, and they do so by changing the relations of things in time or space.... The merchant is producing utility as truly as is the farmer or the manufacturer (1893, p. 127).

Thus a solution to the problem of productive and unproductive labor was to regard anyone who produced utilities as creating economic value. The four utilities concept offered a pedagogical means to demonstrate that particular kinds of utility were created by different types of labor. Elementary utility was produced by extractive industries, form utility by manufacturing, and place and time utility by merchants. By creating utilities, each of the various branches of labor produced value and hence were productive.

III. INFLUENCE ON PIONEERS IN MARKETING

Institutional economists, particularly Clark and Ely, directly influenced such early marketing pioneers as Paul Nystrom, Ralph S. Butler, E.D. Jones, Fred Jones, and Paul Converse, among others (Bartels 1951). Consequently, the concept of four utilities was carried over into marketing.

Neoclassical economists, on the other hand, argued to the contrary. Breaking down utilities into component parts to explain the productivity issue, they asserted, provided far more baggage than it was worth; these economists also influenced a number of marketing pioneers. For example, Taussig (1915, p. 19) wrote, "no conclusions of importance for economics flow from the mere distinction between those who shape material wealth and those who bring about utilities of other kinds." Taussig had a major influence on such pioneers as Cherington and Copeland among others (Bartels 1951). Not surprisingly, their work does not refer to the four utilities concept.

The foremost neoclassic economist of the period, Alfred Marshall, also thought the subdivision of utility into component parts was unnecessary to the argument of productive labor. Regarding it not only as arbitrary to divide up labor by their utilities, Marshall (1920, p. 63) also argued: "There is no scientific foundation for this distinction." He compared a cabinetmaker creating furniture with a furniture dealer selling it:

They both produce utilities, and neither of them can do more: the furniture-dealer moves and rearranges matter so as to make it more serviceable than it was before, and the carpenter...re-adjusts matter...as when he makes a log into a table does no more (1920, p. 63).

After Marshall's statement resolving the problem of productive and unproductive labor in terms of the unity of utility, whole, without the necessity for breaking it into component parts, most economists appear to have lost interest in the four utilities concept. Even to the few American economists who continued to discuss the concept it was a minor issue that paled in significance to the far more relevant discovery of the marginal utility concept; the topic to which economists devoted their primary attention.

While many economists became disenchanted with and even dismissed the four utilities concept, early marketing writers for the most part adopted it.

Jones and Monieson (1987) argue that contrary to Bartels' (1962, p. 195) supposition that early marketing writers were largely influenced by neoclassical economists, the men under whom most early marketing scholars studied were predominantly institutional economists; and therefore "the philosophy of early marketing thought may well be quite different from what we currently understand it to be" (1987, p. 154).

This proposition regarding dominant influence is supported in the case of the four utilities concept. Those pioneers in marketing influenced by J.B. Clark, Ely, and other institutional economists carried over the four utilities concept into marketing, while marketing pioneers influenced by Taussig, Marshall, and other neoclassical economists generally did not. The institutional influence was apparently greater, because ultimately the four utility concept emerged as a fundamental precept of early marketing thought.

IV. THE NATURE AND SCOPE OF MARKETING

Most of the earliest marketing scholars either implicitly implied or explicitly expressed the four utilities concept as the foundation of the newly emerging discipline of marketing. The utilities concept originally served two related purposes. One was to delimit the scope of the field by separating marketing activity (producing time, place, and possession utilities) from farming and manufacturing activities (creating form utility). The second purpose was to demonstrate that because it created value the nature of marketing was productive, like other economic activity, as could be shown by the various marketing utilities.

Even before the name "marketing" emerged from the term "distribution," the earliest writers in the field implied the four utilities concept to describe the nature and scope of middlemen and later all of marketing. In retailing, for example, E. D. Jones (1905, p. 11) writes: "The task of the retailer is to furnish the consumer goods wanted, at the time and in the quantity and place desired." Nystrom (1915, p. 1) extends the utilities concept to distribution as a whole: "To move goods from where they are, to places where and when they are wanted; ... and to get the goods from the producers and place them in the hands of the consumers—this is the problem of the distribution of goods." Both writers clearly suggest the various utilities.

To separate manufacturing from marketing activities, Shaw (1912, p. 764) implies two types of utility. In an article on "Some problems of market distribution," he writes: "Industry is concerned with the application of motion to matter to change its form and place. The change in form we term production; the change in place, distribution." In his subsequent book, *An Approach to Business Problems*, Shaw (1915, p. 7) expands his matter in motion metaphor to "times, places, forms and conditions." Of these four motions, production caused changes by altering the form of materials, while distribution caused changes by transporting the goods to create place utility, storing the goods to create time utility, and transferring ownership of the goods to create possession utility (p. 7). Again, Shaw separates manufacturing and marketing by including form in the former, and adding the creation of possession utility to time and place utilities in the latter.

Including marketing in his definition of production as "the creation of utilities," Weld (1916, p. 5) explicitly states "utility may be divided [into] form, time, place, and possession utilities." Form is related to "manufacturing or crop raising" and the last three utilities are related to marketing activities. In a theme that came to permeate the marketing literature, Weld concludes: "Marketing begins where the manufacturing process ends" (p. 6).

From this point onward, the four utilities concept emerges as a cornerstone of marketing. Time, place, and possession utilities are implied in the definitions of the field by most of marketing's earliest textbook authors (Ivey 1921; Clark 1922; Moriarty 1923; etc.). For example, Clark (1922, p. 1) states: "Marketing consists of those efforts which effect transfers in ownership of goods and services and care for their physical distribution." Implying the utility concept in his definition of marketing, he continues "sellers must know what buyers want, and buyers must know what is for sale;...goods must be physically moved to places at which they are wanted by the time they are wanted" (p. 1). In discussing the "great division of business activities," Clark writes about: "The activities of production which change the form of materials" and "the activities of distribution which changes the place, time and ownership of the commodities thus produced" (p. 7). He also recognizes a potential semantic problem and is careful to distinguish between the meaning economists and businessmen attach to the term production:

> To the economists the creation of utilities, such as...time, place, and possession utility is included in the process known as production. [To the businessman] production is generally used in a narrower sense which excludes these activities and includes only the creation of elementary and form [utilities] (1922, p. 9).

It is important to bear in mind the distinction in the meaning of the term production, between the economists from whom marketing pioneers learned, on the one hand, and the businessmen who they taught, on the other hand. This variation in meaning frequently caused confusion in the literature and often required clarification.

Moriarty includes all utilities in production, in the economists' sense of the term. In describing "the conditions under which things of value are produced," he writes (1923, p. 13): "all material products contain in greater or less measure four different kinds of utilities: (1) elementary or raw materials..., (2) form..., (3) place..., and (4) time." Note the economic influence on some marketing writers in retaining the original version of the four utilities concept that includes elementary and excludes possession utility. Moreover, Moriarty makes no distinction between marketing and non-marketing types of utility.

On the other hand, most marketing writers highlight the difference between marketing and non-marketing utilities. Butler (1923, p. 21), for example, uses the utility concept quite emphatically to define the scope of the field: "With elementary and form utility the marketing organization has nothing to do, but with place and time utility it has very much to do." He also introduces the labor productivity issue to describe the nature of marketing. Noting that middlemen, like farmers and manufacturers, are also productive, Butler offers the example: "The men who grow wheat and the men who grind it into flour are not the only producers, we must also class as producers those who transport the flour to the place where it is needed and those who hold it there until it is needed" (p. 22). Again, the term producers is used in the economic sense.

A few marketing authors, for example Moriarty (1923) and Butler (1923), favored the economic version of the four utilities concept that includes elementary utility and excludes possession utility. Still fewer writers, such as Macklin (1924), favored five utilities which includes both elementary and possession utility along with the other three utilities of form, time, and place. The vast majority of thinkers in the field, however, preferred to exclude the term elementary utility, but include the concept (farm products) as a part of form utility (that originally only dealt with manufactured products).

This modern treatment of the four utilities concept and its use in describing the nature and scope of marketing are found in the original textbooks, and subsequent revisions, of two groups of marketing scholars whose views were particularly influential on later marketing writers. In *Principles of Marketing*, Maynard, Beckman, and Weidler (1927, p. 5) write: "While the farmers and manufacturers create form utilities, traders, transportation companies, and other marketing agencies create place, time and possession utilities. All of these activities are productive in the same sense as are changes in form."

The separation of utilities to describe the scope of the field was also emphasized in the definition found in the opening sentence of the *Elements of Marketing* by Converse and Huegy (1930, p. 1): "Marketing includes all the activities involved in the creation of place, time and possession utilities." Furthermore: "The fabrication, or change of form, which occurs in the factory, farm, forest, fishery, or mine is called production by many businessmen" (p. 1). These authors also carefully distinguish between the businessman's view of factory and farm workers as production from the economists use of the term. (Subsequent writers, however, do not always make such meticulous distinctions.)

The 1930 Converse and Huegy version of the four utilities concept continued to be found in the six later editions of their texts (including Mitchell as an author), going up to 1965. It is also found in all nine editions of the marketing textbooks written by Beckman and his various coauthors from 1927 to 1969. Because the textbooks of Beckman and Converse and others dominated the marketing discipline for more than forty years, their influence on succeeding generations of marketing writers was profound.

Since its introduction by the pioneers and refinement by subsequent marketing scholars, the overwhelming majority of marketing textbook writers, decade by decade and generation by generation, included a description of the four utilities concept to describe the nature and scope of marketing. (see among many others: Agnew, Jenkins, and Drury 1936; Alexander, Surface, Elder, and Alderson 1944; Phillips and Duncan 1951; Matthews, Buzzell, Levitt, and Frank 1964; Stanton 1975; Kotler 1988). Their treatment of the four utilities concept is essentially similar, but without the meticulous distinctions in terminology suggested by Beckman and Converse.

In a typical example, an AMA-published textbook describes the nature of "marketing as a productive process." Yet in defining the scope of the field it notes, "creating possession, place, and time utilities are marketing activities" whereas the creation of "form utility is production" (AMA Committee 1961, p. 3). The problem is that the terminology is not just inconsistent, it is contradictory. If marketing is productive, then something is being produced; if something is produced, then marketing is involved in production. Such a lack of precision in terminology, lead Beckman and Davidson (1967, p. 7) to complain that the term "production has been narrowly construed." In this larger economic meaning of producing utility, many marketing writers regard marketing as an element of production. For example, Alexander, Surface, Elder, and Alderson observe:

> The student should be careful to remember that the word "production" is almost never used in its technical economic sense...of creating want-satisfying power. Writers.-..habitually use the term in the sense in which it is employed by the average layman or businessmen (1944, p. 10, N. 10).

Using the four utilities to define the scope of marketing, by differentiating it from manufacturing, has caused confusion in recognizing that marketing is productive because it is part of the production process. Indeed, Alderson (1965, pp. 37-8) recognized the productive nature of both firms *and* households as "organized behavior systems" using inputs to produce outputs. Modern writers now speak of the household as a productive entity organized around a production function (Muth 1965). The problem of what is production arises because of the early use of the terms production and distribution. When the term marketing evolved from distribution the complimentary term production was not replaced by manufacturing, leading to the present confusion. Replacing the term production with manufacturing, which is what is usually meant when distinguishing "production" from marketing, would provide considerable precision in terminology.

Aside from the semantic confusion in defining the scope of the field based on types of utilities, a stronger argument than the four utilities concept can be made to demonstrate the productive nature of marketing. The argument is based on the concept of value added (Beckman 1955). Simply, marketing activity is productive, because it is work that adds value to goods as part of the process of producing utility. Its advantages are noted by Beckman and Davidson (1967, p. 813): "The value added concept is consistent with...consumer-oriented concepts of marketing management...measuring the economic values created in the marketing process,...and...*emphasizes the productive character of marketing*" (italics in original).

Using the four utilities concept to define the nature and scope of marketing has been shown to have difficulties. Next we turn to its use in organizing marketing functions.

V.   THE MARKETING FUNCTIONS

Another application of the four utilities concept was its use in identifying the functions of marketing. Although there are similarities and considerable overlap in various authors' lists of marketing functions, there are almost as many lists as there are authors. Lists of between six and twelve functions are the most common (Faria 1983), but a list of over one hundred marketing functions was also proposed (Ryan 1935). The problem this creates for marketing thought is that if writers can argue lists ranging from six to over one hundred functions based on the same four utilities concept, then the relationship between functions and utilities is tenuous at best.

The most comprehensive examination of marketing functions was made by Ryan (1935), who reviewed more than two dozen prior studies of the subject. His analysis showed that all lists of marketing functions were based on two implied questions. The more important question was: "What functions add time, place, ownership, and other kinds of utilities to physical goods as they gradually move toward the point where they are sold to final consumers?" (p. 212). The second question was what functions do businesses perform to "carry on the work of distribution?" (p. 212).

Much of the confusion in the various lists of functions could be attributed to the secondary question, the functions related to operating a business. Nevertheless, with respect to the primary question, those functions adding utility, the four utilities concept still does not offer much basis for clarity. To match a number of the functions proposed, Ryan (1935, p. 222) was forced to add more than a half dozen new utilities. Some of the confusing terminology this creates is illustrated by comparing the traditional utilities along with several new ones as shown on the next page:

Function	Utilities Added
Transforming Materials, Packaging	Form
Storage	Time
Transportation	Place
Buying and Selling	Ownership (Possession)
Dividing (Breaking Bulk)	Size
Branding and Trade-Marking	Distinction
Special Services to Customers	Goodwill
Credit	Credit
Guarantees	Confidence

The difficulty with relating functions and utilities is that lists of functions appear limited only by an author's imagination making them extremely arbitrary, which also renders any relationship at least as capricious. More recently the four utilities concept has been related to the four P's of marketing management (e.g., McDaniel and Darden 1987; Mason and Ezell 1987; Kotler 1988; among many others). This application of the concept is perhaps the most problematic.

VI. THE FOUR P's OF MARKETING MANAGEMENT

The four utilities concept has a certain intuitive appeal to marketing management because of its long history and correspondence with some identifiable elements of the marketing mix. The product "P" is linked to form utility, the place "P" to time and place utilities, even the price and promotion "P's" are sometimes vaguely associated with possession utility. Despite its intuitive appeal, however, the concept contains a number of inherent problems for marketing management.

Bucklin (1966, p. 8) was one of the first to recognize there might be difficulties. He notes that by linking "production and consumption" within a trade channel, the four utilities concept "has much merit;" but he also observes: "From the point of view of marketing management, this distinction among utilities makes little sense." Bucklin regards this point as so obvious as not to require further explanation; but other writers explain.

Apparently based on Alderson's (1957, p. 199) view of marketing as "matching a small segment of supply with a small segment of demand," Dixon and Grashof (1979, p. 1) argue that attempting to align the four utilities offered to consumers with the four P's provided by marketing management results in a mismatch:

It is difficult to identify the 'match' between form, time, place and possession utilities which represent the demand side, and the product, price, promotion and place variables manipulated by the seller which represent the supply side. The problem is complicated

further by the common view that marketing is not associated with 'form' utility, even though
the 'product' which is manipulated by the marketing manager does seem to have a form
element. Moreover, it is not at all clear in what sense buyers demand 'price and promotion.'

From the marketing management perspective, time and place utility result from
the physical distribution functions of transportation and storage, what is
known as the place "P". Attempting to relate the other P's and U's raise more
questions than they answer.

A. Form Utility

Of the four utilities the most problematic in marketing management is
dealing with form utility. There are two problems. One is specifying what
constitutes form utility, and a second problem is who creates it: manufacturing
or marketing?

The first problem involves whether form utility includes products only or
both products and services. Early writers regarded form utility as relating to
tangible goods alone. Modern thinkers in marketing management generally
conclude that form utility includes both; however, examples almost always
discuss products and almost never mention services. The four utilities is
deficient if it fails to adequately deal with services. To exclude something as
important as the utility created by services from marketing would render the
four utilities concept impotent. Yet to include services in form utility appears
to be a contradiction in terms, since by its very nature services lack corporeal
form. The problem is clear: if form utility is created on the farm or the factory
floor by fashioning materials into the products desired by consumers, then what
do service workers produce?

Although marketing management authors seldom elaborate on the product-
service issue, a few production economists have. John D. Black (1926), for
example, argues that form utility embraces both products and services. With
products satisfaction results from human effort applied to material things, and
in the case of service production satisfaction results from human effort applied
to people; and he argues that both produce changes in form. The form element
is easy to visualize in some of the service examples Black provides, such as
"the barber produces changes in form" (1930, p. 38). Similarly, in one of the
few examples relating services to form utility in a marketing management text,
Pride and Ferrell (1985, p. 260) note that "service retailers, like hair styling
and dry cleaning provide aspects of form utility that are usually associated with
the production process."

In some service production, however, the form element is less apparent. Even
Black (1930, p. 30) realized some of his examples appeared over-extended: "It
is refining a good deal to say that a singer is producing changes of form in
the ear membranes of his audience; or that a lecturer is producing changes

of form in the brain cells of his students." Rather than stretching to fit services into the category of form utility, another production economist suggests service as a fifth type of utility. Paul F. Gemmill (1935, p. 68) argues: "There are persons engaged in creating service utility...those who are rendering personal service rather than dealing in concrete goods." Thus, some authors believe that services produce form utility, while others hold that what they produce is service utility. Still another view is that it may not matter. Alderson (1965) argues that consumers want neither products nor services per se, but "bundles of utilities." These bundles are produced by the utility inherent in an assortment of products and services.

The second problem of form utility involves the category in which it belongs—manufacturing or marketing (Shaw 1988). Historically, most marketing writers in attempting to distinguish marketing functions from manufacturing activities included form in the latter. A few marketing authors, however, have recognized that form utility is at least sometimes created by marketing.

As previously noted, J. B. Clark (1886) who conceived the four utilities concept considered merchants breaking bulk as producers of form utility along with manufacturers. A modernized version of this aspect of utility appears in Kotler (1988, p. 138) who renames the process of breaking bulk the creation of "quantity utility;" Ryan (1935, p. 222) called it "size utility." Apparently, following Alderson's (1965) concept of discrepancy of assortment, Kotler also terms the building up of a collection of products the creation of "assortment utility." Although not stating it, if Kotler regards these "new" utilities as attributes of products, as earlier authors did, this would imply that he believes marketing creates at least some aspects of form utility.

Other writers have also seen marketing's hand in the creation of form utility. For example, Breyer (1934, p. 13) observes "that marketing creates possession, time and place utilities and, incidentally, some form utilities." Ryan (1935, p. 207) was even more emphatic in arguing that form utility is always created by marketing activity: "The creation of form utility, as a matter of fact, is merely one of the many elements of the marketing process." Further, Ryan emphasizes that marketing is an element of production: "The only scientific definition of production is the 'creation of utilities or want-satisfying powers.' Production never stops until the goods are used by final consumers.... all the elements of the marketing process are production" (p. 224). It has also been argued by Tousley, Clark, and Clark (1962, p. 5) that marketing does not exclusively produce any of the four utilities: "the creation of time, place and possession utilities does not always involve marketing." They also note that "marketing is a part of production" (p. 5).

Most authors generally accept the idea of marketing and non-marketing utilities, and the inclusion of form in the latter. Yet some writers are critical of separating utilities into two categories. After originally embracing the four utilities concept, Alderson (1944, 1954) ultimately came to a diametrically opposite conclusion: "It is a highly arbitrary procedure to divide the utilities provided to the consumer into two parts and to say one part [form utility] is created by production and the other part by marketing" (1957, pp. 68-9). Holding stock in inventory, drop shipping, and even moving plants closer to customers by manufacturers create time and place utilities; and factory outlets and direct catalog mailings offer possession utility. On the other hand, retail clothing stores providing alterations, automobile dealers making repairs, and bakeries or restaurants preparing foods, for example, are creating form utility.

Many marketing management writers have also experienced difficulties in attempting to exclude form utility from marketing. For example, McCarthy (1960, p. 30) recognizes that form utility is at least partly related to marketing. Time, place, and possession utility are definitely created by marketing, and...the creation of form utility, usually considered a production activity, should be directed by marketing." Rather than marketing directing the creation of form utility, however, McCarthy later falls back on the standard treatment, begun by Weld (1916), of taking the form utility created by a manufacturer as the starting point for marketing. He writes that the task of marketing management is "to provide the product already possessing form utility with time and place utility. When this is accomplished, the consumer will enjoy possession utility" (pp. 314-15). This treatment is repeated in revisions of his text over the next thirty years.

There is no apparent logic for regarding form utility an exclusive element of manufacturing operations rather than considering it a component of marketing management, since a major purpose of market research is to provide brand specifications of what consumers presumably want. Manufacturing may make products but marketing management is responsible for identifying what is wanted in the same sense that transportation agencies may move products but marketing management is responsible for identifying where they are wanted.

In sum, to have relevance for modern marketing management, service utility requires the same recognition and consideration as form utility. Moreover, relevance requires both utilities be regarded as elements of marketing management, rather than manufacture or service production, per se, since marketing management is responsible for specifying the quality and quantity of the service or product "P". In addition to these issues there are other problems relating P's and U's.

B. Possession Utility

Possession utility is apparently the catch-all category for various missing elements of the marketing mix. Hasty and Will (1975, p. 6), include price, promotion and research in possession utility, but do not explain how they are related. Similarly, price and promotion are linked to possession utility by Boone and Kurtz (1980, p. 291), who discuss promotion as enhancing the price of acquiring possession utility: "Promotion can provide more ownership utility to buyers, thereby accentuating the value of a product." The argument is that promotion may enhance consumer perceptions of the status of a product allowing prestige pricing.

There is a more direct argument relating the price "P" to possession utility, without the necessity of entangling it with promotion. Simply, price represents the exchange value of transferring ownership or use rights to market goods. Price is therefore a measure of what consumers will spend to obtain possession utility. Nevertheless, few marketing writers mention any relationship between the price "P" and possession utility and still fewer provide any rationale.

On the other hand, many authors relate the promotion "P", to possession utility. For example, Schewe and Smith (1983, p. 7) write: "learning that a product is available and then gaining ownership is called possession utility." Similarly, McDaniel and Darden (1987, p. 5) note: "advertising facilitates possession;" and Mason and Ezell (1987, p. 14) state that "creating awareness helps create [possession] utility." The argument is essentially a two step process. Information is inherent in possession utility because if consumers have possession of a product, then logically they must have had the information necessary to acquire it (Hasty and Will 1975, p. 6). Simply, information is a prerequisite to purchase.

The rationale for promotion as an element of possession utility, however, raises a larger problem than it resolves. It could also be said that form, time and place utilities are included in possession utility. For consumers to derive satisfaction from possession utility then by definition form, time, and place utility are present, just as information must be present. But if promotion is not related to possession utility, then where does it fit?

C. Information Utility

One way to handle at least part of the promotion "P" is to relate it to information utility. Hotchkiss (1933, pp. 67-68) observes that "advertising adds utility," and he used the term "information utility," recognizing: "the value of any commodity depends on knowledge of its existence and uses." Although the cost and value of information search has been identified (Stigler 1961), the utility of information has not gained much recognition in the marketing management literature.

A failure to consider the utility of information was not an oversight by the economists who originally developed the utilities concept. Using a model of perfect competition, people were assumed to have perfect information. Marketing management writers using a model of imperfect competition, however, acclaim the value of promotional activities in reducing buyer search costs, but have not developed a corresponding concept of information utility to explain it. And yet, unless the value of information utility is explicitly postulated there cannot logically be any perception of what exists in the environment; hence, no knowledge of what is wanted, nor where, when and from whom it is wanted. Therefore, the other four utilities all become irrelevant.

In summary, to make the four utility concept relevant to marketing management it is at least necessary to bring it up to date. This requires patching-up problems with form utility by adding services utility to the product "P", and including both in the domain of marketing management. Possession utility should be explicitly related to the price "P". It is also necessary to postulate information utility to justify the promotional "P". Yet even after bringing the utilities concept into closer alignment with the variables manipulated by the marketing manager, a more fundamental problem remains.

VII.   THE GENERAL PROBLEM OF THE FOUR UTILITIES CONCEPT

The various difficulties in applying the four utilities concept in marketing are symptomatic of a more generic problem. The four (or more) utilities concept is not based on an underlying conceptual framework. The various utilities represent, ultimately, an ad hoc classification. The categories are neither mutually exclusive (as evidenced by form and possession utilities) nor collectively exhaustive (as evidenced by assortment, service, information, and other proposed utilities).

The weaknesses of the categories in the four utilities concept has not gone unnoticed. Black (1926, p. 30) regards these categories as only pedagogically useful and in no sense final. He notes that "some [activity]...is hard to fit into any...category" and it is "not necessary that all [work] shall fit into these four groups." Black concludes that the categories were "introduced only for the sake of convenience in discussion, and if it confuses more than it helps to force a particular [activity] into one of these groups, it had better not be done." Gemmill (1935, p. 69) also expresses reservations about regarding the various classes of utility as a final conceptual scheme. He writes: "The classifications...are not necessarily hard and fast," and he also concludes: "they are made largely on an arbitrary basis."

Alderson's (1954) reservations about the arbitrary nature of separating utilities into marketing and non-marketing types were previously noted. A stronger objection, similar to the unity of utility point raised by Menger (1871), is based on Alderson's (1957, p. 69) reasoning that "there is a fallacy...in breaking down utilities into separate aspects, since it is an all or none proposition." That is, if one of the four utilities is missing, say for example wrong place, then the right product, at the right time, for the right customer all become irrelevant. This is even more apparent in the case of personal services, form, time, place, and possession are often aspects of the service that occur contemporaneously with use by the consumer.

The difficulties of attempting to patch up the four utilities concept appear insurmountable. Separating utilities into four, five, six, or more types is arbitrary at best and misleading at worst. Because of the weakness of the categories and the fallacious all or nothing logic, the usefulness of the concept to explain future marketing phenomena is also questionable.

VIII. CONCLUSION

Early on, the four utilities concept was used to describe the nature and scope of marketing. Its productive nature was shown because marketing provided time, place, and possession utilities, which were as important as the form utility provided by manufacturing or farming. The value added concept, however, provided a stronger argument for explaining the productive nature of marketing than the four utilities concept. The scope of marketing was described by separating the field from other productive activities on the basis of marketing and non-marketing utilities. In defining marketing's scope, however, semantic confusion occurred over the term production.

Moreover, the four utilities concept was applied to identifying marketing functions, but this relationship was also shown to be tenuous. It was noted that lists of utilities, like lists of functions, are limited only by the imagination of the author. Hence, early applications of the four utilities concept can at best be described as problematic.

The four utilities concept is currently being used to provide a foundation for the four P's of marketing management. However, this application was shown to result in a mismatch. There are problems with the utilities included in the concept, such as form and possession, and the utilities excluded from the concept, such as service and information. Therefore, the concept offers little benefit for marketing management.

Even if these difficulties could be resolved, a more general problem remains. The categories are neither mutually exclusive nor collectively exhaustive making them arbitrary at best, and the all-or-nothing fallacy in the logic of the concept makes it misleading at worst. Thus, the four utilities concept appears to offer little potential for explaining future marketing phenomena.

It is difficult to assign a concept to the scrap heap of history, especially one as old as the discipline itself. The lack of utility for the four utilities concept, however, argues for its demise. Significantly, more than a century after the origination of the concept modern writers are still tinkering with it, adding new elements (e.g., information, quantity, and assortment utilities) and blurring old ones (e.g., form and possession utilities). The tinkering has not lead to any consensus arguing that it is the idiosyncratic opinions of individual authors rather than improvements on the basic idea, which further argues the lack of an adequate conceptual foundation underlying the four utilities concept.

When problems appear in a conceptual framework, and attempts at resolving them raise more questions than are answered, the paradigm itself must undergo a shift (Kuhn 1970). Ultimately, as Alderson (1957, p. 69) suggested: "What is needed is not an interpretation of the utility created by marketing, but a marketing interpretation of the whole process of creating utility." Moreover, Alderson recommended the rudiments of a solution: "Progressive differentiation is the key to defining the values created by marketing" (p. 70). Progressive differentiation is the continuous process of shaping and fitting, extension, modification or refinement in assortments, from original sellers of raw materials, through intermediate purchases and sales to final buyers of finished goods, so that they more closely approximate consumer requirements for an assortment of products and services. Thus, because of its lack of utility, the four utilities concept should be abandoned in favor of developing a more tenable explanation of marketing's role in the production of utility.

REFERENCES

Agnew, H. E., R. B. Jenkins, and J.C. Drury. (1936). *Outlines of Marketing*. New York: McGraw-Hill.

Alderson, W. (1954). "Factors Governing the Development of Marketing Channels." In *Marketing Channels*, edited by R. M. Clewett. Homewood, IL: Irwin.

Alderson, W. (1957). *Marketing Behavior and Executive Action*. Homewood, IL: Irwin.

Alderson, W. (1965). *Dynamic Marketing Behavior*. Homewood, IL: Irwin.

Alexander, R. S., F. M. Surface, R. Elder, and W. Alderson. (1944). *Marketing*. New York: Ginn and Company.

AMA Committee on Marketing. (1961). *Principles of Marketing*. New York: Pitman Publishing.

Bartels, R. (1951). "Influences on the Development of Marketing Thought, 1900-1923." *Journal of Marketing*, 16; pp. 1-14.

Bartels, R. (1962). *The Development of Marketing Thought*. Homewood IL: Irwin.

Beckman, T. N. (1955). "The Value Added Concept as Applied to Marketing and its Implications." Pp. 83-99 in *Frontiers in Marketing Thought*, edited by S. Rewoldt. Bloomington IN: Indiana University Press.

Beekman, T. N. and W. R. Davidson. (1967). *Marketing* (8th ed.). New York: Ronald Press.

Black, J. D. (1926). *Production Economics*. New York: Henry Holt Company.

Boone, L. E. and D. L. Kurtz. (1980). *Contemporary Marketing*. Hinsdale, IL: Dryden Press.

Breyer, R. F. (1934). *The Marketing Institution*. New York: McGraw-Hill.

Bucklin, L. (1966). *A Theory of Distribution Cost Structure*. IBER, University of California-Berkeley Press.

Butler, R. S. (1923). *Marketing Merchandising*. New York: Alexander Hamilton Institute.

Clark, F. E. (1922). *Principles of Marketing*. New York: Macmillan.

Clark, J. B. (1886). *The Philosophy of Wealth*. Boston: Ginn & Company.

Converse, P. D. and H. W. Huegy. (1930). *The Elements of Marketing*. New York: Prentice-Hall.

Dixon, D. F. and J. F. Grashof. (1979). *"An Alternative View of Marketing Management."* Unpublished manuscript, Temple University.

Ellis, D. S. and L. W. Jacobs. (1977). "Marketing Utilities: A New Look." *Journal of the Academy of Marketing Science*, 5(1); pp. 21-26.

Ely, R. T. (1889). *An Introduction to Political Economy*. New York: Chautauqua Press.

Ely, R. T. (1893). *Outlines of Economics*. New York: Hunt and Eaton.

Faria, A. J. (1983). "The Development of the Functional Approach to the Study of Marketing to 1940." Pp. 160-169 in *Proceeding of the First North American Workshop on Historical Research in Marketing*, edited by S. C. Hollander and R. Savitt. East Lansing: Michigan State University Press.

Franklin, B. (1767 [1906]). "Notes." In *The Collected Writings of Benjamin Franklin* Volume 5, 102, edited by A. H. Smyth. New York: MacMillan, 1906.

Gemmill, P. F. (1935). *Fundamentals of Economics*. New York: Harper & Brothers.

Hasty, R. W. and T. R. Will. (1975). *Marketing*. San Francisco: Canfield Press.

Hotchkiss, G. B. (1933). *An Outline of Advertising*. New York: MacMillan.

Ivey, P. W. (1921). *Principles of Marketing*. New York: Ronald Press.

Jones, E. D. (1905). "The Manufacturer and the Domestic Market." *The Annals of the American Academy*, 25; pp. 1-20.

Jones, D.G. and D. D. Monieson. (1987). "Origins of the Institutional Approach in Marketing. Pp. 149-168 in *Marketing in Three Eras*, edited by T. Nevett and S. C. Hollander. East Lansing: Michigan State University Press.

Kotler, P. (1988). *Marketing Management*. Englewood Cliffs, NJ: Prentice Hall.

Kuhn, T. S. (1970). *The Structure of Scientific Revolutions*. Chicago: University of Chicago Press.

Macklin, T. (1924). *Efficient Marketing for Agriculture*. New York: MacMillan.

Mason, J. B. and H. F. Ezell. (1987). *Marketing Principles and Strategy*. Plano, TX: Business Publications.

Marshall, A. (1920). *Principles of Economics*. New York: MacMillan.

Matthews, J. B., R.D. Buzzell, T. Levitt, and R. E. Frank. (1964). *Marketing: An Introductory Analysis*. New York: McGraw-Hill.

Maynard, H. H., W. C. Weidler, and T. N. Beckman. (1927). *Principles of Marketing*. New York: Ronald Press.

McCullock, J. R. (1844). *The Principles of Political Economy*. Edinburgh: Adam and Charles Black.

McCarthy, E. J. (1960). *Basic Marketing: A Managerial Approach*. Homewood, IL: Irwin.

McDaniel, C., Jr. and W. R. Darden. (1987). *Marketing*. Boston: Allyn & Bacon.

Menger, C. (1871[1950]). *Principles of Economics*. Glencoe, IL: The Free Press.

Moriarty, W. D. (1923). *The Economics of Marketing and Advertising*. New York: Harper & Brothers.

Muth, R. F. (1965). "Household Production Theory." *The American Economic Review* (Dec); pp. 997-1003.

Nystrum, P. H. (1915). *The Economics of Retailing*. New York: Ronald Press.

Phillips, C. F. and D. J. Duncan. (1951). *Marketing Principles and Methods*. Chicago: Richard D. Irwin.

Pride, W. M. and O. C. Ferrell. (1985). *Marketing: Basic Concepts and Decisions*. Boston: Houghton Mifflin.

Ryan, F. W. (1935). "Functional Elements in Market Distribution." *Harvard Business Review*, (2); pp. 205-224.

Schewe, C. D. and R. M. Smith. (1983). *Marketing Concepts and Applications*. New York: McGraw-Hill.

Schumpeter, J. A. (1968). *History of Economic Analysis*. New York: Oxford University Press.

Shaw, A. (1912). "Some Problems in Market Distribution." *Quarterly Journal of Economics*, 26; pp. 703-765.

Shaw, A. (1915). *An Approach to Business Problems*. Cambridge: Harvard University Press.

Shaw, E. H. (1988). "An Historical Analysis of Form Utility: Is it Created by Manufacturing Operations or Marketing Management?" Pp. 105-107 in *Proceedings of the AMA Winter Educators' Conference*,edited by S. Shapiro and A. H. Walle. Chicago: AMA Press.

Smith, A. (1776[1937]). *The Wealth of Nations*. New York: The Modern Library.

Stanton, W. J. (1975). *Fundamentals of Marketing*. New York: McGraw-Hill.

Stigler, G. (1961). "The Economics of Information." *Journal of Political Economy*,LXIX(3); pp. 213-224.

Taussig, F. W. (1915). *Principles of Economics*. New York: MacMillan.

Tousley, R. D., E. Clark, and F. Clark. (1962). *Principles of Marketing*. New York: MacMillan.

Turgot, A. R. J. (1766[1958]). "Reflections." Reprinted in *Early Economic Thought*. New York: The Modern Library.

Weld, L. D. H. (1916). *The Marketing of Farm Products*. New York: MacMillan.

BIOGRAPHY AND THE HISTORY OF MARKETING THOUGHT:

HENRY CHARLES TAYLOR AND EDWARD DAVID JONES

D. G. Brian Jones

ABSTRACT

This article outlines a biographical approach to the study of the history of marketing thought and illustrates that approach with biographical essays on two pioneer marketing scholars—Henry Charles Taylor and Edward David Jones. Both Taylor and Jones began their academic careers at the University of Wisconsin, one of the earliest centers of development in marketing thought.

So let great authors have their due, as time, which is the author of authors, be not deprived of his due, which is further and further to discover the truth.
—Francis Bacon

Research in Marketing, Supplement 6, pages 67-85.
ISBN: 1-55938-187-6

I. INTRODUCTION

Between 1956 and 1962 the *Journal of Marketing* featured 23 biographical sketches of "Pioneers in Marketing." This series was distinctive in its focus on some of the earliest and most distinguished marketing scholars—pioneers in the marketing discipline. Several of these sketches were later revised and two others added in a compilation by Wright and Dimsdale (1974). A further series of biographical sketches was also included in Paul Converse's (1959) *The Beginning of Marketing Thought in the United States with Reminiscences of Some of the Pioneer Marketing Scholars*. This collection of biographical work provides many insights into the development of marketing thought.

Biography can contribute in many ways to our understanding of the history of ideas. It can help explain the genesis of a scholar's work, how it came to include certain ideas, the ideological underpinnings of a subject's thought, and the social, economic, and political context that gave rise to certain ideas (Jaffe 1965; Walker 1983). Biography can also shed light on the sociology of knowledge by examining the transmission of ideas (Stigler 1976) and their acceptance by a scholar's contemporaries (Jaffe 1965). Finally, in recognizing important, interesting scholars, biography can be valuable for its own sake.

Biography, like other forms of historical research, is a very time-consuming process involving the careful study of vast quantities of information (Nevett 1983) from a wide variety of sources. Personal biography deals with where the subject was born, raised, and lived, family influences, and personal traits. Professional biography includes the academic, government, and business positions a subject held, as well as professional affiliations and activities. Environmental biography refers to the economic, social, and political conditions in which a subject lived. Finally, intellectual biography includes the ideas and information, the literature (both published and unpublished), studied by the individual (Walker 1983).

The biographical essays on Edward David Jones and Henry Charles Taylor presented herein make use of all of these types of data, although the focus is on professional and intellectual biography, especially in the essay on Jones. More specifically, the primary sources of data for this work included unpublished correspondence, manuscripts, and autobiographical materials, records of scholarly organizations, as well as publications (some of which have nevertheless gone unrecognized by marketing historians) by the two scholars in question. The archival sources were found in various collections listed in the reference section of this article. The Taylor collection, for example, is a rich source of some 67 boxes of manuscripts covering the period from 1896 to 1967.

The two scholars whose lives and careers are examined here, have been recognized by marketing historians, but the depth of their contributions has not yet been appreciated. Jones, whose academic career extended from 1895 to 1901 at the University of Wisconsin, and from 1901 to 1919 at the University of Michigan, is credited only for teaching the first university course in marketing in North America (Bartels 1951, p. 3; Maynard 1941, p. 382). However, his contributions to the marketing literature included the development of a functional approach to the study of marketing, articulation of a primitive version of the marketing concept, and what he referred to as a "moral conception of the merchant."

Taylor's academic career extended from 1901 to 1919 at the University of Wisconsin, and from 1925 to 1928 at Northwestern University. Paul Converse made the first known reference, if only in passing, to Taylor as an early contributor to marketing ideas (1945, p. 19). Converse suspected that Taylor might have preceded Arch W. Shaw (1912) in originating a functional approach to the study of marketing (Converse 1944). However, widely recognized as the father of agricultural economics in North America, at a time when the commodity approach in marketing was at its peak, Taylor's full contributions to the development of marketing thought have not been appreciated.

However else this paper may contribute to our understanding of the history of marketing thought, its primary purpose is to give two pioneer marketing scholars their due.

II. HENRY CHARLES TAYLOR: 1873-1969

Henry Taylor was born on April 16, 1873 on a farm in southeast Iowa. His recollections of childhood focused on lessons in the "art of farm management" taught by his father, the values of a good Christian life instilled by his mother, and on grade-school teachers who recognized in young Henry a sharp mind and who encouraged him to pursue an education (1960, chap. 1). Taylor described those lessons learned in the home and on the farm as "fundamental to all of the [subsequent] education received from universities and from life's activities" (1960, p. 17).

Taylor's father was a successful farmer. However, during the 1890s the U.S. economy was in the depths of a depression and farmers seemed to be hit particularly hard. Taylor's father became a member of the Grange which was pressing for legislation to improve prices of farm products. From these conditions Henry Taylor derived inspiration and an ambition that guided his education and career. He decided to "get an education, become a successful farmer and then go to Congress to promote legislation which would help farmers" (1960, p. 18). Eventually, Taylor accomplished all three of these goals.

The first step in that direction was taken in 1891 when Taylor entered Drake University to study agriculture. In 1893, he transferred to Iowa State College (later Iowa State University at Ames) where his studies "had to do with the material side of agriculture" (1960, p. 21). He completed a Bachelor degree in agriculture in 1896 and that same year received a Master of Science in agriculture for a thesis on "Tenancy and Farm Ownership."

Having studied the physical side of farming, Taylor felt a need to learn about the social sciences in relation to agriculture. In 1896, he was drawn to the University of Wisconsin and to Richard T. Ely, director of the School of Economics. In Taylor's words:

> Professor Ely was a social economist. He gave emphasis to John Stuart Mills' view that while in the production of wealth, man must keep step with natural laws, human institutions were the determining factor in the distribution of wealth. Ely taught that the distribution of wealth could be improved by modifying economic institutions. He stressed that in modifying social economic institutions the general welfare is always to be kept in mind as the goal. He taught that private property is not absolute; it is a 'social trust' and may be modified in the interest of the general welfare (1960, p. 26).

Ely had been looking for a student to specialize in agricultural economics. However, that subject was not yet well developed in North America, so he advised Taylor to spend some time studying in Europe "where [the studies of] agricultural problems were in a more advanced stage" (Taylor 1960, p. 31). In general, it was Ely's habit to encourage his graduate students to spend time studying in Germany where he himself had studied under Karl Knies, Ernst Engel, and Johannes Conrad of the Historical School of Economics. Ely admired the Historical School for its inductive, statistical, comparative methodology, a positivistic epistemology, pedagogical pragmatism, and its explicit concern with ethics, sometimes manifested in social activism (Herbst 1965; Myles 1956).

Following Ely's advice, in 1899, Taylor went to England, then to Germany where he studied agricultural economics under Johannes Conrad at the University of Halle and under Max Sering at the University of Berlin. At the latter institution, Taylor also took courses from the notable historical economists, Wagner and Schmoller. At Halle, Conrad's courses in agricultural economics were described by Taylor as "historical and descriptive in character" concentrating on the political economy of agriculture rather than on the technical aspects of farming (Taylor 1941, p. 95).

Taylor returned to Wisconsin from Germany in 1901 to complete his doctoral thesis on "The Decline of Landowning Farmers in England." It was a historical, comparative study of land tenure that drew upon archival materials from the British Museum, personal observations made while visiting farmers and estate agents in England, and from the works of Roscher, Conrad, Sering, and Brentano, all of the German Historical school. Taylor later cited this thesis, along with B.H. Hibbard's (1902), "The History of Agriculture in Dane County," M.B. Hammond's (1897), "The Cotton Industry: An Essay in American Economic History," and J.G. Thompson's (1907), "The Rise and Decline of the Wheat Growing Industry in Wisconsin," as major contributors to the University of Wisconsin's reputation as the leading center in the use of the historical approach (Taylor and Taylor 1952, p. 287). He credited Ely as the primary stimulus for the use of this historical method but acknowledged that "the roots of that Wisconsin background may lead back to the German Historical school" (Taylor 1939, p. 2).

A. Teacher and Scholar of Agricultural Marketing

On his return to Wisconsin in 1901, Taylor began teaching economic history and economic geography, taking over the latter from Edward David Jones who was departing for the University of Michigan. The course in economic geography, offered in 1901, was a significant beginning for Taylor's contributions to marketing education. For example, one of his first steps was to give the course in economic geography more emphasis on agriculture and marketing:

> From two-thirds to three-quarters of the time in the course in economic geography was spent in describing where each of the important agricultural products was grown, where it was consumed, and the transportation, merchandising, and processing which it underwent as it passed from producer to consumer (1941, p. 23).

The text Taylor used in this course was Volume VI of the Report of the United States Industrial Commission of 1900, entitled, "Distribution and Marketing of Farm Products" (1941, p. 23). This report has been cited by marketing historians as the first "text" used in marketing courses (Bartels 1962; Hagerty 1936) and its impact as an early marketing text has been discussed at length by Johnson and Hollander (1987). It provided descriptions of the distribution of cereals, cotton, and dairy products, and of the marketing of livestock as well as a discussion of the significance of cold storage and refrigeration in the marketing of perishable products. In Taylor's words, Volume VI was:

> by all odds the best book on agricultural economics at the beginning of the twentieth century.... The facts assembled and the methods of presentation made it possible for the reader to develop in his mind a fairly clear picture of marketing processes and price-making forces (1952, p. 517).

Taylor went so far as to state that this report marked the very beginning of "scientific study of marketing" (1952, p. 13). Other government publications that described the marketing process were also assigned in Taylor's 1901 course. They included "The Grain Trade of the U.S." and "The Cotton Trade of the U.S.," both in *Monthly Summary of Commerce and Finance* (1900), as well as several bulletins of the U.S. Department of Agriculture's Bureau of Statistics (Taylor 1908).

The materials developed by Taylor for that early course in economic geography dealing with agricultural economics later formed the basis of his seminal book, *An Introduction to the Study of Agricultural Economics*, published in 1905. This was probably the first book dealing with agricultural economics to be published in the English language and would have been one of the first to deal with agricultural marketing, had it not been for the time pressures of Taylor's tenure clock. Taylor described the omission of marketing content in this way:

> It will be noted that the first edition of *Agricultural Economics*, published in 1905, did not include the subject of marketing, although there was a chapter on prices. My interest in the fields of farm management and land tenure was greater at that time than my interest in marketing. I had not written up my ideas on marketing so carefully as I had those on these other subjects, and since, for practical reasons, it was necessary to publish the book in the spring of 1905 in order to get the promotion to an assistant professorship, I published the material on the economics of farm management and land tenure which was ready, omitted the discussion of marketing, and called the book *An Introduction to the Study of Agricultural Economics* (1941, p. 2).

The next edition (1919) incorporated a substantial discussion of marketing with specific emphasis on the relation between the farmer and middlemen.

If we trace Taylor's ideas for that book, an intriguing path is revealed to earlier German courses in agricultural marketing. In responding to a survey in 1906 by Henry W. Farnam on the influence of the German Historical school, Taylor stated that many of the subjects covered in his book were lectured on by Sering at Berlin and by Conrad at Halle while he was studying in Germany (Farnam 1906). In addition, a report sent to Benjamin Hibbard at the University of Wisconsin from the American Consulate-General in Berlin indicates that courses in agricultural marketing were offered as early as 1912 at the Universities of Berlin, Halle, and others (Thakara 1913). For example, the calendar of the University of Berlin for 1912-1913 included the following course description:

> General course in business management. Includes credit, competition, speculation, the methods and psychology of advertising, selling methods and organization tariff technique, etc. Organization of commercial establishments in particular branches. The grain trade and the marketing of grain (quoted in Thakara 1913, p. 5).

The report by the Consulate-General concluded, "in most, if not all, of the universities there are, of course, opportunities for the study of various phases of economics bearing in a broad way on the subject of marketing" (1913, p. 2). One is also left wondering how much of Taylor's lecture material dealing with marketing might have been borrowed from such courses offered earlier in Germany. Whatever its sources of influence, his course in economic geography almost certainly marked the beginning of instruction in agricultural marketing at Wisconsin.

Gradually, Taylor was able to expand the number of courses on agricultural economics offered by the Department of Economics. In 1904-1905, he taught "The Elements of Agricultural Economics," "Historical and Comparative Agriculture," and "Agricultural Industries" (University of Wisconsin Calendar, p. 117), in addition to the course on economic geography. In 1907, he added a course on "Commercial Geography" that was described as:

> A description of the production and marketing of the principle agricultural products, and a study of the conditions which determine the geographical distribution of the centers of production of each of these products; a discussion of the production and consumption of the leading products of mines and of forests (Extension Division 1907).

This was the same year that Taylor was promoted to the rank of associate professor.

Then, in 1908, Taylor's expanding efforts in agricultural economics were rewarded with the promotion to full professor and an appointment as head of a new department. A Department of Agricultural Economics, the first such department to be established in an American university, was formed within the College of Agriculture in 1908 and Taylor was appointed the first director. As a result, work in agricultural economics in general, and in marketing in particular, received additional emphasis. Taylor had already encouraged several of his students in economics to work on marketing topics (Taylor 1907). When the Department of Agricultural Economics was formed, however, a new emphasis was evident in thesis work and in research published through the Agricultural Experiment Station's Bulletin Series.

A phrase that became popular in agricultural circles after the turn of the century was "the marketing problem." This had to do with the suspected manipulation of prices for farm products by middlemen. One significant result of this widespread concern was the formation, in 1903, of the American Society of Equity, with the purpose of securing for farmers a fair share of the national income (Taylor 1941, p. 4). The Society was very critical of a "price-making system" which was "tyrannical," and reduced farming to "commercial slavery" (Everitt, quoted in Taylor 1941, p. 5). Taylor's attitude was much more moderate:

> I was tolerant towards but not enthusiastic about the Equity movement in Wisconsin. I had read [Everitt's] *The Third Power* when it first came out with the feeling that Everitt was an agitator and that many of his statements were wild exaggerations. While I was fully aware of the opportunity for dishonesty in the middleman service, I believed that hired men of cooperative associations working in central markets, remote from the farmers, might also succeed in being dishonest. I believed that, so far as the central market was concerned, the best control the farmers could exert was by understanding clearly what took place. (Taylor 1941, p. 6).

In 1906, as the interest of Wisconsin farmers in the activities of middlemen grew, Taylor began studying the cooperative creameries and cheese factories in southern Wisconsin. In 1910, he published a bulletin through the Agricultural Experiment Station on "The Prices of Farm Products." In it, Taylor's conclusions about the prices of eggs, butter and cheese were consistent with the notion that middlemen served an essential function for which a price had to be paid (Taylor 1941, p. 8).

The following year, in 1911, two of Taylor's senior students in agricultural economics, W.A. Schoenfeld and G.S. Wehrwein, were given the task of studying the marketing of Wisconsin cheese. Together with Taylor in 1913, they published the results of their investigations as "The Marketing of Wisconsin Cheese." Using descriptive statistics and maps, the article illustrated where cheese was produced and where it was consumed. It described the middlemen processes, the advantages and disadvantages of a cheesemaker versus a sales agent carrying out the selling function, the various types of retailers and wholesalers, the operation of dairy boards, retail prices, and the services rendered by various middlemen. Taylor commented that, "while our findings tended to sober those persons who had been speaking excitedly about the marketing problem, they made it perfectly clear that, in certain stages in the marketing of Wisconsin cheese, the agencies were not functioning satisfactorily" (1941, p. 16).

This early research dealing with the marketing of Wisconsin cheese was significant in a number of ways. It signified the beginning of a specialization by the Department of Agricultural Economics in marketing and cooperatives which, today, is considered its single most important contribution to the study of agriculture (Pulver 1984, p. 7). Also, a flurry of graduate research started with this initial study and led to numerous theses in agricultural marketing, including: G.S. Wehrwein's (1913), "The Dairy Board of Wisconsin," W.A. Schoenfeld's (1914) "Seasonal and Geographical Distribution of Wisconsin Cheddar Cheese for the Year 1911," J.H. Dance's (1915) "The Distribution, Marketing and Value of Milk, Cream and Butter Produced on 222 Wisconsin Farms," H.R. Walker's (1915) "The Cooperative Marketing of Livestock in Wisconsin," and E.T. Cusick's (1916) "The Raising and Marketing of Wisconsin Tobacco."

As the Department of Agricultural Economics grew, Taylor recruited two University of Wisconsin alumni to specialize in agricultural marketing. In 1913, Benjamin Hibbard was persuaded to join the faculty, having taught at the University of Iowa since graduating from Wisconsin in 1902. Then in 1917, Theodore Macklin returned to Wisconsin from Kansas State College. Macklin had been a student of Taylor's and Hibbard was a classmate of the latter. Under these three, the University of Wisconsin became a leading center of research in agricultural marketing.

Hibbard, Taylor, and several of the graduate students in the department published a series of studies including (1914) "Agricultural Cooperation,"

(1915) "Markets and Prices of Wisconsin Cheese," (1915) "The Marketing of Winconsin Butter," (1915) "The Marketing of Wisconsin Potatoes," (1917) "Cooperation in Wisconsin," and (1917) "Marketing of Wisconsin Milk." The latter study led to a thesis and subsequent book on *The Marketing of Whole Milk* (1921) by H.E. Erdman. That book, as well as Hibbard's (1921) *Marketing of Agricultural Products* and Macklin's (1921) *Efficient Marketing for Agriculture* were seminal contributions to the marketing literature.

Commenting on the series of articles published between 1913 and 1917, Taylor observed that they followed a common pattern. Each study was designed "to picture the marketing process clearly in order that the true character of the problems of marketing might be discovered" (1941, p. 22). Each study proceeded from a perceived marketing problem and followed the same method, to observe the facts, to look and see, with the objective of formulating principles and recommendations afterwards.

Another characteristic of that collection of research was that it "followed through stage by stage the different [marketing] functions ... not using the term functions although studying functions" (Taylor 1944). It was in recognition of that work that Paul Converse thought Taylor might have been the originator of the functional approach in marketing (Converse 1944). In his efforts to understand the discrepency between prices paid to the farmer and by the consumer, Taylor discovered that there were valuable functions being performed by middlemen in the marketing process.

However, he never lost his compassion for the farmer. To the extent that there was a "marketing problem," it seemed to Taylor that it was one of educating farmers in the techniques of marketing so that they might perform those functions and collect for themselves the value added.

B.   Social Activism and the Effects of Marketing on Society

Taylor also experienced a tension between wanting to maintain scholarly detachment, and his desire for social activism. When he hired Hibbard in 1913, Taylor expressed these views to the Dean of the College of Agriculture:

> The function of the University, in the field of marketing, became clearly defined in my mind. As I see it, our function is to investigate and educate and not to agitate or organize marketing institutions.... It is especially important just at this time because Hibbard will be called upon to go before the public on various occasions dealing with the subject of marketing. It seems to me entirely proper for him to give an historical and descriptive lecture on cooperation, pointing out its strengths and its weakness, but not his function to go to a given place to tell people specifically how to organize for a specific purpose (1913).

Taylor felt that the work in the university on agricultural cooperation and marketing should be scientific—inductive, historical, and descriptive.

Nevertheless, he also believed that research and teaching should result in practical programs for state and federal legislation.

In 1917, with Richard T. Ely, Taylor helped found the American Association for Agricultural Legislation for the purposes of studying agricultural legislation and making recommendations on policy matters to government. In a study program distributed to founding members, the following topics were included:

- the history of state marketing bureaus and departments
- the essentials of an efficient state marketing bureau
- the present status of standardization and grading laws
- the relation of state marketing organizations to national regulation
- cold storage legislation
- laws governing cooperative organizations of producers and consumers
- federal marketing legislation (Ely 1917)

This study program reflected a concern for land use, prices and credit, transportation, and the role of education in improving farm lifestyle. More importantly, it explicitly addressed marketing as an area of concern and study, specifically, the role of the state in the marketing process. Two years later, in 1919, the AAAL moved toward becoming a more scholarly, and less political, organization when it was consolidated with the American Farm Management Association to form the American Farm Economics Association (Taylor 1939). That same year, 1919, marked the end of Taylor's academic career.

His views on marketing and marketing education were made most clear in the *Journal of Farm Economics* (1924), five years after leaving the University of Wisconsin. In reflecting on his teaching career, Taylor gave the following definition of marketing:

> Marketing may be viewed in the very narrow sense of selling what one has produced for sale. It may be broadened to include all those activities and institutions involved in the handling, storing, transferring, transforming and ultimate sale to consumers of specific products. To this enlarged concept may be added that of finding ways and means of improving the present marketing system. These may include standardization, a better adjustment of shipments to the demands for the specific products in the various markets at a given time and a better equalization of shipments throughout the season. It may include methods of sale and methods of settling disputes such as public inspection services, systems of arbitration, and in this day of movements for self help among farmers in their efforts to solve their marketing problems, the science and the art of cooperative marketing comes in for a large share of the time and attention of the student of agricultural marketing (1924, p. 20).

In essence, Taylor held a very broad view of marketing, one concerned with the general welfare of society. In some ways it was a view which, today, we would associate with macromarketing.

C. A Continuing Commitment to Public Service

Except for a brief stint at Northwestern University from 1925 to 1928, Taylor spent most of his remaining years working as a civil servant. From 1919 to 1925, he worked for the U.S. Department of Agriculture. He served as chief of the Office of Farm Management and Farm Economics for two years, then became chief of the Bureau of Markets and Crop Estimates for the same length of time. In 1922, those two divisions were combined into the Bureau of Agricultural Economics, which was headed by Taylor until 1925. During these years he gave new impetus to the research work in these government organizations, emphasizing the need for historical work (Taylor 1939). He also coordinated research on problems of marketing, production, and farm management, revised the work in crop estimates, and negotiated agreements between the U.S. Department of Agriculture and nine European cotton associations for the establishment of universal standards for American cotton (1939, p. 1).

In 1935, at the age of 62, Taylor became managing director of the Farm Foundation, an organization established to manage funds for the improvement of rural living conditions. Remarkably, he held that position for ten years and added another seven as agricultural economist for the same organization.

In retirement, and 47 years after writing his seminal book on agricultural economics, Taylor published his only other major work, *The Story of Agricultural Economics in the United States, 1840-1932* (1952), with the help of his wife, Ann Dewees Taylor. It is a wonderfully detailed history of agricultural economics and marketing, and essential reading for any student of marketing history.

As a young man Henry Charles Taylor's goals were to become a successful farmer and to lobby Congress for legislation that would help farmers. Whatever else he accomplished, he succeeded in helping students of agriculture to better understand the marketing process.

III. EDWARD DAVID JONES: 1870-1944

Edward David Jones was born on May 15, 1870 in Orfordville, Wisconsin. After completing public school, he attended Lawrence University for one year and switched to Ohio Wesleyan University at Delaware where he completed a Bachelor of Science degree in 1892. He then enrolled as one of the first graduate students in the newly formed School of Economics at the University of Wisconsin. Thus, he shared with Taylor much the same midwestern upbringing and educational influences.

At Wisconsin, Jones studied economics under Richard T. Ely. Of course, this also meant a period of time spent studying in Germany, at the Universities of Halle and Berlin in 1894 and 1895. At the University of Halle Jones attended lectures in *Nationalokonomie* (economics), *Statistik* (statistics), and *Staatswissenschaft* (political science) by Johannes Conrad, and was especially impressed by Conrad's habit of taking his students on weekly excursions to various manufacturing institutions in the vicinity (Jones 1894). Conrad had suggested to Jones a thesis on agriculture. However, Jones had in mind several comparative, historical studies including a "History of Economic Crises," which he eventually settled on and completed at the University of Berlin. Following this, in 1895, Jones returned to Madison and married Annabelle White (whose family's business Jones would later work for) and accepted an appointment in the School of Economics.

A.   First University Teacher of Marketing

For the next six years, from 1895 to 1901, Jones taught economic geography and statistics at the University of Wisconsin. In 1901, however, Jones was approached by Henry C. Adams, formerly a colleague of Ely's at Johns Hopkins University and now head of the Department of Economics at the University of Michigan, to teach a course in commercial geography. The course was originally to have been entitled, "The Physical Basis of Industrial Organization," and subsequently came to be called "Industrial Resources of the United States." Adams himself had proposed a similar course at Johns Hopkins University as early as 1880 (Dorfman 1969, p. 14). Ultimately these plans led to what has been recognized as the first university course in marketing (Bartels 1951, p. 3; Maynard 1941, p. 382) and was taught by Jones, now assistant professor of Commerce & Industry at the University of Michigan. That course was entitled "The Distributive and Regulative Industries of the United States" and was described in the University of Michigan catalogue as follows:

> A description of the various ways of marketing goods, of the classification, grades, brands employed, and of wholesale and retail trade. Attention will also be given to those private organizations not connected with money and banking, which guide and control the industrial process, such as trade associations, boards of trade and chambers of commerce (1901).

In 1903-1904 Jones was promoted to junior professor and his course in marketing was expanded into three others. "The Distribution of Agricultural Products" focused on the various systems of marketing agricultural products and included a discussion of commission selling, cooperation, public and private market contracts, and speculation. A second course, "The Wholesale Trade," looked at "the requirements of marketing as they affect the technique of manufacturing...the principles governing the determination of price and quality...the outlets employed in direct and indirect selling and the methods of stimulating trade" (University of Michigan Calendar 1903-04). Finally, "The Retail Trade" covered:

> The general position of the retailer followed by an analysis of location, stock-keeping, selling and advertising. Special attention is paid to the principle of departmentizing [sic]. Department stores, mail-order stores and special stores are studied" (University of Michigan Calendar 1903-04).

Thus, in their focus on commodity and institutional analyses, these seminal courses dealt with two of the three classic schools of thought in marketing. In addition, Jones taught courses in "Techniques of Foreign Trade" and "The Domestic Market," suggesting an early recognition of international marketing in the curriculum.

B. Scientific Investigations

Jones felt that these marketing courses, along with the study of administration and accounting/finance, were basic to an education in business (1913a, p. 188). Yet he also recognized that in order to teach business, research was first needed so that the general principles of these subjects could be discovered. In fact, he observed that the "chief function of this generation of college men associated with business administration will be recognized to be, not teaching, but scientific investigation" (1913a, p. 190). In that connection Jones gathered historical, statistical data on the costs of marketing activities and wrote descriptive case studies of marketing institutions and practices. He became deeply concerned with improving marketing efficiency and with distributive justice.

In 1903 the Carnegie Institution of Washington undertook the writing of a multivolume history of the American economy. The project was divided into eleven sections, one of which was the history of foreign and domestic commerce. Jones felt that a related topic which had been ignored was the "evolution of methods of marketing products—wholesaling, retailing etc." and was eager to contribute materials on this subject (Jones 1903). Unfortunately, responsibility for the work on foreign and domestic commerce was given to E. R. Johnson of the Wharton School. Nevertheless, Jones later became involved with a division of the project dealing with the history of agriculture and forestry. He assumed responsibility in 1907 for writing a chapter on the "American Domestic Market Since 1840" (Carnegie Institution of Washington 1907, p. 78). Interestingly, his plan included having some students of Henry Charles Taylor's at the University of Wisconsin, work on various aspects of the history of marketing agricultural products (Taylor 1907). Although the volume on agriculture and forestry, as originally planned, was never completed, Jones did publish a series of articles in 1911 and 1912 which were to have served as a trial of the material designated for the Carnegie project. These articles became part of a series of 20 which Jones published between 1911 and 1914 on marketing-related topics. (See reference list for 1911a-k, 1912a-g, 1913b-e, and 1914.) This collection of work had a common thread running throughout—an analysis of the efficiency of the marketing system. It was quite remarkable for the critical tone in which it was presented, as well as for the principles and concepts of marketing it identified. To my knowledge, none of this work has previously been examined by marketing historians.

In the first article, entitled "The Larger Aspects of Private Business,"(1911a) Jones stated that his purpose in presenting this work was to examine "some marketing problems." The most general of these, in his estimation, was the apparent inefficiency of the marketing process. He called for a "cost of living movement" to "reform the distributive system to secure efficiency in the merchandising of products from producer to consumer" (1912d, p. 284). Greater efficiency, he believed, could be achieved through the application of scientific management principles to industrial purchasing and consumer buying, through the organization of industrial and consumer cooperatives, and through the standardization of products.

In retailing, Jones had determined that marketing activities added 50 percent to the cost of goods and he felt that much of this added cost was wasteful (1912f). For example, the ratio of population to the number of stores was decreasing and this seemed to him an unnecessary trend. His strongest criticisms, though, were targeted at advertising expenditures:

A distributive expense of great importance is the modern advertising campaign. Although I am willing to grant what the modern business man says about the necessity of advertising for his individual business it is true in my opinion that advertising is one of the great blood-suckers of modern industry. Very largely it is a waste of money so far as the customer is concerned, as it is merely a usurption by the manufacturer of the function of recommending and guaranteeing products which previously the local retailer performed. And in the change there is waste, for the retailer is still necessary and the manufacturer must spend immense sums to gain the attention of the customers (1910, p. 139).

Jones' overriding concern in his analysis of the efficiency of marketing processes was with distributive justice. This concern was very much directed by a critical view of the structure of marketing systems. For example, he felt that the emergence of large department store retailers had set different distribution channels—the local jobber-small retailer system and the general jobber-department store system—against each other as representatives of rival systems (1911f, p. 245).

He was also critical in his general assessment of the performance of markets (1912c). He described the function of a market as providing an opportunity for purchasing a good assortment of reliable merchandise in the required quantity at a fair price. However, his observations led him to conclude that markets were unstable, unsafe for traders, and, that the system of distribution was excessively expensive (1912c, p. 121).

Greater efficiency was only part of the solution to the distributive injustices Jones perceived in the marketing system. He also advocated the education of consumers and of certain classes of producers in the techniques of marketing. For example, he suggested that consumers should study and learn the differences in quality between brands and determine the "appropriate service level" at which goods should be purchased (1912e, p. 408). Farmers, he felt, were particularly in need of education in marketing techniques and of the "development of a theory of the choice of crops and products from the market side" (1912d, p. 248). Like Taylor, Jones believed that part of the "marketing problem" was due to naive participants in the marketing process, who needed education in the techniques of marketing.

In dealing with the subject of ethics in marketing, Jones' ideological perspective became quite clear. He suggested the need for a code of ethics for business in the belief that the majority of businessmen would do the "fair and honorable thing"—if they knew what that was (1911g). Such conduct was essential to what he called the "moral conception of the merchant":

> The moral conception of the merchant as one who selects his stock of goods in the spirit of a friend selecting a present for a friend; who preserves the merchandise as one who feels that it already belongs to another, and is held in trust; who awaits trade with the spirit of accomodation in his heart; who charges for his service with that justice tempered with humanity which characterizes the best class of physicians; and who advises with that fidelity which makes the best attorneys, is the only conception which will attract the highest talent into this profession and will leave the pathway open for growth in functions and in efficiency (1912e, p. 577).

In addition to his observations on marketing efficiency and his philosophy of distributive justice, Jones made some important conceptual contributions. Perhaps the most significant idea to emerge from his writing about marketing was a relatively well-developed conception of marketing functions. A functional approach was evident in at least three of Jones' articles (1911k; 1912g; 1913b). However, the principal marketing functions were most clearly and explicitly outlined in his "Functions of the Merchant" (1912g). These included transportation, bulk-breaking, assorting, storage, buying, selling, and risk taking which, he stated, were carried out in order to provide time, place, and quantity utility (1912g, p. 575).

Although Arch W. Shaw is generally credited with originating the functional approach (Hunt and Goolsby 1988), it seems that Jones might share in that distinction. Jones' article, "Functions of the Merchant," was published (October, 1912) two months after Shaw's. However, Jones had written about marketing functions as early as December of 1911 and appears to have developed the idea quite independently of Shaw's work. In any case, both of these scholars recognized that certain essential functions were performed in the marketing process and that these functions added value to goods and products. Jones went even further in his 1912 article by articulating a primitive version of the marketing concept, a focus on serving customers' needs and not simply on sales:

> Many merchants narrow their field of enterprise by placing undue emphasis on the sale itself as the object of study and the field of retail activity. The field of the retail expert is self-training, the establishment of the principles and policies of action, proper equipment, selection of stock etc.; and the establishment of a reputation for reliability and efficiency. Sales are the natural consummation of these things; and sales only come steadily, and in satisfactory amount, as consummations. In short, then, the proper thing for the merchant to emphasize, as an expert, is preparation for service, rather than the act of sale itself (1912g, p. 577).

After teaching and writing about marketing for over a decade of his university career, Jones was promoted, in 1913, to Professor of Commerce and Industry. At that time his attention shifted somewhat to the broader field of business administration. This was marked by his publication of *Business Administration–The Scientific Principles of a New Profession* (1913), *Business Administration, Its Models in War, Statecraft, and Science* (1914), and, *The Administration of Industrial Enterprises* (1916). His teaching responsibilities also included courses in "Principles of Industry," "Business Organization and Management," and "The Chief Executive and Underlying Principles of Administration." Jones believed that the principles of military administration could be generalized to business, including marketing, which could be studied and taught as a science and practised by professionals guided by the highest ethical standards and by a concern for the general welfare of society. He summarized these beliefs in a letter to his colleague, friend, and former teacher, Richard T. Ely in 1918:

> I want to tell you how your advanced thinking in so many lines (which American social evolution has since confirmed) and your matchless productivity have been an inspiration to me. My own program can be briefly told....I hope to see industry made more just and generous not only through a democratic process, but by the formation of a code of ideals of professional competence for administrators....I hope to see the general welfare promoted, not only by the use of the national dividend outside of industry but by the transformation of the life in industry itself, by fitting men to their tasks, interpreting the tasks in terms of service and elegance of method, by control of fatigue, by the sociability and aesthetics of welfare work etc.... What I should like from Providence, more than anything else, is the opportunity to push the development along these main lines in which, chiefly, business administration is capable of being deepened and worked into something of a philosophy (Jones 1918).

Soon after that statement, however, Jones left academia to test his ideas in industry. In 1919 he resigned from the faculty of the University of Michigan and, except for a year spent as supervisor of foreman training courses in the Division of Education at Harvard University, served the balance of his working days as a vice president of the Z.L. White Company in Columbus, Ohio. Jones died on January 9, 1944.

Edward David Jones was one of the first scholars in North America to teach and study marketing. Throughout his academic training and career, there were constant influences from empirically-oriented, reform-minded economists that helped give him a critical perspective on the marketing system. This was an unusual ideological position for a teacher of business to adopt. Like Henry Charles Taylor, Jones was concerned with the effects of marketing on society and believed that education in the techniques of marketing was a necessary part of the solution to "marketing problems." However, Jones went far beyond Taylor's more limited commodity approach, to examine in detail marketing institutions and the functions they performed. This led him to many conceptual insights that were not well recognized until decades later.

IV. EPILOGUE

As the science of marketing evolves there is a natural progression from concepts to theories, and then to schools of thought, each with its own history. Indeed, theories and schools of thought have become the most popular topics for historians of marketing thought (Jones and Monieson 1990, p. 271). In the process, however, there is the danger that ideas can become disembodied spirits. Yet each new theory is the contribution of a distinctive individual; it is, to some extent, an expression and reflection of the personality and experiences of its innovator. Each school of thought developed as a result of the transmission and acceptance of ideas among scholars. Truly important and original ideas are the product of intricate combinations of conditions and influences, the study of which helps us to understand how and why those ideas emerged. Just as history adds depth and texture to the study of marketing, biography can add a similar richness to the history of marketing thought.

REFERENCES

Bartels, R. (1951). "Influences on the Development of Marketing Thought, 1900-1923." *Journal of Marketing,* 16; pp. 1-17.
Bartels, R. (1962). *The Development of Marketing Thought.* Homewood, IL: Irwin.
Carnegie Institution of Washington. (1907). *Annual Report.*
Converse, P. D. (1944). *Correspondence, Converse to Henry Charles Taylor, May 29.* Henry Charles Taylor Papers. Madison: The State Historical Society of Wisconsin.
Converse, P. D. (1945). "The Development of the Science of Marketing." *Journal of Marketing,* 10; pp. 14-23.

Converse, P. D. (1959). *The Beginning of Marketing Thought in the United States*. Austin TX: Bureau of Business Research, University of Texas.

Dorfman, J. (1969). *Two Essays by Henry Carter Adams*. New York: Augustus M. Kelley.

Ely, R. T. (1917). *Study Program for the American Association for Agricultural Legislation, Topics for Theses and Other Publications*. Unpublished manuscript, Richard T. Ely Papers. Madison: The State Historical Society of Wisconsin.

Extension Division, University of Wisconsin. (1907). *Courses in Political Economy*. Madison.

Farnam, H. W. (1906). *Correspondence, Henry Charles Taylor to Farnam*. Farnam Family Papers. New Haven: Yale University Library Archives.

Hagerty, J. E. (1936). "Experiences of Our Early Marketing Teachers." *Journal of Marketing*, 1; pp. 20-27.

Herbst, J. (1965). *The German Historical School in American Scholarship*. Ithaca, NY: Cornell University Press.

Hunt, S. D. and J. Goolsby. (1988). "The Rise and Fall of the Functional Approach to Marketing: A Paradigm Displacement Perspective. Pp. 35-52 in *Historical Perspectives in Marketing: Essays in Honor of Stanley C. Hollander*, edited by Terence Nevett and Ronald A. Fullerton. Lexington: Lexington Books.

Jaffe, W. (1965). "Biography and Economic Analysis." *Western Economic Journal*, 3; pp. 223-232.

Johnson, S. D. and S. Hollander. (1987). *The United States Industrial Commission of 1898-1902: The Formation of Early Marketing Thought*. Paper presented at the 12th annual Macromarketing Conference, Montreal.

Jones, D. G. B. and D. D. Monieson. (1990). "Historical Research in Marketing: Retrospect and Prospect." *Journal of the Academy of Marketing Science*, 18; pp. 269-278.

Jones, E. D. (1894). *Correspondence, E.D. Jones to Ely, January 23*. Ely Papers.

Jones, E. D. (1903). *Correspondence, E.D. Jones to Ely*. Richard T. Ely Papers. Madison: State Historical Society of Wisconsin.

Jones, E. D. (1910). "The Causes of the Increased Cost of Agricultural Staples and the Influence of this Upon the Recent Evolution of Other Objects of Expenditure." *Michigan Academy of Science 12th Report*; pp.137-142.

Jones, E. D. (1911a). "The Larger Aspects of Private Business." *Mill Supplies*, 1; p. 3.

Jones, E. D. (1911b). "What Goods are Worthy of Manufacture." *Mill Supplies*, 1; pp. 57-58.

Jones, E. D. (1911c). "Standardization: Its Effect on Quality." *Mill Supplies*, 1; pp. 99-100.

Jones, E. D. (1911d). "Cost Accounting and Efficiency." *Mill Supplies*, 1; pp. 149-152.

Jones, E. D. (1911e). "Buyers' Specifications: Scientific Purchasing." *Mill Supplies*, 1; pp. 209-21.

Jones, E. D. (1911f). "Quantity Prices Versus Classified Lists." *Mill Supplies*, 1: pp. 245-246.

Jones, E. D. (1911g). "The Cancellation of Orders." *Mill Supplies*, 1; pp. 291-292.

Jones, E. D. (1911h). "The Restriction of Prices." *Mill Supplies*, 1; pp. 339-340.

Jones, E. D. (1911i). "Advertising and Trade Brands." *Mill Supplies*, 1; pp. 391-392.

Jones, E. D. (1911j). "Our System of Weights and Measures Indefensible." *Mill Supplies*, 1; pp. 430-432.

Jones, E. D. (1911k). "Functions of a System of Grades." *Mill Supplies*, 1; pp. 529-530.

Jones, E. D. (1912a). "Some Problems of Price." *Mill Supplies*, 2; pp. 9-10.

Jones, E. D. (1912b). "List Prices and Discounts." *Mill Supplies*, 2; pp. 59-62.

Jones, E. D. (1912c). "The Perfect Market Outlined." *Mill Supplies*, 2; pp. 115-121.

Jones, E. D. (1912d). "Cost of Living and Marketing of Farm Products." *Mill Supplies*, 2; pp. 283-285.

Jones, E. D. (1912e). "Cost of Living and the Retail Trade." *Mill Supplies*, 2; pp. 406-408.

Jones, E. D. (1912f). "Principles of Modern Retail Merchandising." *Mill Supplies*, 2; pp. 461-462.

Jones, E. D. (1912g). "Functions of the Merchant." *Mill Supplies,* 2; pp. 575-577.

Jones, E. D. (1913a). "Some Propositions Concerning University Instruction in Business Administration." *Journal of Political Economy,* 21; pp. 185-195.

Jones, E. D. (1913b). "Function of Trade Marks." *Mill Supplies,* 3; pp. 69-70.

Jones, E. D. (1913c). "The Purchasing Department." *Mill Supplies,* 3; pp. 130-132.

Jones, E. D. (1913d). "History of American Machine-tool Manufacture." *Mill Supplies,* 3; pp. 623-628.

Jones, E. D. (1913e). "History of American Machine-tool Manufacture, Part II." *Mill Supplies,* 3; pp. 684-686.

Jones, E. D. (1914). "Evolution of Accuracy in Manufacture." *Mill Supplies,* 4; pp. 23-24.

Jones, E. D. (1918). *Correspondence, E.D. Jones to Ely, February 3.* Ely Papers.

Maynard, H. H. (1941). "Marketing Courses Prior to 1910." *Journal of Marketing,* 6; pp. 382-384.

Myles, J. C. (1956). *German Historicism and American Economics–A Study of the Influence of the German Historical School on American Economic Thought.* Unpublished doctoral dissertation, Princeton University.

Nevett, T. (1983). "Blood, Sweat, Tears and Biography." Pp. 20-29 in *Proceedings of the First North American Workshop on Historical Research in Marketing,* edited by Stanley Hollander and Ronald Savitt. Lansing, MI: MSU.

Pulver, G. C. (1984). "Improving Agriculture and Rural Life." *Achievements in Agricultural Economics 1909-1984.* Madison: University of Wisconsin.

Shaw, A. W. (1912). "Some Problems of Market Distribution." *Quarterly Journal of Economics,* 26; pp. 703-765.

Stigler, G. J. (1976). "The Scientific Uses of Scientific Biography, With Special Reference to J.S. Mill." Pp. 55-66 in *James and John Stuart Mill / Papers of the Centenary Conference,* edited by John Robson and Michael Laine. Toronto: University of Toronto Press.

Taylor, H. C. (1907). *Correspondence, E.D. Jones to Taylor, March 16.* Henry Charles Taylor Papers. Madison: The State Historical Society of Wisconsin.

Taylor, H. C. (1908). *Correspondence, Taylor to B.H. Hibbard, March 18.* Taylor Papers.

Taylor, H. C. (1913). *Correspondence, Taylor to H.L. Russell, January 18.* Taylor Papers.

Taylor, H. C. (1924). "Courses in Marketing." *Journal of Farm Economics,* 6; pp. 20-27.

Taylor, H. C. (1939). *Statement with Regard to the Development of Agricultural History in the U.S. Department of Agriculture.* Unpublished manuscript. Taylor Papers.

Taylor, H. C. (1940). "Early History of Agricultural Economics." *Journal of Farm Economics.*

Taylor, H. C. (1941). *The Development of Research and Education in Agricultural Cooperation and Marketing at the University of Wisconsin, 1910-1920.* Unpublished manuscript. Taylor Papers.

Taylor, H. C. (1944). *Correspondence, Taylor to Paul D. Converse, June 1.* Taylor Papers.

Taylor, H. C. (1960). *Plus Ultra.* Unpublished autobiography. Taylor Papers.

Taylor, H. C. and A. D. Taylor. (1952). *The Story of Agricultural Economics in the United States, 1840-1932.* Westport, CT: Greenwood Press.

Thakara, A.M. (1913). *German Educational Courses in Cooperation and Marketing.* Unpublished Report. Benjamin H. Hibbard Papers. Madison: The State Historical Society of Wisconsin.

University of Michigan. (1901-02, 1902-03, 1903-04, 1917-18). *Calendars.*

University of Wisconsin. (1904-05, 1907-08). *Calendars.*

Walker, D. A. (1983). "Biography and the Study of the History of Economic Thought." *Research in the History of Economic Thought and Methodology,* 1; pp. 41-59.

Wright, J. and P. B. Dimsdale. (Eds.). (1974). *Pioneers in Marketing.* Atlanta: Georgia State University.

THE ADOPTION OF STATISTICAL
METHODS IN MARKET RESEARCH:
THE EARLY TWENTIETH CENTURY

Richard Germain

ABSTRACT

The goal of this research is to determine, whether or not, known, readily available statistical methods were discussed in market research textbooks during the 1915-1937 time period. A content analysis of market research and statistics texts indicates that basic statistical concepts were omitted from market research books of the period. An adoption of innovation framework is used to identify and discuss possible causes of the delay. Three potential factors that could have slowed the adoption of statistics were identified: the personality of Ronald Fisher; statistics as a discipline; and market research practices of the period.

I. INTRODUCTION

As recently observed, the marketing discipline was somewhat slow in adopting statistical methods during the mid-twentieth-century:

Research in Marketing, Supplement 6, pages 87-101.
Copyright © 1994 by JAI Press Inc.
All rights of reproduction in any form reserved.
ISBN: 1-55938-187-6

Survey design, statistical sampling, and related methodologies developed at Rothemstead
Experimental Station in England [by Sir Ronald Fisher] and at the U.S. Census Bureau
in the 1920s and 1930s—and as extended for marketing in the 1940s and 1950s—provided
important stimuli for market research (Charnes, Cooper, Leaner, and Phillips 1985, p. 96).

The purpose of this study is to examine the transference of statistical methods
to the market research discipline. The specific research questions addressed
are, (a) did market research textbooks published during the early part of the
twentieth century include readily available statistical techniques that are now
routinely included in today's market research texts?, and (b) if so, then how
rapidly were they adopted, or if adopted after considerable delay, what seems
to have caused the delay?

In the following section, a content analysis of twenty-five texts published
between 1913 and 1937 demonstrates that a considerable number of routine
statistical methods were not incorporated by market research textbook authors.
The section that follows discusses the personality of Sir Ronald Fisher, the
discipline of statistics, and market research practices of the period as potential
causes of the delay. The discussion of potential delay causes is cast in an
adoption of innovation framework. The discussion of market research practices
will in part focus on the *relevance* of statistical methods to market research
during the period, an issue that has received little attention (Bartels 1976).

II. IDENTIFICATION OF
UNUSED STATISTICAL METHODS

Fifteen statistics texts from various disciplines and ten market research books
published prior to 1940 were selected for a content analysis. The books were
reviewed to identify statistical topics, yielding a total of fifty-two items. As seen
in Table 1, major topic headings include measures of central tendency,
graphical methods, data collection, probability, correlation and regression,
analysis of variance, as well as others. The twenty-five books were then content
analyzed on these topics.

A.   The Statistics Texts

The results of the content analysis of the fifteen statistics texts is summarized
in Table 1. Each book falls into one of three categories. The first category
consists of books that treated statistics as an abstract or generic subject as
evidenced by a reliance on calculus and a lack of a specific application area
(Forsyth 1924; Kelly 1924; Bowley 1926; Camp 1930). The second type is
comprised of sophisticated, application books (Fisher 1925; Snedecor 1937—
both in biology) and the third is comprised of less sophisticated, application-
oriented texts (the remaining nine books).

Table 1. Content Analysis of Fifteen Statistics Books

	King (1913)	Forsyth (1924)	Kelly (1924)	Kent (1924)	Secrist (1925)	Crum and Patton (1925)	Thurstone (1925)	Fisher (1925)	Bowley (1926)	Dittmer (1926)	Elmer (1926)	Camp (1930)	Day (1932)	Davis (1937)	Snedecor (1937)
Measures of central tendency and dispersion — mean	×	×	×	×	×	×	×	×	×	×	×	×	×	×	×
— mode	×	×	×	×	×	×	×	×	×	×	×	×	×	×	×
— median	×	×	×	×	×	×	×	×	×	×	×	×	×	×	×
— geometric mean	×	×	×	×	×				×		×	×	×	×	×
— weighted mean	×	×	×	×	×				×		×	×	×	×	×
— standard deviation	×	×	×	×	×	×	×	×	×	×	×	×	×	×	×
— skewness	×	×	×	×	×	×		×	×	×	×	×	×	×	×
— moments		×	×	×	×			×		×	×	×	×	×	
— grouped data (mean/variance)			×	×	×	×	×	×	×		×	×	×	×	×
Graphs, tables and time series — graphical methods	×	×	×	×	×	×	×	×	×	×	×	×	×	×	×
— tabular interpretation	×		×	×	×	×	×	×	×	×	··	×	×	×	··
— interpolation	×	×	×	×	×	×			×		×		×	×	×
— index numbers	×		×	×	×	×			×	×	×	×	×	×	
— moving averages	×		×	×	×	×			×	×	×			×	
— other advanced time series methods	×		×		×	×							×	×	
Data collection — collection of secondary data	×			×	×	×			×	×	×				
— survey methods	×				×	×				×	×				
— collection of internal/company data	×			×	×	×		×	×						
— experimentation								×							
Probability and probability distributions — simple probability theory		×			×		×		×					×	×
— normal distribution		×		×	×	×	×	×	×		×	×		×	×
— binomial distribution		×	×	··	×		×	×	×	··	··	×		×	×
— variance of proportions		×						×	×		×	×		×	×
— poisson distribution		×						×						×	×
— student t distribution								×						×	×

(continued)

Table 1. (Continued)

	King (1913)	Forsyth (1924)	Kelly (1924)	Kent (1924)	Secrist (1925)	Crum and Patton (1925)	Thurstone (1925)	Fisher (1925)	Bowley (1926)	Dittmer (1926)	Elmer (1926)	Camp (1930)	Day (1932)	Davis (1937)	Snedecor (1937)
Correlation and regression (strictly estimation of coefficients) — simple linear correlation	×	×	×	×	×	×	×	×	×	×	×	×	×	×	×
— simple linear regression		×	×	×	×	×	×	×	×			×	×	×	×
— multiple correlation		×	×					×	×			×		×	×
— multiple linear regression		×	×				×	×	×			×		×	×
— rank order correlation			×			×						×	×	×	
— correlation ratio			×	×	×	×			×			×	×	×	
— correlation in time series studies									×			×	×	×	
— coefficient of contingency			×						×			×			
— advanced correlation methods			×	×	×			×	×			×	×	×	×
χ^2 tests — goodness of fit test								×	×		i	×		×	×
— test of independence								×							×
Probability distribution tables — standardized normal							×	×	×			×	×	×	×
— student t								×						×	×
— χ^2												i		×	×
— F-distribution															×
Use of sampling distribution (degrees of freedom)								×	i			i		i	×
Test of two statistics — test of two means								×				i			×
— two variances								×				i			×
— paired means												i			×
Use of significance rather than probable error								×							×
Analysis of variance — analysis of variance								×							×
— analysis of variance and regression								×							×
— experimental design								×							×
— analysis of covariance												×			×
Accuracy of proportions			×						×						
Internal reliability of proportions		×													
Reliance on calculus															

Notes: ×: discussion of topic   i: incomplete discussion of topic   blank: no discussion of topic

90

The Fisher (1925) and Snedecor (1937) texts were designated sophisticated because, as seen in Table 1, they were the only ones to discuss: (1) experimental design, (2) the χ^2 test of independence, as presented in most contemporary texts, and the χ^2 goodness of fit test; (3) the student t and χ^2 distributions; (4) tests of two means, two variances and paired means; and (5) analysis of variance including advanced methods of analyzing experiments. Among the many innovations in Fisher's book was his introduction of analysis of variance, and his focus on significance (or the use of a small α value) as opposed to probable error (or the use of a 50 percent alpha level). Snedecor, in addition to covering these topics, also discussed the F-distribution and analysis of covariance.

As seen in Table 1, most books adequately covered measures of central tendency, dispersion, and graphs, tables, and time series. Secondary data sources, survey methods, and/or internal (to the firm) time series data were treated in the majority of less sophisticated texts. Only Bowley (1926) among the calculus-based textbook authors covered some data collection methods. The most complete treatment of probability theory and the normal, binomial, Poisson, and student t distributions were in the calculus-based and the two sophisticated application texts. Among the less sophisticated books, Davis (1937) deserves mention as an exception because of his coverage of some of these topics.

While the majority of authors adequately discussed simple linear correlation and regression, treatment of more advanced correlation and regression methods such as coefficient of contingency and rank order correlation were in the calculus-based books.

B.   The Market Research Texts

Table 2 presents the results of the content analysis of ten market research texts published between 1916 and 1937. The Starch (1923) and White (1927) books focused on advertising research, while the remaining eight were general market research texts.

A comparison of Tables 1 and 2 reveals that the statistics texts in general covered a larger number of topics than did the market research books. The market research textbook authors adequately covered measures of central tendency, but not dispersion. Wheeler's (1937) discussion of dispersion was incomplete since he stated it was important, but without explication of formulae or interpretation. Five out of ten texts covered two or more topics within graphs, tables, and time series.

The market research texts emphasized data collection, and in this area their coverage was more comprehensive than that of the statistics texts. Eight of ten authors discussed secondary data, survey methods, and internal firm data. In addition, Starch (1923), White (1927) and Reilly (1929) discussed

Table 2. Content Analysis of Ten Market Research Books

	Shaw (1916)	Copeland (1917)	Duncan (1922)	Starch (1923)	White (1927)	Reed (1929)	Reilly (1929)	White (1931)	Brown (1937)	Wheeler (1937)
Measures of central tendency and dispersion										
— mean		×	×	−	×		×	×		×
— mode		×	×	−	×		×	×		×
— median		×	×	−	×		×	×		×
— geometric mean										
— weighted mean		×	×		×			×		×
— standard deviation										−
— skewness										
— moments										
— grouped data (mean/variance)					−	−				
Graphs, tables and time series										
— graphical methods		×	×	−	−			×	×	×
— tabular interpretation		×	×	−	×			×	×	×
— interpolation										
— index numbers		×	×		×					×
— moving averages										
— other advanced time series methods	−		×	×	×	×	×			−
Data collection										
— collection of secondary data	−	×	×	×	×	×	×	×	×	×
— survey methods	−	−	×	×	×	×	×	×	×	×
— collection of internal/company data	−	×	×	×	×	×	×	×	×	×
— experimentation				×	×		×		−	−
Probability and probability distributions										
— simple probability theory										
— normal distribution										
— binomial distribution										
— variance of proportions							×			
— poisson distribution										−

92

Correlation and regression (strictly estimation of coefficients)	— simple linear correlation
	— simple linear regression
	— multiple correlation
	— multiple linear regression
	— rank order correlation
	— correlation ratio
	— correlation in time series studies
	— coefficient of contingency
	— advanced correlation methods
χ^2 tests	— goodness of fit test
	— test of independence
Probability distribution tables	— standardized normal
	— student t
	— χ^2
	— F-distribution
Use of sampling distribution (degrees of freedom)	
Test of two statistics	— test of two means
	— two variances
	— paired means
Use of significance rather than probable error	
Analysis of variance	— analysis of variance
	— analysis of variance and regression
	— experimental design
	— analysis of covariance
Accuracy of proportions	
Internal reliability of proportions	
Reliance on calculus	

Notes: x: discussion of topic   i: incomplete discussion of topic   blank: no discussion of topic

93

experimentation. This finding concurs with the observation that business marketers pioneered many survey methods during the 1920s and 1930s (Converse 1987).

With the exception of Reilly (1929), the statistical content of these books was rather limited. Reilly discussed: (1) variance of proportions; (2) accuracy of proportions which is a type of confidence interval construction; and (3) a test of "internal reliability" which was a test of the difference between two proportions. Neither the statistics nor the marketing research texts discussed these topics as a whole. Noteworthy is that Reilly placed the latter two tests in Fisher's sampling theory context and used a one percent significance level.

None of the market research books adequately treated variance, probability, probability distributions, correlation or regression, χ^2 tests, two sample tests, or analysis of variance. The late inclusion of the F-distribution in book form precludes its omission from market research texts an example to resistance to innovation (e.g., Snedecor 1937).

The content analysis indicates that basic statistical concepts such as variance and correlation, the latter introduced by Pearson at the turn of the century, were omitted by market research textbook authors. In contrast, all of the fifteen texts analyzed in Table 1 discussed variance and correlation. For this reason, the market research texts can be classified as less sophisticated application texts. This does not imply that market research books lacked redeeming qualities. They were particularly strong in survey methods and in nonstatistical research areas. For example, the sections in these books on questionnaire design and cost versus benefit analysis were unparalleled. Nor does the classification of market research texts as less sophisticated imply that authors from other disciplines were any quicker at adopting innovative statistical methods. For instance, Day (1932) did discuss variance and correlation, but not Fisher's sampling theory, tests of two statistics, χ^2 tests, experimental design, or analysis of variance.

Two recently published market research books were examined (Aaker and Day 1983; Churchill 1987) to allow comparisons to be drawn with earlier texts. Both authors covered the two foundations of market research; data collection and data analysis. Approximately 40 and 35 percent of the Churchill, and Aaker and Day texts are respectively devoted to data collection and related topics. This points out that data collection is still the backbone of market research methodology. Both texts covered tests of two means, correlation, dispersion and χ^2 tests. Churchill treated analysis of variance, but only in an appendix. Nonrigorous treatment of advanced methods such as factor analysis and clustering methods were in both texts.

III. FACTORS LIMITING ADOPTION OF STATISTICAL METHODS

A. Sir Ronald Fisher

In 1925, Ronald Fisher's *Statistical Methods for Research Workers* broke the mold in which texts of the period were typically cast. In a review of the text, the eminent statistician Harold Hotelling (1927, p. 41) wrote that "most books on statistics consist of pedagogic rehashes of identical material.... [This book] summarizes for the non-mathematical reader the author's independent codification of statistical theory and some of his brilliant contributions to the subject." Perhaps Fisher's greatest contribution was analysis of variance.

Although Fisher's contributions were monumental, he did little to smooth the way for their acceptance. He was well known for a volatile temper that led to "titanic battles" with Pearson and Gosset, two leading statisticians of the period (Tankard 1984, p. 116). The battles centered around the merits of methods each had introduced. Fisher's introduction of degrees of freedom to Pearson's extant χ^2 formula is one example of a topic over which he and Pearson disagreed, in spite of the fact that most statisticians sided with Fisher. For his book, Fisher developed the now widely accepted format for the χ^2 distribution. This was because Pearson, *Biometrika*'s editor at the time, denied Fisher permission to use W.P. Elberton's tables which had been published previously by the journal, and were under copyright protection.

After 1918, Fisher refused to publish in *Biometrika*, and some of his most distinguished works appeared in obscure outlets such as the *Proceedings of the International Congress of Mathematics, Toronto*. He frequently omitted assumptions, and constantly failed to reference work done by others (Tankard 1984). He also wrote enigmatically. Mantel stated (1976, p. 125): "Once we had the sense to understand, we could appreciate the preciseness of writing in R.A. Fisher's texts—but then wonder how mysterious it could still be to the novice." Thus it should not be surprising that many of his ideas became popular after other authors *translated* them (Tankard 1984). One of the best examples of a text that made Fisher's ideas more accessible is the one written by Snedecor (1937).

The discussion illustrates two factors that could have slowed adoption of Fisher's notions by *all* potential users, not just those in marketing. First, conflicting opinions over an innovation by experts retards adoption (Gatingnon and Robertson 1985, p. 857). Second, ineffective communication of the existence of an innovation hampers adoption. Fisher's "battles," his tendency to publish in obscure outlets, and his puzzling writing style could have slowed the adoption of his ideas.

Some market researchers recognized that ineffective communication was delaying the transfer of more advanced statistical methods to the market research discipline. Reilly (1929), for instance, was one such individual:

True, some statisticians have done notable work in the theory of sampling, but little has
been done to adapt this sampling theory to the study of market problems in such a way
that the adaptation might be understood and used by one unschooled in higher mathematics
(p. 136).

Reilly's discussion of accuracy and internal reliability of proportions could have
been an effort on his part to address this shortcoming.

While this discussion helps explain why Fisher's notions were omitted from
market research texts, it does not address the omission of simpler statistical
methods. The following two subsections present more encompassing factors
that could have delayed the adoption of statistical methods.

B. Statistics as a Discipline

Three properties of statistics as a discipline could have impeded the adoption
of statistical methods: (1) the extent of an educational infrastructure; (2) the
properties of statistics as a body of mathematics; and (3) symbolic
inconsistency.

First, statistics was a relatively new discipline in American colleges and
universities during the early part of the twentieth century. The courses that
existed appear to have focused on descriptive and not inferential statistics.
Determining the exact content of each course at various institutions and exactly
which institutions were offering which courses is beyond the scope of this
research. But some trends can be found in the work of Glover (1926) and
Walker (1927). They discussed the results of a 1925 survey in which 40 out
of 125 responding colleges and universities reported offering no statistics
courses. Thus, in at least one third of responding institutions, students had
no opportunity to be exposed to statistics. In providing a list of what is most
needed in market research, Reilly (1929, p. 213) included "academic training
of men in mathematics and experimental methods."

As for content, King (1926) and Chaddock (1926) proposed similar "ideal"
introductory courses. Their suggested courses focused on: (1) interpretation of
charts, diagrams, and simple statistics such as the mean, mode and median; (2)
sources of data; (3) problem definition; and (4) units of analysis. King (1926) felt
introductory courses should be titled "Interpretation of Statistics," and objected
to the often used and misleading title of "Elementary Statistical Method."

A one-term market research instructor may not have had the time, nor
perhaps the ability or student capabilities, for developing skills in advanced
statistics. Market research textbook authors, themselves being marketers, and
their publishers, were probably aware of these potential deficiencies and may
have taken them into account when designing market research texts. An
educational infrastructure able to provide a market of sufficient size and
sophistication may not have existed.

Second, statistics is a complex body of mathematics and its relative trialability and observability are low. If trialability and observability are positively related to the speed of diffusion, and complexity is inversely related (Gatingnon and Robertson 1985, p. 862), then the properties of statistics could have slowed the rate at which the notions of the discipline were adopted.

Third, and last, some critics claimed statistics lacked symbolic uniformity, which is still true to some extent today. Walker (1927, p. 170) observed that statistics: "has not yet secured any considerable uniformity of language, symbolism, and certainly any uniformity of teaching aims." If standardization is associated with more rapid diffusion of an innovation (Robertson and Gatingnon 1986, p. 5), then a lack of symbolic uniformity may have been a barrier toward absorption of statistical methods. However, the symbolism within the reviewed texts did not appear to be any more inconsistent than that of contemporary texts. On balance, this last factor does not appear to have been a major barrier to diffusion.

C. Market Research Practices

By the 1920s and 1930s, market researchers were addressing a wide range of questions. During the early 1930s, the Norge division of the Borg-Warner Corporation, a maker of electric refrigerators, engaged in competitor analysis and assessed consumer buying intentions, brand recognition, volume per dealer, and the relative importance of price in consumer purchase decision making (Blood 1935). Trade journals forecasted annual sales in particular industries (*Sales Management* 1930a). IBM initiated a "Future Demands Department" with the mandate to "discover new needs in the business machine field and locate promising markets, then to build devices to meet specific demands" (Ehret 1929, p. 9). How to determine the profitability of individual items in a product line using internal data was demonstrated (McNiece 1929). The International Silver Company employed a survey to aid management in product design (Dowd 1931). As a last example, Westinghouse test marketed a new electric iron in Rochester, and a year later, about 1,000 users were surveyed to help name the product and identify directions for advertising copy and merchandising plans (White 1930).

In addition, in a vein more akin to marketing research rather than market research, marketing processes were researched. How advertising budgets of industrial firms were distributed across various expenditures such as conventions and house organs (*Sales Management* 1929), and how consumer demand for specific brands at point-of-purchase differed across products such as paints versus automobiles and buying situations such as grocery versus drugstores were investigated (Smith 1934).

Of the concerns of market researchers during this period, two are predominant. The first relates to the determination of sample sizes. Market researchers relied on an odd variety of quota sampling and experience, as opposed to probability sampling methods. Clark (1929) suggested the scope of the investigation, influential factors such as whether geographical differences exist, quantitative versus qualitative factors, and the number of important dependent variables could all be used to determine the required sample size.

Sample sizes were sometimes calculated by adding observations until estimates of percentages or means stabilized to an acceptable level. This often led, by contemporary standards, to exorbitant sample sizes. For example, the International Silver Company surveyed 15,000 consumers in one study, asking each respondent to select his or her first and second most preferred silverware design from among ten alternatives (Dowd 1931). In a study of brand preferences in Milwaukee, 6,700 housewives were surveyed *Sales Management* 1936). Some suggested that 10,000 responses were required before estimates stabilized in consumer studies, while only 250 were required in dealer research (Blood 1935).

Market researchers of the period tended to rely on what can be called the "eyeball" method, or the focus on obviously large differences among group means or proportions. However, statistical theory states that increasing sample size leads to decreasing sampling error. It follows that when the "eyeball" method is used, the likelihood of Type I error decreases as sample size increases. This implies that the relevance of inferential statistics to market research was limited during this period. One could even conclude that inferential statistics was incompatible with the dominant market research paradigm, leading to the possibility that market research procedures were an obstacle, or a perceived obstacle, to the adoption of techniques.

The second predominant concern revolved around question wording. Market researchers stressed the importance of making questions easy to understand and of not asking misleading or biased questions. Most of the reviewed market research texts discussed question wording (e.g., Reilly 1929, p. 82; White 1927, pp. 62-63). Articles also appeared in the trade press on how to write unbiased questions (Franken 1927; Sales Management 1930b).

During the 1920s and early 1930s, the objectives of the American Statistical Association focused on collecting and combining data (Harshbarger 1976). A similar emphasis was found in the reviewed market research texts. The purpose of collecting data is to aid management in marketing decision making. As the current study has shown, market researchers were addressing a wide variety of basic questions associated with the identification of markets, sales forecasting, product design, product line analysis, new product test marketing, and competitor analysis. Obviously, new technologies and methods allow researchers to ask new questions, but in many cases, the new questions are more complex formulations of the basic questions that were already being asked by 1940. Thus the adoption of inferential statistics apparently represents a refinement of decision-making processes. Its adoption does not represent any change in basic market research objectives. This supports the contention that the period of marketing since 1930 is an era of refinement and formalization (Fullerton 1988).

The skills that market research texts passed along to readers were closely linked to the collection and interpretation of data. These skills, coupled with a thorough understanding of measures of central tendency, proportions and tabulation, would allow a researcher to correctly answer important, meaningful market-related questions, especially in conjunction with large sample sizes. Therefore, the texts of the period appear to have passed along precisely what was needed. Apparently not required was knowledge of advanced inferential statistics.

As a final note, Reilly (1929) was the first American market research textbook author to adopt inferential statistics. It is interesting that he applied inferential statistics only to proportions. This is probably more than mere coincidence since the market research texts and articles examined here used proportions more often than any other summary measure, including mean and mode, to convey survey results.

IV. SUMMARY AND CONCLUSION

This research sought to determine the degree to which known, readily available statistical methods were being expounded by market research textbook authors during the early part of the twentieth century. A content analysis indicated that market research textbook authors did not include much beyond measures of central tendency.

The omission of more complex methods was examined within an adoption of innovation framework. Three factors were examined. First, Fisher's battles with other leading statisticians, his enigmatic writing style, and his tendency to publish in obscure outlets may all have slowed that rate at which his innovations were adopted.

Second, the teaching of statistics at the university level appears to have been limited and the introductory courses that were taught focused on descriptive statistics. An infrastructure able to provide a market large enough to digest advanced statistics in market research textbooks may not have existed. Also, the complexity and lack of observability and trialability that characterize statistics could be important factors that affected the adoption rate.

Lastly, market research practices could have precluded the need for widespread use of inferential statistics. There is evidence that market researchers relied on large sample sizes and large differences in estimates thereby alleviating the need for inferential statistics. The decision-making objective of market research has changed little over the years and the ultimate adoption of inferential statistics may represent more efficient decision making.

REFERENCES

Aaker, D.A. and G.S. Day. (1983). *Market Research*, Chicago: The Dryden Press.

Bartles, R. (1976). *The History of Marketing Thought* (2nd ed.). Columbus, OH: Grid, Inc.

Blood, H. (1935). "Comparative Research." *Printers' Ink*, 172. (August 22); pp. 37.

Bowley, A.L. (1926). *Elements of Statistics* (5th ed.). London: P.S. King & Sons, Ltd.

Brown, L.O. (1937). *Market Research and Analysis*. New York: The Ronald Press Company.

Camp, B.H. (1930). *The Mathematical Part of Elementary Statistics*. New York: D.C. Heath & Company.

Chaddock, R.E. (1926). "The Function of Statistics in Undergraduate Training." *Journal of the American Statistical Association*, 21 (March); pp. 1-8.

Charnes, A., W.W. Cooper, D.B. Learner, and F.Y. Phillips. (1985). "Management Science and Marketing Management." *Journal of Marketing*, 49 (Spring); pp. 93-105.

Churchill, G.A. (1987). *Market Research*. New York: John Wiley & Sons.

Clark, S.I. (1929). "How Many Questionnaire Replies Give an Accurate Answer?" *Printers' Ink*, 148 (July 18); pp. 17-20.

Converse, J.M. (1987). *Survey Research in the United States: Roots and Emergence 1890-1960*. Los Angeles: University of California Press.

Copeland, M.T. (1917). *Business Statistics*. London: Oxford University Press.

Crum, W.L. and A.C. Patton. (1925). *An Introduction to the Methods of Economic Statistics*. New York A.W. Shaw & Company.

Davis, H.T. (1937). *Elements of Statistics with Application to Economic Data* (2nd ed.). Bloomington, IN: The Principa Press.

Day, E.E. (1932). *Statistical Analysis*. New York: The Macmillan Company.

Dittmer, C.G. (1926). *Introduction to Social Statistics*. New York: A.W. Shaw Company.

Dowd, L. (1931). "How International Silver Pre-tested Product Designs." *Sales Management*, 25 (January 17); p. 112.

Duncan, C.S. (1922). *Commercial Research*. New York: The Macmillan Company.

Ehret, C. (1929) "International Business Machines Inaugurates a Future Demand Department." *Sales Management*, 18 (April 6); pp. 9-10.

Elmer, M.C. (1926). *Social Statistics: Statistical Methods Applied to Sociology*. Los Angeles: Press of Jesse Ray Miller.

Franken, R.B. (1927). "How to get Unprejudiced Market Data." *Printers' Ink*, 139 (April 21); pp. 127-28.

Fisher, R.A. (1925). *Statistical Methods for Research Workers*. Edinburgh: Oliver & Boyd.

Forsyth, C.H. (1924). *An Introduction to the Mathematical Analysis of Statistics*. New York: John Wiley & Sons.

Fullerton, F.A. (1988). "How Modern is Modern Marketing? Marketing's Evolution and the Myth of the "Production Era". *Journal of Marketing*, 52 (January); pp. 198-225.

Gatingnon, H. and T.S. Robertson. (1985). "A Propositional Inventory for New Diffusion Research." *Journal of Consumer Research*, 11 (March); pp. 849-67.

Glover, J.W. (1926). "Statistical Teaching in American Colleges and Universities." *Journal of the American Statistical Association*. 21 (December); pp. 519-524.

Harshbarger, B. (1976). "History of the Early Developments of Modern Statistics in America (1920-1944)." In *On the History of Statistics and Probability*, edited by D.B. Owen. New York: Marcel Dekker, Inc.

Hotelling, H. (1927). "Statistical Methods for Research Workers." Review of book by R.A. Fisher. *Journal of the American Statistical Association*, 22 (September); pp. 411-2.

Kelley, T. (1924). *Statistical Method*. New York: The Macmillan Company.

Kent, F.C. (1924). *Elements of Statistical Method*. New York: McGraw-Hill Book Company.

King, W.I. (1913). *The Elements of Statistical Method*. New York: The Macmillan Company.

King, W.I. (1926). "Content and Purpose of Training in Elementary and in Advanced Statistics." *Journal of the American Statistical Association,* 21 (December); pp. 430-5.

Mantel, N. (1976). "Statistical Techniques for Quasi Experiments." In *On the History of Statistics and Probability,* edited by D.B. Owen. New York: Marcel Dekker, Inc.

McNiece, T.M. (1929). "Are There Profitless Black Sheep in Your Lines of Products?" *Sales Management,* 18 (June 22); pp. 591-92.

Reed, V.L. (1929). *Planned Marketing.* New York: The Ronald Press Company.

Reilly, W.J. (1929). *Marketing Investigations.* New York: The Ronald Press Company.

Robertson, T.S. and H. Gatingnon. (1986). "Competitive Effects of Technology Diffusion." *Journal of Marketieng,* 50 (July); pp. 1-12.

Sales Management. (1929). "New Survey Shows How Technical Advertising Budget is Spent." 20 (October 5); pp. 20.

Sales Management. (1930a). "Building Forecasts Show Seven to Nine Billion Dollars for 1930." 21 (February 8); p. 246.

Sales Management. (1930b). "The ABC's of Casting a Sales Research Questionnaire." 23 (September 20); p. 430.

Sales Management. (1936). "Four-Year Analysis Shows Changes in Brand Preferences in Milwaukee." 38 (April 20); pp. 648-49.

Secrist, H. (1925). *An Introduction to Statistical Methods.* New York: The Macmillan Company.

Shaw, A.W. (1916). *An Approach to Business Problems.* Cambridge, MA: Harvard University Press.

Smith, E.R. (1934). "Brand Selection at Counter in 36.9% of Sales." *Printers' Ink,* 169 (December 27); pp. 35-36.

Snedecor, G.W. (1937). *Statistical Methods Applied to Experiments in Agriculture and Biology.* Ames, IO: Collegiate Press.

Starch, D. (1923). *Principles of Advertising.* New York: A.W. Shaw Company.

Tankard, J.W. (1984). *The Statistical Pioneers.* Cambridge, MA: Schenkman Publishing Company, Inc.

Thurstone, L.L. (1925). *The Fundamentals of Statistics.* New York: The Macmillan Company.

Walker, H.M. (1927). *Studies in the History of Statistical Method.* Baltimore: The William & Wilkins Company.

Wheeler, F.C. (1937). *The Technique of Marketing Research.* New York: McGraw-Hill Book Company.

White, P. (1927). *Advertising Research.* New York: D. Appleton & Company.

White, P. (1930). "Don't Plunge Wildly on New Products—Test Your Market." *Sales Management,* 24 (November 8); p. 225.

White, P. (1931). *Marketing Research Technique.* New York: Harper & Brothers.

THE DEVELOPMENT OF SPATIAL THEORY IN RETAILING AND ITS CONTRIBUTION TO MARKETING THOUGHT AND MARKETING SCIENCE

Barry J. Babin, James S. Boles, and Laurie Babin

ABSTRACT

This paper takes a historical look at contributions to marketing thought made by scholars studying spatial behavior by emphasizing the work of "retail gravitationalists." These researchers are applauded for their work based on its parsimony, scientific rigor, theoretical contribution, and its ability to provide normative guidelines to marketing practice.

I. INTRODUCTION

The reason that the people of a society need some form of marketing is that producers and consumers are separated....The separations of producers and consumers however, are of many types: spatial, temporal, informational, and financial. Whatever is done in the marketing process must contribute to the removal of these and other separations (Bartels 1968, p. 32).

Research in Marketing, Supplement 6, pages 103-116.
Copyright © 1994 by JAI Press Inc.
All rights of reproduction in any form reserved.
ISBN: 1-55938-187-6

The inclusion of a theory of market separations within Bartels' outline of a general theory of marketing clearly indicates the importance of research aimed at removing separations between producers and consumers. A paramount question raised by the issue of market separations concerns locating business enterprises in such a manner as to be attractive to as many prospective customers as possible. During the relatively brief history of marketology, retailing scholars and practitioners have contributed a significant body of knowledge to resolving this question (Craig, Ghosh, and McLafferty, 1984; Hollander 1980). Therefore, it seems fitting that any account of the development of marketing thought, science, or theory acknowledges these contributions.

Marketing scholars have often criticized consumer and marketing research for their lack of a scientific approach or their inability to make substantive theoretical contributions (Alderson and Cox 1948; Anderson 1983; Bartels 1951; Calder and Tybout 1987; Maholtra 1988; Olson 1981). Prominent among the leaders in theoretical and scientific advances within our discipline have been the retailing scholars (Bartels 1962; Hollander 1980; Sheth 1983). More specifically, retailing scholars toiling to advance knowledge related to removal of market separations have been singled out for their contribution to marketing science (Schwartz 1963). Perhaps an even greater accolade for these researchers has been their ability to produce practical normative guidelines concerning locational decisions that could easily be employed by large numbers of retailing practitioners (Lilien and Kotler 1983; Nelson 1958).

As in other areas of marketing and consumer research, retailing scholars addressing locational concerns have made advances by both borrowing from other disciplines and by developing specific knowledge. While Brown (1989) has recently reviewed the contributions of numerous economists to locational theory, the purpose of this paper is to focus on historical advancements made by retail researchers and practitioners studying market separations and to demonstrate how researchers working within a spatial framework may remain on the forefront of advancement within marketing science. In doing so, this paper is not only a tribute to the scientists who have made these advances, but also an acknowledgment of the durability of locational decisions and the generalizability of a spatial framework.

II. DEVELOPMENT OF EARLY
SPATIAL BEHAVIOR MODELS

Interest in studying spatial behavior appears to have increased in prominence during the early decades of the twentieth century (e.g., Chamberlin 1935; Hotelling 1929; Reilly 1929a). It is perhaps more than coincidental that this increased interest coincided with dramatic increases in transportation alternatives and in urban and rural infrastructures necessary to support them. In addition to marketers, scholars from other disciplines participated in studying spatial behavior as well.

Brown (1989) has recently noted the contribution of Harold Hotelling (1929) to location theory. Hotelling advanced the principle of minimum differentiation as an attempt to explain why stores of one type tend to locate in a central location. Taking an opposing view, Ed Chamberlin also contributed to spatial theories of behavior (1935). In his much heralded text, *The Theory of Monopolistic Competition,* Chamberlin advances a normative theory of spatial behavior that demonstrates how product differentiation can be accomplished by changing locations so as to be nearest to the greatest number of consumers (Dickson and Ginter 1987)—even if your ice cream is all alike. The result would be firms spatially dispersed in a configuration approaching social optimality. Other economists, certainly, contributed much to location theory. However, their contributions neither predate, nor are they clearly more important to, the advancement of marketing knowledge than are the contributions made by those involved in the practice and study of retailing. Perhaps most prominent among these contributors is William Reilly.

III. GRAVITY MODELS (SPATIAL INTERACTION THEORY)

William Reilly was one of the earliest retailing scholars to study spatial consumer behavior and was self-described as a "Sometime Marketing Specialist and Professor of Business Administration" (Reilly 1929a). The work of Reilly deserves mention on several accounts. First, he is recognized as among the earliest marketing scientists (Bartels 1962; Schwartz 1963). His interest in developing the scientific method of marketing research is clear in his text on survey research entitled *Marketing Investigations* (1929b). Second, he was dedicated to developing a culpable body of theory, but only after it met rigorous empirical and conceptual standards (Reilly 1931). Third, Reilly was capable of providing research that spanned the boundary between market and marketing research. His work not only provided a rich theoretical basis for basic research, but it also provided useful information to marketers in the field. Indeed, for fear of appearing too complex for retailers of his era, he suggested the use of newspaper subscription tracing as proxy for the Law of Retail Gravitation; "...since retailers who will use this law are, as a rule, not mathematicians, the application of the law has been simplified" (Reilly 1929a, p. 16). Since his main contribution to the study of market separations is the Law of Retail Gravitation, further discussion is warranted.

Table.1   Evolution of the Gravity Model

Equation	Year	Description
(1) $(B_a/B_b) = (P_a/P_b)^N (D_b/D_a)^n$	1929	The general form of the "law" as first proposed by Reilly.
(2) $BPD = (D_{a-b}) / [1 + (P_a/P_b)^{-5}]$	1948	A mathematical restatement of Reilly's "law" determining "Breaking Point Distance" between competing towns, a and b (Converse).
(3) $(B_a/B_b) = (P_a/P_b)(4/d)^2$	1948	Converse introduces the "inertia factor" in this form which allows for the determination of trade shares between towns a and b.
(4) $p_{ab} = (S_b/T_{ab}^n) / (\sum_{b=1}^{m} S_b/T_{ab}^n)$	1964	Huff uses shopping center size as a measure of attraction and travel time as a deterrence measure in a model which determines the likelihood of travel from a to shopping center b, considering m alternative centers.
(5) $p_{ab} = \dfrac{(\pi A_{ab}^N * \pi D_{ab}^n)}{(\sum_{k=1}^{m} \pi A_{abk}^N * \pi D_{abk}^n)}$	1985	A multiplicative interaction model reflecting multiple measures of attraction (A) and deterrence (D) allowing probabilities to be computed as above (Black 1987).

IV.   THE LAW OF RETAIL GRAVITATION

The general form of the law of retail gravitation as proposed by Reilly is Equation (1) in Table 1 where B represents business from an intermediate town to cities a and b, P represents the population of the cities, and D represents the distance of cities a and b from the intermediate town. The values of N and n represent the sensitivity of the dependent variable, business, to the individual predictors. Reilly states that unpublished studies support a value of one for N. He does, however, publish the results of a frequency analysis that supports a value of n equal to two when shopping goods are involved. Thus the more familiar representation of Reilly's Law:

$$B_a/ B_b = (P_a/ P_b)^1 (D_b/ D_a)^2$$

While economists and geographers working in this area were not influenced by Copeland's (1923) influential work on classification of goods, it is evident Reilly's work was. He was very clear about the limitations of this specific form of the relationship. The familiar form of the law, as expressed previously, pertained only to shopping, or "style" goods, and, in his original work (1929a), the state of Texas. He later (1931) conducted tests that led to the conclusion that, *on average*, this relationship would hold for the entire country.

Reilly (1929a) was also careful to point out that there are many factors that influence the actual decision of place of patronage, and he provides a rather exhaustive list. However, he feels these factors are very closely related to population and density, thus the use of these measures as composite indicators.

A. Basic Extensions of the Law

Another marketing researcher, Paul Converse (1948), contributed to spatial interaction theory by conducting studies to test and to extend the scope of the general form of Reilly's Law. Using this general relationship, he developed modifications of the law represented by Equations (2) and (3) given in Table 1. Equation (2) determines the breaking point distance (BPD) between two towns, thus representing the distance at which someone is indifferent concerning which town to patronize. The division of business between two towns can also be determined by Equation (3), where B represents the proportion of trade going to an outside town (a) and the proportion of trade retained by the home town (b). P represents population of the respective towns, and d represents distance to the outside town. The inertia factor, which was found to be usually close to 4, represents what must be overcome to visit any store.

Converse used these relationships to determine the breaking point distance for and the division of business between a small town and a large metropolitan center as well as for a small town versus Chicago. In each application he recognized how the parameters can change, thus implying the inherently probabilistic nature of his work. Thus, he reiterated that these relationships hold on the *average* and not necessarily in every instance. Extending to other classes of goods may not provide similar results.

David Huff (1964) extended the gravitational concept to intra-urban applications. He altered the general form of Reilly's Law to Equation (4) in Table 1 where P_{ab} is the probability of a consumer at point a traveling to shopping center b, T_{ab} is the time required to travel from a to b, S_b is the size in square feet of center b, and n, once again, is an empirically derived sensitivity factor.[1] This model allows for the evaluation of probabilities associated with someone selecting a particular location to patronize over a multitude of other alternatives, not just one. Using this idea, overlapping stochastic market areas can be configured for a number of locations, which provides for the capability of mapping market areas, even in an urban setting. Huff also suggests using size of stores to measure the amount of selection offered at a center. He considers size to be the predominant factor comprising attractiveness in urban settings.

Further extensions of Reilly's general model have resulted in a multiplicative interaction model (Black 1987). Equation (5) represents multiple measures of attraction (A), such as store size and appearance, and deterrents (D), such as travel time and travel cost, that are used to determine patronage probabilities. The main contribution of this work is that multiple indicants of attraction and deterrence are used instead of simply the single proxies of population and distance.

The substitution of other surrogates became quite common as other researchers attempted to extend the gravity concept. This suggests that the general form of Reilly's Law may be restated as:

$$(B_a/B_b) = (A_a/A_b)^N (C_b/C_a)^n$$

Where A represents attractiveness and C costs associated with the selection of a center. In applying this equation one has to decide on the appropriate measures of cost and attractiveness for that application. The result is a quite general relationship that is capable of accounting for a wide range of phenomena.

B.   The Versatility of the Gravity Model

Just as Newton's Law of Gravity proved to be a quite versatile relationship, spawning numerous forms explaining various related phenomena (force, inertia, momentum, etc.), it could be argued that Reilly's behavioral application of the physical concept of gravity to retailing is multifaceted as well. It appears, for example, that the general form of the gravity model is consistent with, or provides the basis for, a number of other advances in location theory.

As an illustration, it would appear that the gravity model has something to offer the principle of minimum differentiation. Brown (1989) cites the Canadian fur trading industry of the eighteenth and nineteenth centuries as a prototypical case of agglomeration. Rather than locating in a dispersed fashion, as Chamberlin (1935) would suggest, the two fur trading competitors, the Hudson's Bay Company and the North West Company, tended to locate their wilderness trading post within close proximity of one another. In an effort to gain competitive advantage, posts began offering incentives (mainly firewater) to their customers (mainly Indians) in return for their patronage. Given no real differences in distance to the posts, the Indians patronized posts perceived as being most attractive depending upon the incentives offered. Although economic theory would imply this to be a less than optimal economic arrangement, it may be that the incentives increased the attractiveness of the two-post centers to a far greater extent than would have been the attractiveness of two one-post centers. The gravity model would seem to be able to account for this phenomena by deriving and applying the appropriate sensitivity factors.

Similarly, Brown (1989) notes how Hotelling's model can be used to explain the agglomeration of retailers with similar product offerings, however, the introduction of a store with a different assortment of goods considerably complicates things.

If the apocryphal ice-cream sellers cluster together today, it is...because they realize that sunbathers prefer to compare prices and flavors before purchase. The arrival of a hot-dog seller, however, considerably complicates the competitive landscape (p. 462).

However, a straight forward application of a gravity model can easily accommodate the hot-dog vendor. In particular, Huff (1964) employed a gravity framework to study this problem. The hot-dog vender increases a consumer's probability of patronizing the center in proportion to the increase in attractiveness created by having a larger and more encompassing center.

Likewise, the gravity model implicitly underlies many principles of central place theory (Christaller 1966; Losch 1954). For example, the familiar hexagonal arrangement of centers, in the absence of certain geographic constraints, can be explained using Reilly's Law (Mason and Mayer 1990). Also, the concept of threshold indicates that a store has a minimum level of attractiveness that must be achieved given the population of an area. In addition, other central place concepts (Kivell and Shaw 1980), such as the greater patronage associated with higher order centers (those with a wider assortment of goods) and the threshold of a good, are also consistent with the law or retail gravitation.

Perhaps more familiar to retailing practitioners are the numerous heuristics and checklist methods used to guide them in selecting a retail site. Strohkarck and Phelps (1948) developed a shopping goods "market area map" showing the marketing areas for each market center in the continental United States. The basis of this map was the Law of Retail Gravitation. Likewise, most typical checklists (e.g., Nelson 1958) include a rather exhaustive inventory of indicators of a center's cost and attractiveness. Factors commonly considered are traffic patterns, what side of the street a center is on, how protected is it from the weather, what other shops are in the area, and so forth. Another popular locational technique, known as the analog technique (Applebaum 1966), also implicitly represents some of the gravity model's principles. A major component of the analog method is that as the distance of a trade area from a center increases, the proportion of consumers a retailer could hope to attract from those centers decreases. Applebaum's method demonstrates a fairly straightforward way of determining what could be thought of as various "breaking points."

These examples provide further evidence of how versatile and encompassing, particularly from a behavioral standpoint, the gravity framework has proven to be. In addition, it is worth noting that the law of retail gravitation predates most economic and geographic location theory, and has been around the same length of time as Hotelling's theory of minimum differentiation. The remainder of the paper briefly reviews what has happened since the early days of the retail gravity model, and suggests reasons for this framework's past, and perhaps, future success.

V.   RECENT ISSUES IN
SPATIAL INTERACTION MODELS

Interest in spatial behavior models, or models of separations, has continued since the period of substantive revelations offered earlier in this century. However, the popularity of this research has fluctuated in both quantity and content within the retailing and marketing literature. Recently, two interesting issues have gained the attention of spatial researchers. First is the issue of various estimation techniques used to uncover model parameters. A second concern is decomposition of attractiveness and deterrents (cost), composites into actual variables that they may represent, thus increasing specificity of the 'model. On both of these issues it is clear that this group of scholars continues on the forefront of advancement in marketing science and continues to make substantive contributions to other areas of marketing, consumer behavior, and other disciplines as well.

A.   Modeling Issues

The most common form of the original law of retail gravitation assigns parameters of one to population (attractiveness) and two to distance (deterrents) in a multiplicative model (Engel, Blackwell, and Miniard 1990). However, these parameter values were expected to hold only under specific conditions outlined by Reilly (1929a). Reilly obtained these values through statistical regression analysis. In doing so, his work represents one of the earliest applications of regression in marketing research. Later, Converse (1948), also using regression analysis, specified parameter values for a variety of conditions not covered in Reilly's original work.

However, as gravity models evolved increasingly into explicit choice axioms (e.g., Luce 1959), the statistical assumptions normally associated with linear regression, and least squares parameter estimation, became inadequate in many instances. To be more precise in estimating parameters, store choice researchers were among the first researchers to apply both the multinomial logit (Arnold, Roth, and Tigert 1978) and probit (Maholtra 1983) models in consumer or marketing research. While logit seems to have become the model of choice, primarily because of its simplicity (Maholtra 1984), current research is underway testing the appropriateness of its assumptions to store choice phenomena. The assumption called most into question is one that forces cross-elasticities to be equal (Maholtra 1988). It is likely that researchers striving for applications of gravity type models will play a role in resolving this and similar issues, and perhaps, contribute to the advancement of all of marketing science.

Like Reilly, other gravitationalists have demonstrated a great concern for scientific precision and rigor. However, the real strength of the gravity model is not so much in its techniques or mathematics, but rather, its simplicity is its greatest virtue.

B. Weaknesses

Along with its many strengths, gravity models have often been criticized for their limitations in serving as a general location tool (Mason, Mayer, and Ezell 1991). Reilly (1929a) himself acknowledged that, in practice, it may be too mathematical to apply. Thus, he offered a useful heuristic involving measurement of newspaper subscriptions to aid retail practitioners in location decisions.[2] Also in practice, it is more often applied successfully in rural rather than urban settings. Perhaps its greatest disadvantage as a locational tool is its inability to explicitly take into account numerous competitive and logistical forces that could greatly determine the success of a marketing operation (Porter 1990). For example, a conglomeration of similar industries may often lead to economies of scale. Thus, formal gravity models may be more useful as an explanatory tool, rather than as a general locational device.

C. Specification Issues

What is often overlooked when considering gravity models is that they do not limit us to studying behavior related only to geographic or actual physical distances (Stanley and Sewall 1976). Reilly's (1929a) original work clearly recognized that distance and population were merely composite indications of various other factors that make a shopping alternative either attractive or unattractive. As previously indicated, more recent research has attempted to increase model specificity by decomposing surrogates into their individual components (Black 1987; Hubbard 1978). This decompositional approach, while having similar aims, is an attractive alternative for studying consumer behavior because it avoids many of the problems associated with traditional multiattribute models of retail patronage (Darden, Erdem, and Darden 1983).

Other attempts at increasing specification have led to the development of novel concepts. Thompson (1963) introduced the concept of "subjective distance." He felt that subjective, rather than actual, distance increased the precision of gravity models because individual perceptions better captured consumer inclinations. Thus, shopping centers that are more attractive are likely to be perceived as geographically closer than they actually are.

An interesting application of this concept has recently appeared in the *Journal of the Academy of Marketing Science*. Mayo, Jarvis, and Xander (1988), in applying a gravity model to vacation alternatives, have demonstrated how increased subjective distance can actually make an alternative more attractive. Applications of subjective distance in this vein may be useful in explaining outshopping or "shopping vacations" (Darden and Perreault 1976), which comprise a substantial segment of new retail developments in major urban markets. In part, subjective distance may capture the "pull" associated with sensory qualities associated with these new shopping alternatives (Grossbart, Hampton, Rammohan, and Lapidus 1989; Meoli andd Feinberg 1989).

Other applications of future research can be envisioned. The inertia factor first introduced by Converse (1948) is worthy of further attention (Mayo, Jarvis, and Xander 1988). Given dramatic increases in in-home shopping alternatives, a study of how these alternatives have affected consumer inertia may be warranted. If consumer inertia is increasing due to increased in-home shopping opportunities, it may mean that traditional retailers will have a more difficult time motivating consumers to leave the comfort of their homes to do their shopping. Also, the inertia factor may provide a useful segmentation variable to help in separating those consumers who enjoy shopping from those that do not. Another area of future research that may greatly improve studies of market separations lies in greater use of longitudinal studies. Since spatial theories in marketing research deal with consumer behavior through both time and space, longitudinal studies would seem an appropriate avenue for extending knowledge in this important area.

Thus, study of market separations has proven to be a very useful method for uncovering important concepts and techniques that have found widespread acceptance across market as well as marketing research. Based on recent studies like those briefly described previously, this trend can be expected to continue in the future.

VI. CONCLUSIONS

An argument has been made in this paper that the study of spatial market separations has led to many advances in the state of knowledge of marketing. Among researchers studying related phenomena, "retail gravitationalists" can be singled out as responsible for numerous major contributions to both marketing science and marketing theory. Early gravitationalists, such as Reilly and Converse, provided us with a conceptually simple, yet, scientifically rigorous framework for studying consumer behavior through time and space.

Despite its apparent simplicity, the gravity framework appears to be one of the few models in marketing worthy of the label "theory" (Hunt 1983).

As time has progressed there have been many more complex models advanced in marketing. It is perhaps safe to say that many of these have not enjoyed the success of the gravity framework in providing a useful tool for both research and application. If it is true that simplicity is a virtue, then it is clear why the gravitationalists have been successful. The simplicity and usefulness of the theory are made clear when it is summarized.

Gravitationalists provide a framework for studying market separations that simply says consumers make patronage decisions by summarizing and comparing the attractiveness and costs associated with each alternative. Mathematically, this simple relation can be expressed as:

$$P_a = f(\, A_a\,) \; X \; f(\, C_a\,)$$

The probability of selecting a shopping alternative, a, is equal to some function of a's attractiveness times some function of costs associated with choosing a. Figure 1 pictorially represents this simple framework and various individual measures that may comprise attractiveness and costs.

Future research should recognize that the designation of variables as contributing to an alternative's attractiveness or costs is somewhat arbitrary.[3] Factors may be derived that are a cost to some segment of consumers but contribute to the attractiveness of an alternative to another. Further, some variables may contribute to both an alternative's attractiveness and costs. Image inputs, emotional factors, and individual differences would seem likely to introduce such paradoxes. Additionally, the gravity model provides us with a simple yet versatile framework capable of including both cognitive and emotional considerations in explaining consumer behavior. This capability may allow the model to extend beyond what is considered traditional "rational" consumer behavior. Therefore it seems that this general form of a spatial theory may allow applications involving all types of market separations—not simply geographic ones.

In addition, more work needs to be done specifically demonstrating the similarity of various cross-disciplinary locational theories. Mathematical representations might be developed, at least in some instances, which might accomplish this task.

In conclusion, it is clear that the development of spatial theory in retailing research represents a significant achievement in marketing thought. These researchers have left us with many contributions through the history of marketing. In addition, their impact will almost certainly be seen in the future as well.

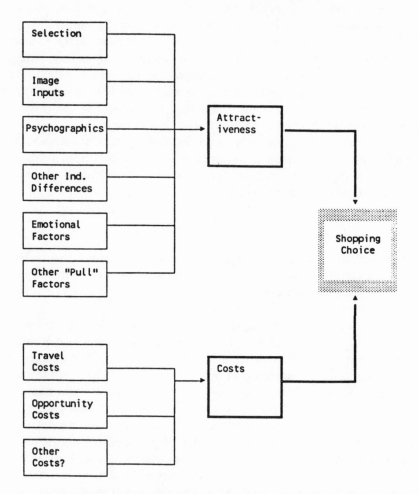

Figure 1.   A Pictorial Representation of a
General Theory of Retail (Consumer) Spatial Behavior

NOTES

1.   This sensitivity factor can be thought of as a measure of the amount of time someone is willing to spend shopping for a particular good. For instance, n would be expected to be higher for convenience goods than style goods (Huff 1964). Small n also recognizes the intuitively obvious geometric properties associated with these relationships. (If the choices are extremely far apart, the attractiveness is not very important.)

2.   Many of the heuristics mentioned earlier may well be explained mathematically by some sort of gravity model.

3. An even more parsimonious representation may be to include only benefits as a construct. In such a representation costs are merely negative benefits while positive benefits make up attractiveness. However, the conceptually rich notion of trading off benefits versus costs is retained by keeping both concepts.

REFERENCES

Alderson, W. and R. Cox. (1948). "Towards a Theory of Marketing." *Journal of Marketing,* 13; pp. 137-152.

Anderson, P. F. (1983). "Marketing, Scientific Progress, and Scientific Method." *Journal of Marketing,* 47(3); pp. 18-31.

Applebaum, W. (1966). "Methods for Determining Store Trade Areas, Market Penetration, and Potential Sales." *Journal of Marketing Research,* 3; pp. 127-141.

Arnold, S., V. Roth, and D. J. Tigert. (1978). "Conditional Logit Versus MDA in the Prediction of Store Choice." Pp. 665-670 in *Advances in Consumer Research,* edited by R. Bagozzi. Ann Arbor, MI: Association for Consumer Research.

Bartels, R. (1951). "Can Marketing be a Science?" *Journal of Marketing,* 15; pp. 319-328.

Bartels, R. (1962). *The Development of Marketing Thought.* Homewood IL: Irwin.

Bartels, R. (1968). "The General Theory of Marketing." *The Journal of Marketing,* 32; pp. 29-33.

Black, W. C. (1987). "Choice-set Definition in Patronage Modeling." *Journal of Retailing,* 63; pp. 63-83.

Brown, S. (1989). "Retail Location Theory: The Legacy of Harold Hotelling. *Journal of Retailing,* 65(Winter); pp. 450-469.

Calder, B. J. and A. M. Tybout. (1987). "What Consumer Research is..." *Journal of Consumer Research,* 14; pp. 136-140.

Chamberlin, E. (1935). *The Theory of Monopolistic Competition.* Cambridge: Harvard Press.

Christaller, W. (1966). *Central Places in Southern Germany* (C. Baskin, Trans.). Englewood Cliffs, NJ: Prentice-Hall.

Converse, P. D. (1948). "New Laws of Retail Gravitation." *Journal of Marketing,* 13; pp. 379-84.

Copeland, M. T. (1923). "The Relation of Consumers' Buying Habits to Marketing Methods." *Harvard Business Review,* 1; pp. 282-289.

Craig, S. C., A. Ghosh, and S. McLafferty. (1984). "Models of the Retail Location Process: A Review." *The Journal of Retailing,* 60; pp. 5-36.

Darden, W. R. and W. D. Perreault. (1976). "Identifying Interurban Shoppers: Multiproduct Purchase Patterns and Segmentation Profiles." *Journal of Marketing Research,* 13; pp. 51-6.

Darden, W. R., O, Erdem, and D. Darden. (1983). "A Comparison and Test of Three Causal Models of Patronage Intention." Pp. 135-143 in *Patronage Behavior and Retail Management,* edited by W. R. Darden and R. F. Lusch. New York: Elsevier.

Dickson, P. R. and J. L. Ginter. (1987). "Market Segmentation, Product Differentiation, and Marketing Strategy." *Journal of Marketing,* 51(April); pp. 1-10.

Engel, J. F., R. D. Blackwell, and P. Miniard. (1990). *Consumer Behavior.* Orlando, FL: Dryden.

Grossbart, S., R. Hampton, B. Rammohan, and R. S. Lapidus. (1989). "Environmental Dispositions and Customer Responsiveness to Atmospherics." Pp. 131-148 in *Proceedings of The Symposium on Patronage Behavior and Retail Strategy: The Cutting Edge,* edited by W. R. Darden. Baton Rouge, LA: Louisiana State University.

Hollander, S. C. (1980). "Some Notes on the Difficulty of Identifying the Marketing Thought Contributions of the 'Early Institutionalists.'" Pp. 45-46 in *Theoretical Developments in*

Marketing, edited by C. W. Lamb and P. M. Dunne. Chicago: American Marketing Association.

Hotelling, H. (1929). "Stability in Competition." *The Economic Journal*, 39(March); pp. 41-57.

Hubbard, R. (1978). "A Review of Selected Factors Conditioning Consumer Travel Behavior." *Journal of Consumer Research*, 5; pp. 1-21.

Huff, D. L. (1964). "Defining and Estimating a Trading Area." *Journal of Marketing*, 28(July); pp. 34-38.

Hunt, S. D. (1983). *Marketing Theory: The Philosophy of Marketing Science*. Homewood, IL: Irwin.

Kivell, P. T. and G. Shaw. (1980). "The Study of Retail Location." Pp. 45-60 in *Retail Geography* edited by J. Dawson. New York: John Wiley and Sons.

Lilien, G. L. and P. Kotler. (1983). *Marketing Decision Making*. New York: Harper and Row.

Losch, A. (1954). *The Economics of Location* (Wolfgang F. Stopler, Trans.). New Haven: Yale University Press.

Luce, R. D. (1959). *Individual Choice Behavior*. New York: John Wiley and Sons.

Maholtra, N. K. (1983). "A Threshold Model of Store Choice." *Journal of Retailing*, 59(Summer); pp. 3-21.

Maholtra, N. K. (1984). "The Use of Linear Logit Models in Marketing Research." *Journal of Marketing Research*, 21(February); pp. 20-31.

Maholtra, N. K. (1988). "Some Observations on the State of Art in Marketing Research." *Journal of the Academy of Marketing Science*, 16(Summer); pp. 4-24.

Mason, J. B. and M. Mayer. (1990). *Retailing: Theory and Practice*. Homewood, IL: Irwin.

Mason, J. B., M. Mayer, and H. Ezell. (1991). *Retailing*. Homewood, IL: Irwin.

Mayo, E. J., L. P. Jarvis, and J. P. Xander. (1988). "Beyond the Gravity Model." *Journal of the Academy of Marketing Science*, 16(Fall); pp. 23-29.

Meoli, J. and R. A. Feinberg. (1989). "Stores as Stimulus Reinforcement: a Learning Theory Approach to Retail Mall Assortment." Pp.149-161 in *Proceedings of The Symposium on Patronage Behavior and Retail Strategy: The Cutting Edge*, edited by W. R. Darden. Baton Rouge: Louisiana State University.

Nelson, R. L. (1958). *The Selection of Retail Locations*. New York: F. W. Dodge.

Olson, J. C. (1981). "Presidential Address—1981: Toward a Science of Consumer Behavior." Pp. 1-10 in *Advances in Consumer Research*, edited by K. B. Monroe. Ann Arbor: Association for Consumer Research.

Porter, M. E. (1990). *The Competitive Advantage of Nations*. New York: Macmillan.

Reilly, W. J. (1929a). *Methods for the Study of Retail Relationships* (Research Monograph ν4). University of Texas: Bureau of Business Research.

Reilly, W. J. (1929b). *Marketing Investigations*. New York: Ronald Press.

Reilly, W. J. (1931). *The Law of Retail Gravitation*. New York: William J. Reilly.

Schwartz, G. (1963). *Development of Theory in Marketing*. Cincinnati: South-Western.

Sheth, J. N. (1983). "An Integrative Theory of Patronage Preference and Behavior." Pp. 178-201 in *Patronage Behavior and Retail Management*, edited by W. R. Darden and R. Lusch. New York: Elsevier Science Publishing.

Stanley, T. J. and M. Sewall. (1976). "Image Inputs to a Probabilistic Model: Predicting Retail Potential." *Journal of Marketing*, 40(July); pp. 48-53.

Strohkarck, F. and K. Phelps. (1948). "The Mechanics of Constructing a Market-area Map." *Journal of Marketing*, 13; pp. 493-496.

Thompson, D. L. (1963). "New Concept: 'Subjective Distance.'" *Journal of Retailing*, 39(Spring); pp. 1-6.

REILLY'S LAW OF RETAIL GRAVITATION:

WHAT GOES ROUND, COMES AROUND

Stephen Brown

ABSTRACT

William J. Reilly's *Law of Retail Gravitation* ranks among the classics of marketing thought. This paper examines the evolution of Reilly's Law, using the well-known wheel of retailing theory as an organizational framework. In line with the wheel (and paralleling the development of the wheel theory itself), the gravity model commenced as a simple conceptualization of consumer spatial behavior, became increasingly sophisticated through time, and thereby created conditions conducive to the re-emergence of the basic interaction model. The wheel theory, however, describes but does not explain the processes of change and a more comprehensive model of the evolution of retail marketing theories is suggested.

I. INTRODUCTION

Approximately sixty years ago, a slim, 75 page volume was published by William J. Reilly, founding member of the Institute for Straight Thinking and

---

Research in Marketing, Supplement 6, pages 117-147.
ISBN: 1-55938-187-6

117

self-professed "sometime marketing specialist." Entitled *The Law of Retail Gravitation*, his text drew an analogy between Newton's law of planetary motion and the geography of retailing. It stated that, "two cities draw trade from any intermediate city or town...approximately in direct proportion to the populations of the two cities and in inverse proportion to the square of the distances from these two cities to the intermediate town" (Reilly 1931, p. 9).

Although it was all but ignored at the time, Reilly's Law, as it became known (along with "gravity model" and in its latterday incarnations "general" or "spatial interaction theory"), has had an enormous influence upon the study of retail marketing and buyer behavior. The concept in its various guises has underpinned significant advances in trade area estimation (Goldstucker, Bellenger, Stanley, and Otte 1978), market share determination (Fotheringham 1988), shopping center impact analysis (Wade 1983), sales forecasting and performance monitoring techniques (Ghosh and McLafferty 1987), site selection procedures (Rogers 1984), and all manner of aggregate and disaggregate models of store choice and patronage behavior (Golledge and Timmermans 1988). It has also been examined in historical, archaeological, and political contexts as diverse as mid-nineteenth century Massachusetts (Rose 1987), the prehistoric Near East (Hallam, Warren, and Renfrew 1976), and the command economies of central Europe (Korcelli 1976). Indeed, in its broader spatial interaction variants, the gravity model has been applied to topics as disparate as air travel, telephone calls, marriage patterns, voting behavior, and rural-urban migration (Fotheringham 1981; Mackay 1958; Kasakoff and Adams 1977; Reynolds 1969; O'Sullivan 1977). Reilly's Law, in short, has proved to be perhaps the most productive of all retail marketing generalizations.

Despite the (literally) thousands of published papers that the gravity model has generated, the development of Reilly's Law has been somewhat neglected by students of marketing thought. True, the gravity formulae are fixtures in most marketing, retailing, and buyer behavior textbooks (Cannon 1986; McGoldrick 1990; Engel, Blackwell, and Miniard 1986), and any number of introductory and advanced expositions on spatial interaction theory are now available (Openshaw 1975a; Haynes and Fotheringham 1984; Fotheringham and O'Kelly 1989). But the evolution of the concept itself has been all but ignored by marketing historians and indeed the few analyses that exist have long since been bypassed by the conceptual development process (Bartels 1962; Shwartz 1962).[1] It is arguable, therefore, that an excursus on the development of William J. Reilly's evergreen insight would be welcomed by the academic marketing community.

This paper, accordingly, will endeavor to encapsulate the evolution of Reilly's Law by using the well-known wheel of retailing theory as an organizational framework. The wheel, after all, is simple, familiar to most readers and, somehow appropriately, an exact contemporary of the *Law of*

Retail Gravitation (McNair 1931). Most importantly, it is singularly apt. The wheel describes the evolution of retailing institutions from cut-price, low-cost operations to sophisticated, service orientated establishments. As many commentators have pointed out, few theoretical institutions in the retailing arena were more basic to begin with than the gravity model—and fewer still have become more sophisticated with the passage of time (Wilkinson 1980; Daniels 1985; Field and MacGregor 1987; O'Brien and Harris 1991). What is more, just as the wheel predicts that the upmarket orientation of mature institutions creates opportunities for a new breed of cut price specialists, so too the recent history of spatial interaction theory has been characterized by a "back to basics" ethos among the modeling community.

The objective of this paper, it must be stressed, is not to contribute to the extant body of spatial interaction theory, nor to provide a treatise on the technicalities of the gravity modeling process. It is simply to examine, in a systematic fashion, the evolution of an especially significant theoretical insight. Moreover, by describing the development of one classic marketing concept in terms of another, it may be possible to gain a deeper understanding of both.

II. ANTECEDENTS

According to Sheth, Gardner, and Garrett (1988 p. 187, 189), both the law of retail gravitation and the wheel of retailing rank among the very few concepts that the marketing discipline can claim to have originated. As a consequence, they should be "nurtured and developed rather than abandoned for borrowed concepts from economics, psychology, or sociology." In point of fact, both the wheel and gravity analogies were in widespread use prior to McNair's and Reilly's respective adaptations to retailing phenomena. The wheel metaphor, in various forms, can be traced back to the dawn of civilization (Brown 1991) and social interpretations of the gravity concept are almost as old as Newton's (1687) law itself (McKinney 1968). Even older, indeed, if one considers the commonplace prehistoric belief that physical laws determine human affairs to be a legitimate precursor of subsequent applications (Tocalis 1978).

It is generally acknowledged, however, that Carey (1858) was the first to describe human interaction in gravitational terms (Carruthers 1956), though McKinney (1968) has made a case for Bishop John Berkeley (1713), among others. The earliest empirical application of the Newtonian principle was arguably Ravenstein's (1885, 1889) extensive studies of internal migration in England and Wales (Grigg (1977) however has demonstrated that Ravenstein did not specifically mention the distance component) and a similar exercise in the midwest of the United States was subsequently undertaken by Young (1924).

Thus, although he is frequently credited with its discovery, William J. Reilly cannot be considered the father of the gravity model. He was, nonetheless, the first to employ a gravitational metaphor to describe the trade-off that consumers make between the attractions of competing shopping areas and the deterrent effects of distance (though Lösch (1954), citing early German studies, has even challenged this achievement) and the first to derive a mathematical statement of the relationship (Tocalis 1978). Contrary to widespread belief, what is more, Reilly's Law was the outcome of extensive empirical investigation—not deductive reasoning—which comprised "hundreds" of interviews with shoppers, retailers and trade associations, detailed analysis of store charge accounts, and the study of newspaper circulation patterns (Reilly 1929,1931). In fact, for a theoretical contribution that is invariably described as "crude" and/or "deterministic" (e.g., Olsson 1966; Kivell and Shaw 1980; McGoldrick 1990), Reilly's empirical investigations were remarkably enlightened. As shall become apparent, he identified many of the shortcomings that were to figure prominently in subsequent critiques. Nevertheless, compared to later developments—and in line with the wheel theory—his book comprised a fairly succinct statement of the gravitational hypothesis (three pages of text and a short appendix).

III. INNOVATION

It is a truism that innovations in retailing tend to be brought to fruition by the adapters not the inventors of the concept (Dickinson 1983). So it is with innovations in retailing thought. Just as the wheel theory was proposed by McNair (1931, 1958) and popularized by Hollander (1960), so too Reilly's Law owes much of its reputation to the work of Paul D. Converse (1948). Like Hollander he not only succeeded in bringing a brace of relatively obscure publications (a Texas University monograph and the text that Reilly produced himself) to a much wider audience, courtesy of the *Journal of Marketing*, but he also added substantially to the original model.[2] By a simple reworking of Reilly's gravitational formula, he succeeded in deriving a "break-point" equasion, which, by specifying the point at which the influence of two competing towns is equal, enabled their respective trading areas to be delimited precisely. In actual fact, Converse (1948) presented no less than six variants of the gravity equation, most of which pertained to the estimation of "outshopping" activity, though it is his break-point formulation that is perhaps best remembered and, even today, remains widely used in trade area determination (Ghosh and McLafferty 1987).

Furthermore, Converse's interpretation of the gravity model, like Hollander's dissemination of the wheel, stimulated a rash of empirical analyses, the results of which were mixed at best. Studies undertaken in Laurel, Maryland (Bennett 1944), Charlotte, North Carolina (Douglas 1948, 1949) and in a number of other U.S. cities (Converse 1943; Strohkarck and Phelps 1948;

Reilly 1953), concluded that the original gravity formulae performed reasonably well in practical situations. Indeed, Douglas (1948, p. 60), and latterly Rose (1987, p. 39), went so far as to describe Reilly's Law as "remarkably accurate." Other examinations, most notably those of Jung (1959) in Missouri, Reynolds (1953a) in Iowa, and Wagner (1974) in Ohio, were much less fulsome in their praise. Even August Lösch (1954), the renowned German economist, was moved to inveigh against Reilly's Law after his empirical investigations of Iowan trading areas.

IV. GROWTH

The principal perceived problem with the original gravity permutation was that its variables, population and road distance, and the parameters on these variables, unity and the inverse square, did not always perform well in practice (Carrothers 1956; Huff 1962). In fairness, both Reilly and Converse recognised that population and road distance were surrogates for attractiveness and deterrence respectively and that a host of factors, including topographical conditions, population density and the marketing activities of individual retailers, could serve to distort the theoretical parameters, especially when the cities under scrutiny were of markedly different size. Nevertheless, the apparent shortcomings of the original conceptualization, as with wheel theory, gave rise to modifications of the gravity model and the advocation of alternative theoretical conjectures.

The early alterations, in essence, involved the introduction of what were considered to be more appropriate attraction and deterrence variables and permitting the parameters to take on alternative values (for detailed discussion see, Sweet 1964; Bucklin 1967; Davies 1970, 1974; Openshaw 1973, 1975b). With regard to the former, population was replaced as an attraction factor by a host of variables, ranging from retail floorspace (Voorhees 1957) and number of employees (Lowry 1964), to total retail turnover (Rhodes and Whitaker 1967) and various composite indices reflecting the types of retailing facility on offer (Manchester University 1966). Similarly, the deterrence variable was substituted, among others, by straight-line distance (Gibson and Pullen 1972), a congestion index (Parry-Lewis and Traill 1968), and travel time (Brunner and Mason 1968).

With regard to the parameters, the disproportionately greater shopping opportunities that exist in large cities over small encouraged modifications of the attraction coefficient (Pacione 1974). What is more, as the friction of distance manifestly varies between different categories of merchandise (high for convenience goods, low for comparison goods and, as Mayo, Jarvis, and Xander (1988) have demonstrated, potentially negative for exotic holiday destinations) and for different socioeconomic groups of consumers (those with high incomes, being automobile owners, enjoy greater freedom of movement), the distance parameter has been shown to vary considerably from application to application (Garrison 1956; Yuill 1967; Huff and Jenks 1968; Young 1975).

Although adjustments to the original parameters proved unavoidable in practical applications of the gravity model, the very act of doing so undermined the Newtonian analogy upon which the concept was based (Carrothers 1956). However, just as the wheel theory spawned alternative conceptualizations of retail change, so too studies of spatial interaction gave rise to a wide range of theoretical conjectures—Stouffer's (1940, 1960) "intervening opportunities" model, Zipf's (1949) "principle of least effort" and Stewart's (1941) codification of "social physics," to name but three. From a retailing perspective, perhaps the most significant alternatives were Huff's (1963) spatial interpretation of the Luce (1959) choice axiom and A. G. Wilson's (1967) entropy maximization procedure.

Rightly regarded as one of the most important post-war contributions to spatial interaction theory, Huff's (1963, 1964) reformulation of the gravity model, like the earlier contributions of Reilly and Converse, is frequently misrepresented in the retailing literature. Contrary to widespread belief, Huff was not the first to extend the model to more than two competing centers, nor was he the earliest advocate of overlapping trade areas. Both of these issues had been anticipated by Reilly (1929, 1931). In fact, Huff was not even the instigator of a probabalistic approach to spatial interaction (see for example, Dodd 1950; Schneider 1959; Harris 1964), nor the pioneer of intra-urban adaptations (Ellwood 1954). He was, however, the first to focus attention on the choice behavior of *individual consumers* (though, in practice, individual behaviors are aggregated to derive overall patronization probabilities for the residential zones that make up the study area) and, of equal significance perhaps, championed *store specific* applications of gravitational principles (Huff 1966).

Huff maintained that consumers patronize competing shopping centers (or stores) on the basis of their overall "utility," which, for the purposes of his model, comprised an amalgam of attraction (center size) and deterrence (travel time) factors. After Luce (1959), moreover, he posited that the probability of patronizing a particular center could be determined from the relative utilities of all competing centers. Each center, in other words, had a probability of being patronized, which was directly related to its size, inversely related to its distance, and directly related to the utility of competing shopping areas. Trade areas, as a consequence, could not be conceived as bifurcating at a specific breakpoint but rather overlapping and intermingled in a more realistic fashion. What is more, by combining projected patronage behaviors with estimated start-up costs at specified sites, Huff (1966) argued that it was possible to identify that holy grail of retailing research, the optimal store location.

Although it represented a significant conceptual advance, which was later reinforced by Niedercorn and Bechdolt's (1969, 1972) derivation of the gravity model from utility maximization theory, the operationalization of Huff's model required consumer survey research. As a rule, such information was not available to, nor sought by, early analysts of spatial interaction behavior and recourse was more usually made to another multicenter, intra-urban model that was developed for the Baltimore metropolitan area (Lakshmanan and Hansen 1965). Essentially an attempt to estimate future shopping potential, Lakshmanan and Hansen (1965) introduced a variable representing projected retail expenditure in the various residential zones that made up the study area. This was then allocated, on the basis of spatial interaction principles, among existing and proposed shopping centers. Albeit more of a modification than a true theoretical departure, the Lakshmanan and Hansen model had enormous empirical influence and variations of the framework underpinned numerous regional and subregional shopping models, manifold shopping center impact studies, and, indeed, retailers' estimates of relative market share (Gilligan, Rainford, and Thorne 1974; Davies 1977; Craig, Ghosh, and McLafferty 1984; Berry and Parr 1988; Penny and Broom 1988).

Besides providing a much-used methodological framework, the Baltimore model, in some respects, represents a bridge between Huff's multicenter, intra-urban application and Wilson's (1967) contrasting theoretical standpoint based on entropy maximization. By limiting their model to the allocation of potential retail expenditure, Lakshmanan and Hansen provided an early example of what Wilson (1971) was to term "production constrained" gravity models. Indeed, he demonstrated that, depending upon the available interaction data, a "family" of interaction models, ranging from the traditional (unconstrained) gravity model, through production and attraction constrained, to doubly constrained variants, could be specified. More significantly, perhaps, he showed how the original gravity formula could be derived, not merely from the increasingly abused Newtonian analogy, but from another branch of the physical sciences, the entropy maximization methods of statistical mechanics. However, in complete contrast to Huff's reliance upon microscale behaviors of individual consumers, Wilson's approach was highly aggregate in orientation.

Basically an exercise in statistical averaging, entropy maximization rests upon the assumption that any aggregate pattern of spatial interaction can be attained by a very large number of combinations of individual behaviors. The *most likely* combination of all possible combinations, however, is compatible with the gravity model. Or, as Wilson (1967, p. 258) put it, "given total numbers of trip origins and destinations for each zone... given the costs of travelling between each zone, and given that there is some fixed total expenditure... then there is a most probable distribution of trips between zones, and this distribution is the same as the one normally described as the gravity model distribution" (for detailed discussion see, Gould 1972; Webber 1977; Senior 1979).

V. TRADING UP

Prior to Wilson's, Huff's, and, to a lesser extent, Niedercorn and Bechdolt's insights, gravity modeling was a comparatively unsophisticated process—the mathematics were straightforward and a basic calculating ability was the analyst's principal requirement. Since the early 1970s, however, spatial interaction modeling has become highly elaborate and increasingly reliant upon complex, nonlinear algebra which, despite the existance of several excellent introductory expositions (e.g., Senior 1979; Beaumont 1982), remains all but inaccessible to the uninitiated. While this statistical and conceptual trading up process was not without its contemporary critics—Sayer (1977, p. 188), in a memorable phrase, dubbed it "mathematization beyond the call of duty"— it is undeniable that the sophistication of interaction modelling increased substantially in the post-entropy era. Indeed, few marketing concepts, not even the wheel of retailing, more clearly demonstrate the conceptual trading-up process than spatial interaction theory after Wilson and Huff.

Broadly speaking, this upgrading process comprised three distinct, but by no means unrelated, components. In the first instance, a variety of long-standing theoretical shortcomings in the aggregate (Wilsonian) modeling approach were tackled with considerable vigor and some success. Secondly, the disaggregate perspective pioneered by Huff opened the way for all manner of detailed analyses into the choice behaviors and patronization patterns of consumers.[3] Thirdly, a number of technical issues arising from empirical applications of the gravity model had to be addressed and, as a consequence, the standards of the spatial interaction debate were raised substantially.

A. Aggregate Approaches

Although it is widely employed in practice, the traditional gravity model and its theoretical underpinnings have been subject to substantial scholarly stricture (e.g., Carruthers 1956; Olsson 1965, 1970; Sheppard 1978, 1979; Golledge 1983). Its inherent lack of dynamism, for example, has been roundly condemned on many occasions (Parry Lewis and Traill 1968; Thorpe 1975; Shepherd and Thomas 1980). Albeit frequently used in a predictive capacity (ten- to twenty-year planning horizons in some instances) and for the generation of "what if" retailing scenarios (Davies 1970; Rogers 1984; 1987), the model assumes that existing spatial relationships, spending patterns, parameters, and so forth, will be maintained over the planning period. However as shopping opportunities, retailing formats, personal mobility, and so on, are all in a constant state of change, the model—no matter how successful the initial calibration—cannot be extrapolated with any confidence beyond the short to medium term (Jensen-Butler 1972; Openshaw 1976; Beaumont 1988).

The standard gravitational perspective, what is more, has been castigated for its continuing focus on the allocation of consumer demand rather than on the increasingly important forces of retailer supply (Gibson and Pullen 1972; Ducca and Wilson 1976; Field and MacGregor 1987). Even consumer demand, determined critics point out, has been misrepresented in the traditional model. Contrary to the assumption that shopping trips are home based and single purpose, and that total consumer expenditure is fixed, research reveals that multipurpose and ancillary (e.g., work based) shopping activities are a commonplace (O'Kelly 1981; Lord and Mesimer 1982; Fotheringham 1985) and that the provision of shopping facilities can generate additional, not simply redistribute existing, expenditure (Breheny 1983; Ingene 1983). Furthermore, the model's basic premise that consumers are free to choose from a range of shopping opportunities of various sizes and distances apart, does not necessarily accord with reality. Many consumers, especially those with low incomes and lacking mobility, are effectively constrained in their shopping behaviors and enjoy little in the way of choice (Curry 1972; Kivell and Shaw 1980; Herbert and Thomas 1990).

The foregoing shortcomings of the spatial interaction model are regularly highlighted by its critics, but such condemnations overlook the significant conceptual refinements that have occurred, especially in recent years. The forces of supply were introduced by Harris and Wilson (1978), when they developed a spatial interaction model with a variable that described the cost of the provision of retail floorspace. Their lead has since given rise to interaction models that embrace, among others, store size and location (Miller and Lerman 1979; Jayet 1990a,1990b), multiple retail organizations (Williams and Kim 1990a,1990b), retailer pricing policies (Oppenheim 1990), the participation of the planning system and property development industry (Roy and Johansson 1984), and, indeed, to empirical analyses of the foregoing (Kohsaka 1989). Similarly, the trip chaining and multipurpose shopping behaviors of consumers have been incorporated (Mazurkiewicz 1985; Huriot, Smith, and Thisse 1989; Roy 1990), as have constraints on consumer interaction behavior (Lakshmanan and Hua 1983; Batten and Nijkamp 1990), though the issue of the expenditure generation role of retail development still remains to be tackled effectively (Wilson 1988,1989).

Perhaps the greatest achievement of the aggregate interaction modelers, however, has been the development of dynamic perspectives (e.g., Poston and Wilson 1977; Beaumont, Clarke, and Wilson 1981a, 1981b; Clarke and Wilson 1983; Rijk and Vorst 1983; Kaashoek and Vorst 1984; Muench 1988). These have shown how smooth changes in deterrence and attraction parameters can induce sudden, catastrophic changes in the structure of the retail system, as for example from corner store to hypermarket (Wilson and Oulton 1983) and from spatially dispersed to highly clustered distributions of activity (Fotheringham and Knudsen 1986). Most importantly, however, these illustrations of catastrophe, bifurcation, and, latterly, chaos theory demonstrate that when underlying interaction relationships change, even in an orderly fashion, a multiplicity of outcomes is possible. Predicting the future, in short, remains fraught with difficulty.

B. Disaggregate Approaches

Despite the elegant and undeniable achievements of Wilson and his coworkers (not to mention those of the Rotterdam group), their aggregate approach to spatial interaction, like that of the basic gravity model from which it was derived, is ultimately flawed. As many critics have pointed out, it *describes* behavioral patterns—often very effectively—but does not *explain* why such behaviors occur (Garner 1970; Guelke 1971; Hudson 1976; Walmsley and Lewis 1984). Although the original gravitational metaphor may have been eschewed, its replacements (entropy, catastrophe, chaos, etc.) represent mere substitutions of one analogy from the physical sciences for another. Some modelers, accordingly, have sought refuge in neo-Marxism interpretations, which see spatial outcomes in terms of class conflict and the exploitative nature of capitalist society (Sayer 1977; Wilkinson 1980). Others have espoused the disaggregate approach pioneered by Huff, which, by focusing attention on the choice decisions of individual consumers has given rise to all manner of insightful elaborations of the gravity postulate.

The initial refinements of the Huff model involved, in essence, behavioral and cognitive interpretations of his original utility measures. Store size and distance were replaced, with varying degrees of success, by measures of consumers' store image (Stanley and Sewall 1976, 1978), center image (Spencer 1978; Nevin and Houston 1980), cognitive distance (Cadwallader 1975; Mackay and Olshavsky 1975), attitudes to available transportation alternatives (Gautschi 1981; Bucklin and Gautschi 1983), and, of course, variations in the foregoing from individual to individual and among different ethnic and socioeconomic groups, and so forth (Hubbard 1979; Howell and Rogers 1983). A full-blown cognitive gravity model, wherein both attraction and deterrence were determined subjectively, was also suggested (Cadwallader 1981).

Subsequently, attention turned away from cognitive interpretations of mass and distance and focused instead on the competitive dimension of the Huff formulation. Most prominent in this respect was the MCI (multiplicative competitive interaction) model of Nakanishi and Cooper (1974). A highly flexible technique that can incorporate manifold subjective and objective measures—both discrete and continuous—of the relative attractiveness and accessibility of competing stores, the MCI model has been applied to a wide range of retailing contexts including food store choice (Jain and Mahajan 1979), branch bank patronization (Hansen and Weinberg 1979), automobile dealerships (Black, Ostlund, and Westbrook 1985), the development of chain store branch networks (Achabal, Gorr, and Mahajan 1983; Mahajan, Sharma, and Srinivas 1985) and scenario planning for retail firms (Ghosh and McLafferty 1982; Ghosh and Craig 1986).

Useful though it has proved in a retailing context, the MCI model is by no means the only disaggregate derivation of the gravity hypothesis. On the contrary, all manner of discrete choice models and decompositional multiattribute preference models are now available (Batsell and Lodish 1981; Golledge and Timmermans 1988; Ahn and Ghosh 1989). The former, most notably the multinomial logit and multinomial probit, assume that an individual's preferences among a choice set can be described by a utility function and that the alternative with the highest utility is selected (e.g., Timmermans and Veldhuisen 1981; Timmermans, van der Heijden, and Westerveld 1984; Weisbrod, Parcells, and Kern 1984). The latter rest upon broadly similar assumptions concerning utility and choice but rely upon data derived from laboratory experiments rather than the real world (e.g., Schuler 1981; Mayer and Eagle 1982; Louviere and Gaeth 1987). As with the aggregate interaction approaches, however, both these perspectives are predicated upon single-purpose, single-stop shopping behaviors, assume that alternatives are *chosen* not merely patronized by default and lack an all-important dynamic dimension (Pipkin 1981; Burnett 1981; Craig, Ghosh, and McLafferty 1984). Once again, this has led to the development of models of trip chaining and activity patterns, studies of choice constraints, and the propagation of choice models based on longitutional data from consumer panels (for detailed discussion see Timmermans 1980; Landau, Prashker, and Alpern 1982; Wrigley and Longley 1984; Williams 1988; Timmermans and Golledge 1990).

C.   Technical Issues

Although latterday contributions to aggregate and disaggregate gravity modeling are mathematically rigorous and, compared to early analyses, highly sophisticated, both approaches have been beset by manifold technical problems. The efforts to address these issues, in turn, have given rise to considerable and often bitter debate and led to a greater awareness of the limits to interaction modeling. Most importantly perhaps, the attempted resolution of technical problems has raised the overall standards of research activity.

Broadly speaking, the technical issues arising from gravity modeling can be divided into two basic, but by no means mutually exclusive, categories: calibration problems and specification problems. The latter refer to the structure of the model and the nature of the study area, whereas the former pertain primarily to distortions in model performance. Calibration, in essence, is the process of fitting the model to the data set. This is achieved by adjusting the parameters on the attraction and deterrence variables until as close a correspondence as possible is obtained between known data (for example, the turnover of shopping centers in the study area) and the model's allocation of estimated consumer expenditure to the centers concerned (see Clarke and Bolwell 1968; Hodges and Kennett 1973; Murray and Kennedy 1973).

While straightforward in theory—Reilly, for instance, *assumed* parameters of unity and the inverse square for attraction and deterrence respectively— the calibration procedure has proved particularly problematical in practice (Hyman 1969; Batty 1971). Besides the possibility of a bogus calibration, where the model's output is a function of the attraction variable (Openshaw 1973; Beaumont 1988), allowing both parameters to vary simultaneously ensures that a single, optimal solution to the calibration exercise is very difficult to obtain, unless of course, trip data are available (Curry 1972; Batty and Saether 1972; Openshaw 1975b). Estimating the closeness of the fit between model and data is no less onerous, as Ordinary Least Squares has been deemed inappropriate, for constrained interaction models at least (Batty and Mackie 1972; Openshaw 1976). It is also the case that the geographical distribution of origins and destinations, and the distances between them, influences the outcome of the calibration exercise (Olsson 1970; Bucklin 1971b; Ewing 1974). The parameters, in other words, not only reflect the nature of interaction behavior but also the morphology, or map pattern, of the study area (Johnston 1973, 1976; Griffith and Jones 1980; Fotheringham and Webber 1980; Baxter 1985).

Just as the calibration process has proved somewhat problematical, so to the specification of gravity models is fraught with difficulty. The aggregate approach, for example, assumes a closed system that can be delimited precisely, that all expenditure is accounted for and that the population is evenly distributed within zones. In reality, however, retailing systems are not closed, nor are they readily delimited and population tends to be unevenly arranged (Roberts 1971; Curry 1972; Davies 1977). Expenditure is not easy to calculate with precision and, in urban planning contexts, difficult to translate into future floorspace requirements (Parry-Lewis and Bridges 1974; Thorpe 1975; Williams and Arnott 1977). Similarly, the size and shape of the zones that make up the study area can influence the output of the model (Davies 1971), as can the "modifiable areal unit" problem (Openshaw and Taylor 1979). This is the variation in results that occurs when the same areal data are combined into progressively larger units of analysis, or when the areal units are combined in different ways at the same geographical scale (Openshaw 1983).

Likewise, the dissaggregate approach, as several commentators have pointed out (Stetzer 1976; Timmermans 1980; Fotheringham 1988), necessitates (often arbitrary) definitions of the relevant choice set (the shopping centers or stores deemed to be in competition), the choice rule (the heuristic employed by decision takers), and the combination rule (the way in which evaluations of individual attributes are integrated). The models also assume—again, erroneously—that the utility of a choice alternative is independent from the attributes of the other choice set alternatives (the IIA property), that parameters are invariant with alterations in choice set attribution levels (the context dependency issue) and that the relative location of choice alternatives does not influence choice probabilities (see Mayer and Eagle 1982; Eagle 1984; Fotheringham 1986; Golledge and Timmermans 1988).

Needless to say, these technical considerations have stimulated numerous expositions of the issues and propositions for their alleviation. There are manifold investigations of optimal calibration procedures (Eilon, Tilley, and Fowkes 1969; Stetzer 1976; Batty and Mackie 1972), copious studies of alternatives and improvements to OLS for estimating goodness of fit (Haines, Simon, and Alexis 1972; Baxter 1983; Openshaw 1976; Knudsen and Fotheringham 1986), more than ample analyses of the map pattern effect (Cliff, Martin and Ord 1974, 1975, 1976; Curry, Griffith, and Sheppard 1975; Fotheringham 1983a, 1983b, 1984; Ghosh 1985), sundry surveys of zone size and shape and the modifiable areal unit problem (Batty and Sammons 1978; Openshaw 1977; Batty and Sikdar 1982), many significant insights into the IIA and context dependencey problems of the disaggregate model (Timmermans 1980; Malhotra 1984, 1988; Eagle 1988), and, not least, several detailed comparisons of model performance (Haynes, Poston, and Schnirring 1973; Parkhurst and Roe 1978; Turner and Cole 1980; van Lierop and Nijkamp 1980; Hubbard and Thompson 1981; Recker and Schuler 1981). Few, if any, of these studies have completely resolved the issues concerned, but the very act of addressing them has significantly raised the tenor of the debate.

VI. MATURITY AND CHANGE

Just as "mature" retailing institutions are difficult to specify with any accuracy (Hollander 1981), so too the identification of maturing conceptual institutions is somewhat problematical. In the case of the wheel of retailing theory, however, its maturity phase was characterized by attempts to integrate the myriad variants of the model, the search for a universal theory of institutional change and applications of the original concept to nonretailing phenomena. This, in turn, was accompanied by evidence of growing dissatisfaction with the progress of the theory, disillusion with its increasingly esoteric accomplishments and, as predicted by the wheel theory itself, the appearance of new, simplified versions of the original model (Brown 1988).

When the recent history of the gravity model is examined, a broadly similar pattern of development is discernible. The 1980s, for example, have witnessed several attempts to synthesize the aggregate and disaggregate approaches to consumer spatial behavior. Most noteworthy among these were the analyses of Bennett, Haining, and Wilson (1985), Fotheringham (1986), and Nijkamp and Reggiani (1987, 1990). Similarly, the search is on for an all-encompassing model of spatial interaction, with Alonso's (1978, 1980) much-vaunted theory of movement being perhaps the prime candidate (e.g., Hua 1980; Fisch 1981; Nijkamp and Poot 1987). While the manifold efforts to operationalize his framework have thus far been less than totally successful (Anselin 1982; Tabuchi 1984; Miller and O'Kelly 1991), all manner of highly flexible interaction models, both aggregate and disaggregate, are now available (see for example, Hallefjord and Jornsten 1985; Louviere and Timmermans 1990).

If the evidence of integration and universality is reasonably clear cut, the case for nonretailing applications is rather more complex. As noted earlier, the gravity model has long been applied outside the retailing arena (indeed many early analysts in transportation and industrial research, for instance Casey (1955), Dunn (1956), and Voorhees (1957), openly acknowledged their debt to the pioneering insights of Reilly). Recent years, however, have been characterized by the advent of *conceptual*, rather than empirical, extensions of the model. In other words, by attempts to demonstrate how long standing but independently derived conceptualizations are compatible with the gravity framework. Central place theory, bid rent theory, economic base theory, spatial competition theory, and even Applebaum's trade area determination techniques, can all be derived from the basic spatial interaction model (Beaumont 1980; Wilson 1984; Clarke and Wilson 1985; Birkin and Wilson 1986a, 1986b; Williams, Kim, and Martin 1990; O'Kelly and Miller 1989; Fik and Mulligan 1990).

Despite these undoubted achievements, the late 1980s also witnessed growing disenchantment with the nature and direction of gravity modeling. Disputation, admittedly, is not a stranger to spatial interaction theory; the evolution of the concept has been punctuated by periodic theoretical and technical upheavals. Yet, in recent years the very purpose of interaction modeling has been widely questioned and, such is the esoterism of some contributions (e.g., Slater 1989) that many believe academic interaction modelers to be increasingly out of touch with the real world (Sheth, Gardner, and Garrett 1988; Breheny 1988; Herbert and Thomas 1990). In fact, as was the case in the maturity phase of the wheel theory, even renouned contributors to the development of the field have expressed severe reservations about its latterday achievements. Batty (1989), for instance, describes the widespread sense of disillusion with modeling. Openshaw (1989a, p. 74, 75) argues that "much of this work is useless... a great gulf exists between theory and practice." And Beaumont (1989, p. 171) recalls an academic-practitioner conference where the latter deemed the former's contributions to be "in a language as widely comprehended as Serbo-Croat."

Although the output of the academic modeling community may have become increasingly divorced from reality, the real world has not abandoned interaction modeling. Quite the reverse. Thanks to the advent and virtual ubiquity of powerful, low-cost computing facilities, a wide variety of sophisticated databases, containing spatially organised (geocoded) information on store locations, tranportation provision, consumer expenditure, and so forth are currently available (see Beaumont 1988; Sleight and Leventhal 1989; Reynolds 1990). As retailers need to make sense of this voluminous material, the spatial interaction model has enjoyed a new lease of life (Rogers 1987; Penny and Broom 1988; McGoldrick 1990). In the main, however, the models employed tend to be very basic variants of first generation developments, such as Lakshmanan and Hansen, albeit with a store specific rather than center specific emphasis (Breheny 1988; Batty 1989; Curry and Moutinho 1990; Moore and Attewell 1991). While any number of more elegant formulations exist, the complex calibration procedures that some require (e.g., Wilson) and the difficulties of operationalizing others (e.g., Alonso) are sufficient to ensure that retailers, as Breheny (1988) rightly points out, prefer to endorse the time-honored adage, "when in doubt, keep it simple."

It thus appears that the wheel of retail gravitation has turned and that the sophistication of academic modeling has been superceeded by a new generation of simple models with a highly practical, company orientated ethos. Indeed, and in line with the wheel theory, this turnaround has been accompanied by attempts on the part of certain academic commentators to disparage consultants' (mis)use of the gravity model and bewail retailers' unwillingness to avail themselves of the conceptual insights of leading-edge modelers (though academics' preparedness to partake at the consultancy trough remains encouragingly unimpared).[4] Others, of course, have argued that modelers must tackle the task of adapting their academic offerings to the marketplace (Beaumont 1986; Openshaw 1986, 1989b; Brail 1990) and yet others have sought to demonstrate that, in practical situations, basic gravity models work quite as well as their more refined counterparts (Roberts 1982; Anselin 1984; O'Kelly and Miller 1989). The fact of the matter, however, is that today's users have abandoned the esoteric for the applicable and, as Reilly's original concern was with developing a practical tool for trade area estimation, he would undoubtably have approved.

VII. DISCUSSION

A model, according to the National Economic Development Office (1970), is a simplified representation of reality that can take the form of either a verbal description or a mathematical statement. These extremes, in many ways, are exemplified by the wheel of retailing theory and the law of retail gravitation. Ever since McNair's (1931) tentative enunciation of the hypothesis some sixty years ago, the wheel has been examined, elaborated, and evaluated in essentially subjective terms. The gravity model, by contrast, has almost always been the preserve of the mathematically inclined. Indeed, as noted earlier, Reilly's principal achievement was the derivation of a mathematical statement of the previously established gravitational interpretation of human interaction.

Yet despite the obvious differences in form, the wheel theory and gravity model are similar in several significant respects. Apart from Sheth, Gardner, and Garrett's (1988) revelation, noted earlier, that they comprise the only two generalizations that the marketing discipline can claim to have originated, both are based upon an analogy with the physical sciences—Newtonian laws in the case of the gravity model and the astronomical observations of the ancient world in the case of the wheel (Brown 1991). Spatial interaction theorists, admittedly, have often sought to circumvent the charge of reasoning by physical analogy (e.g., Wilson 1968; Nijkamp 1975; Fisk 1985), but a perusal of the field reveals that innovative conceptual insights in the physical sciences, be it catastrophe theory, chaos theory or whatever, eventually manifest themselves in the gravity modeling and, for that matter, the wheel of retailing literature.[5]

Most importantly for the purposes of this paper, however, both conceptualizations evolved in a very similar fashion. The wheel theory commenced as a short, simple statement concerning the development of certain department stores and chain stores, burgeoned into a substantial body of esoteric theories of institutional evolution and eventually saw a renaissance of straightforward, company specific analyses of retail change. Similarly, the gravity model began as a crude mathematical formula and developed into a highly sophisticated modeling procedure, which has since been effectively upstaged by simplified versions of the same. Both concepts, in short, evolved in line with the low cost trading-up pattern described by the wheel. Just as a "wheel of the wheel of retailing" can be identified, so too a "wheel of retail gravitation" is discernible.

Another parallel between the wheel theory and the gravity model is that they both have been castigated for describing but failing to explain the retailing phenomena to which they pertain. There is no "semi-mystical" (Curry 1972) gravitational force that attracts consumers inexorably to given shopping areas, nor is there some sort of "natural law" that impels low cost retailing innovations to become bloated and moribund institutions, ripe for the assault of aggressive, price orientated interlopers (Brown 1988). It follows, therefore, that the wheel theory may well describe the development of the law of retail gravitation, but it cannot hope to explain its evolutionary pattern.

In this respect, however, the wheel literature abounds with hypothesised mechanisms of retail change, the most frequently espoused of which are alterations in the external environment (economic circumstances, technological innovation, etc.) and cut-throat competition between rival retail organizations (Brown 1988). If these explanations are accepted, it seems reasonable to surmise that similar forces underpin the evolution of retailing thought. The gravity model, after all, took off—not with Reilly[6]—but in the early postwar period when the notion of "social physics" was being championed by several academic

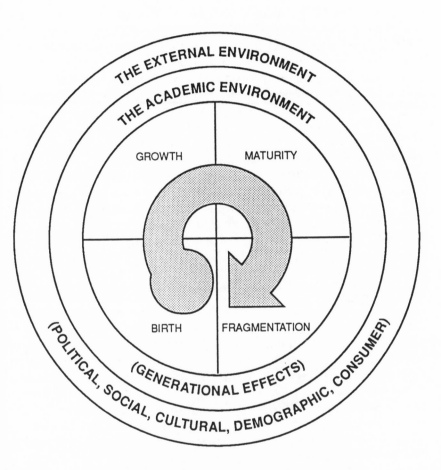

Figure 1. The Wheel of Marketing Thought

disciplines and when there were clear empirical demands in the shape of large scale transportation studies, urban planning exercises and, in the U.S. at least, chain store organizations expanding into undershopped suburbia (Tocalis 1978). The subsequent trading up process stemmed from academic modelers' desire to perfect their conceptual property, to pursue the social sciences' grail of collective intellectual respectability and, not least, to establish personal reputations and enjoy the resultant fruits of their scholarly labors (Batty 1989).

Similarly, the gravity model's comparative fall from grace and its subsequent resurrection can be related to the advent of the retailer database, the gulf that developed between interaction theory and practice and, in the case of the United Kingdom, official disenchantment with the retail modeling process (Rogers 1987; Breheny 1988; Openshaw 1989a).

If the evolution of the gravity model is in any way typical of theoretical developments in marketing science, it is arguable that innovative conceptual insights stem from changes in the external environment (intellectual climate, social need, and the like). These create opportunities for perceptive individuals, who posit simple, often metaphorical, theoretical frameworks of the phenomena in question. Inter-academic rivalry then takes over, which gives rise to alternative conceptual conjectures and, in time, takes the theory to its intellectual limits. An aura of academic veneration subsequently descends, the concept becomes institutionalized and increasingly divorced from its empirical setting. Alterations in the external environment, however, eventually spawn simple adaptations of the original theory, which are disparaged by those with a substantial intellectual stake in the original model. Neverthless, as it serves the needs of society and a new generation of scholars, the novel variant proves successful, only to go through the self-same evolutionary process (Figure 1). Future research will doubtless reveal whether this "wheel of marketing thought" has any real utility, but if nothing else it remins us that academic endeavour, like retailing itself, is in a constant state of change.

VIII.   CONCLUSION

Approximatley sixty years ago, William J. Reilly published a text that ranks among the classics of marketing thought. Widely cited and frequently disparaged, *The Law of Retail Gravitation* drew an analogy between physical laws and human phenomena and thus instigated numerous investigations of spatial interaction behavior. This paper has examined the evolution of Reilly's Law, using the contemporaneous wheel of retailing theory as an organizing framework. In line with the wheel, the gravity model commenced as a basic, uncomplicated conceptualization of consumer patronage behavior and retail trading areas. A number of variants on the original model were proposed, most notably those of Huff and Wilson, and a period of theoretical and technical trading up then transpired. These highly sophisticated spatial interaction models, however, proved difficult to operationalize and, as the wheel theory predicts, a new generation of simple but applicable gravity models emerged. The environmental and competitive causes of this cycle of theoretical development were discussed and a model of conceptual evolution was proposed. It remains to be seen whether the wheel of retail gravitation will continue to turn, but, as both the wheel theory and the gravity model appear to have experienced a similar evolutionary cycle, additional research on the development of retail marketing theories would appear to be necessary.

NOTES

1. Although the development of Reilly's Law has been somewhat neglected in the marketing literature, extensive analyses of the evolution of the gravity model have appeared in cognate disciplines, such as geography (Tocalis 1978), urban planning (Batty 1972), and regional science (Hua and Porell 1979). Such is the pace of progress in spatial interaction theory, however, that even these exercises are now somewhat dated.

2. Converse's "break-point" equation is usually associated with his celebrated 1948 paper in the *Journal of Marketing*. In actual fact, he had been using the formula for more than a decade (Converse 1935) and it was not until the publication of a very similar but independently derived equation (Strohkarck and Phelps 1948), that Converse felt compelled to stake his academic claim (Batty 1978). In his bitter debate with Converse (1953), however, Reynolds (1953b) maintained that the break point equation was actually the work of H.M. Sweet.

3. The terms aggregate and disaggregate tend to be inconsistently applied in the spatial interaction literature. For the purposes of this paper "aggregate" is reserved for models, such as Wilson's entropy maximizing approach, which ignore the behavior of individual consumers and deal instead with gross interaction flows (even though this data is often "disaggregated" into different socioeconomic groups, modes of transport, etc.). The term disaggregate is taken to refer to models, like Huff's, which are predicated upon individual behavior (even though this tends to be aggregated to derive overall estimates for the zones that make up the study area). Some commentators, however, reserve "disaggregate" for models such as the multinomial logit, which deal with individual shopping trips or store choices.

4. The abuse of the gravity model by retailing consultants has attracted considerable academic opprobrium. Rogers (1984) describes a "fiddle factor," where consultants adjust the parameter on the attraction variable in order to suit their nefarious purposes and Whysall (1981) notes an urban planning inquiry where the impact assessments of the opposing parties were inversely correlated. Broadly similar experiences have been described by Couper and Barker (1981) and Dombey (1975) among others.

5. In a recent evaluation of progress in urban modeling, Batty (1990 p.4), somehow appropriately, maintained "that the wheel has turned full circle from the 1950s." With regard to the physical science analogy, moreover, he has aptly described modelers' current infatuation with fractals, chaos theory, etc., as "post-modern social physics" (Batty, Longley, and Fotheringham 1989, p. 1451).

6. Interestingly, Reilly has recently been described as being "ahead of his time." His contributions, as Babin, Boles, and Babin (1991) point out, are often confounded with those of later scholars, most notably Converse (e.g., Field and MacGregor 1987). It thus appears that marketing concepts—like many scholarly achievements—may be circulating for some time before the "intellectual climate" is suitable for their propagation.

REFERENCES

Achabal, D.D., W. L. Gorr, and V. Mahajan. (1982). "MULTILOC: A Multiple Store Location Decision Model." *Journal of Retailing,* 58 (20); pp. 5-25.

Ahn, K.H. and A. Ghosh. (1989). "Hierarchical Models of Store Choice." *International Journal of Retailing,* 4 (5); pp. 39-52.

136   STEPHEN BROWN

Alonso, W. (1978). "A Theory of Movement." Pp. 197-211 in *Human Settlement Systems*, edited by N.M. Hansen. Cambridge: Ballinger.

Alonso, W. (1980). "Alonso's Theory of Movement: A Reply." *Environment and Planning A*, 12 (6); pp. 733-34.

Anselin, L. (1982). "Implicit Functional Relationships Between Systemic Effects in a General Model of Movement." *Regional Science and Urban Economics*, 12 (3); pp. 365-80.

Anselin, L. (1984). "Specification Tests and Model Selection for Aggregate Spatial Interaction: An Empirical Comparison." *Journal of Regional Science*, 54; pp. 165-82.

Babin, B.J., J. S. Boles, and L. Babin. (1991). *"The Development of Spatial Theory in Retailing and its Contribution to Marketing Thought and Marketing Science."* Paper presented at the Fifth Marketing History Conference, East Lansing, April.

Bartels, R. (1962). *The Development of Marketing Thought*. Homewood, IL: Richard D. Irwin.

Batsell, R.R. and L. M. Lodish. (1981). "A Model and Measurement Methodology for Predicting Individual Consumer Choice." *Journal of Marketing Research*, 18 (February); pp. 1-12.

Batten, D. and P. Nijkamp. (1990). "Barriers to Communication and Spatial Interaction." *The Annals of Regional Science*, 24 (4); pp. 233-36.

Batty, M. (1971). "Exploratory Calibration of a Retail Location Model Using Search by Golden Section." *Environment and Planning A*, 3 (4); pp. 411-32.

Batty, M. (1972). "Recent Developments in Land-use Modelling: A Review of British Research." *Urban Studies*, 9 (2); pp. 151-77.

Batty, M. (1978). "Reilly's Challenge: New Laws of Retail Gravitation which Define Systems of Central Places." *Environment and Planning A*, 10 (2); 185-219.

Batty, M. (1989). "Urban Modelling and Planning: Reflections, Retrodictions and Prescriptions." Pp.147-69 in *Remodelling Geography*, edited by B. Macmillan. Oxford: Basil Blackwell.

Batty, M. (1990). "How Can We Best Respond to Changing Fashions in Urban and Regional Planning?" *Environment and Planning B*, 17 (1); pp. 1-7.

Batty, M., P. Longley, and S. Fotheringham. (1989). "Urban Growth and Form: Scaling, Fractal Geometry, and Diffusion-limited Aggregation." *Environment and Planning A*, 21 (11); pp. 1447-72.

Batty, M. and S. Mackie. (1972). "The Calibration of Gravity, Entropy, and Related Models of Spatial Interaction." *Environment and Planning A*, 4 (2); pp. 205-33.

Batty, M. and A. Saether. (1972). "A Note on the Design of Shopping Models." *Journal of the Royal Town Planning Institute*, 58; pp. 303-6.

Batty, M. and R. Sammons. (1978). "On Searching for the Most Informative Spatial Pattern." *Environment and Planning A*, 10 (7); pp. 747-79.

Batty, M. and P. K. Sikdar. (1982). "Spatial Aggregation in Gravity Models. 1. An Information-theoretic Framework." *Environment and Planning A*, 14 (3); pp. 377-405.

Baxter, M. (1983). "Estimation and Inference in Spatial Interaction Models." *Progress in Human Geography*, 7 (1); pp. 40-59.

Baxter, M. (1985). "Misspecification in Spatial Interaction Models: Further Results." *Environment and Planning A*, 17 (5); pp. 673-78.

Beaumont, J. R. (1980). "Spatial Interaction Models and the Location-allocation Problem." *Journal of Regional Science*, 20 (1); pp. 37-50.

Beaumont, J. R. (1982). "Mathematical Programming in Human Geography." *Mathematical Social Sciences*, 2; pp. 213-43.

Beaumont, J. R. (1986). "Modelling Should be More Relevant: Some Personal Reflections." *Environment and Planning A*, 18 (3); pp. 419-21.

Beaumont, J. R. (1988). "Store Location Analysis: Problems and Progress." Pp. 87-105 in *Store Choice, Store Location and Market Analysis*, edited by N. Wrigley. London: Routledge.

Beaumont J. R. (1989). "Applied Geographical Modelling: Some Personal Comments." Pp. 170-73 in *Remodelling Geography*, edited by B. Macmillan. Oxford: Basil Blackwell.

Beaumont J. R., M. Clarke, and A. G. Wilson. (1981a). "Changing Energy Parameters and the Evolution of Urban Spatial Structure." *Regional Science and Urban Economics,* 11 (3); pp. 287-315.

Beaumont, J. R., M. Clarke, and A. G. Wilson. (1981b). "The Dynamics of Urban Spatial Structure: Some Exploratory Results Using Difference Equasions and Bifurcation Theory." *Environment and Planning A,* 13 (12); pp. 1473-83.

Bennett, R. J., R. P. Haining, and A. G. Wilson. (1985). "Spatial Structure, Spatial Interaction, and their Integration: A Review of Alternative Models." *Environment and Planning A,* 17 (5); pp. 625-45.

Bennett, V.W. (1944). "Consumer Buying Habits in a Small Town Located Between Two Large Cities." *Journal of Marketing,* 8 (4); pp. 405-16.

Berry, B. J. L. and J. D. Parr. (1988). *Market Centers and Retail Location: Theory and Applications.* Englewood Cliffs: Prentice-Hall.

Birkin, M. and A. G. Wilson. (1986a). "Industrial Location Models 1: A Review and Integrating Framework." *Environment and Planning A,* 18 (2); pp. 175-205.

Birkin, M. and A. G. Wilson. (1986b). "Industrial Location Models 2: Weber, Palander, Hotelling and Extensions Within a New Framework." *Environment and Planning A,* 18 (3); pp. 293-306.

Black, W.C., L. E. Ostlund, and R. A. Westbrook. (1985). "Spatial Demand Models in an Intrabrand Context." *Journal of Marketing,* 49 (Summer); pp. 106-13.

Brail, R. K. (1990). "Integrating Urban Information Systems and Spatial Models." *Environment and Planning B,* 17 (4); pp. 417-27.

Breheny, M. J. (1983). "Modelling Store Location and Performance: A Review." *European Research,* 11 (3); pp. 111-21.

Breheny, M. J. (1988). "Practical Methods of Retail Location Analysis: A Review." Pp. 39-86 in *Store Choice, Store Location and Market Analysis,* edited by N. Wrigley. London: Routledge.

Brunner, J. A. and J. L. Mason. (1968). "The Influence of Driving Time Upon Shopping Centre Preferences." *Journal of Marketing,* 32 (April); pp. 12-7.

Brown, S. (1988). "The Wheel of the Wheel of Retailing." *International Journal of Retailing,* 3 (1); pp. 16-37.

Brown, S. (1991). *"The Origin of Specious: The Wheel Theory and its Antecedents."* Paper presented at the Fifth Marketing History Conference, East Lansing, April.

Bucklin, L. P. (1971a). "Trade Area Boundaries: Some Issues in Theory and Methodology." *Journal of Marketing Research,* 8 (February); pp. 30-7.

Bucklin, L. P. (1971b). "Retail Gravity Models and Consumer Choice: A Theoretical and Empirical Critique." *Economic Geography,* 47 (4); pp. 489-97.

Bucklin, L. P. and D. A. Gautschi. (1983). "The Importance of Travel Mode Factors in the Patronage of Retail Centres." Pp. 45-55 in *Patronage Behaviour and Retail Management,* edited by W.R. Darden and R.E. Lusch. New York: North-Holland.

Burnett, P. (1981). "Theoretical Advances in Modelling Economic and Social Behaviours: Applications to Geographical, Policy-oriented Models." *Economic Geography,* 57 (4); pp. 291-303.

Cadwallader, M. (1975). "A Behavioural Model of Consumer Spatial Decision Making." *Economic Geography,* 51 (4); pp. 339-49.

Cadwallader, M. (1981). "Towards a Cognitive Gravity Model: The Case of Consumer Spatial Behaviour." *Regional Studies,* 15 (4); pp. 275-84.

Cannon, T. (1986). *Basic Marketing: Principles and Practice.* London: Holt, Rinehart and Winston.

Carey, H. C. (1858). *Principles of Social Science.* Philadelphia: Lippincott.

Carrothers, G. A. P. (1956). "An Historical Review of the Gravity and Potential Concepts of Human Interaction." *Journal of the American Institute of Planners,* 22 (Spring); pp. 94-102.

Casey, H. J. (1955). "The Law of Retail Gravitation Applied to Traffic Engineering." *Traffic Quarterly,* 9; pp. 313-21.

Clarke, B. and L. Bolwell. (1968). "Attractiveness as Part of Retail Potential Models." *Journal of the Town Planning Institute,* 54; pp. 477-8.

Clarke, M. and A. G. Wilson. (1983). "The Dynamics of Urban Spatial Structure: Progress and Problems." *Journal of Regional Science,* 23 (1); pp. 1-18.

Clarke, M. and A. G. Wilson. (1985). "The Dynamics of Urban Spatial Structure: The Progress of a Research Programme." *Transactions, Institute of British Geographers,* 10 (4); pp. 427-51.

Cliff, A. D., R. L. Martin, and J. K. Ord. (1974). "Evaluating the Friction of Distance Parameter in Gravity Models." *Regional Studies,* 8 (3/4); pp. 281-6.

Cliff, A. D., R. L. Martin, and J. K. Ord. (1975). "Map Pattern and Friction of Distance Parameters: Reply to Comments by R.J. Johnston, and by L. Curry, D.A. Griffith and E.S. Sheppard." *Regional Studies,* 9 (3); pp. 285-8.

Cliff, A. D., R. L. Martin, and J. K. Ord. (1976). "A Reply to the Final Comment." *Regional Studies,* 10 (3); pp. 341-2.

Converse, P. D. (1935). *The Elements of Marketing.* New York: Prentice-Hall.

Converse, P. D. (1943). *A Study of Retail Trade Areas in East Central Illinois.* University of Illinois Bulletin, No. 2.

Converse, P. D. (1948). "New Laws of Retail Gravitation." *Journal of Marketing,* 13 (October); pp. 379-84.

Converse, P. D. (1953). "Comment on Movement of Retail Trade in Iowa." *Journal of Marketing,* 18 (2); pp. 170-1.

Couper, M. and A. Barker. (1981). "Joint and Linked Inquiries: The Superstore Experience." *Journal of Planning and Environmental Law,* 3; pp. 631-55.

Craig, C. S., A. Ghosh, and S. McLafferty. (1984). "Models of the Retail Location Process: A Review." *Journal of Retailing,* 60 (1); pp. 5-35.

Curry, B. and L. Moutinho. (1990). "Expert Systems for Site Location Decisions." Pp. 254-73 in *Proceedings of the Marketing Education Group Annual Conference,* edited by T. Watkins. Oxford: Oxford Polytechnic.

Curry, L. (1972). "A Spatial Analysis of Gravity Flows." *Regional Studies,* 6 (2); pp. 131-47.

Curry, L., D. A. Griffith, and E. S. Sheppard. (1975). "Those Gravity Parameters Again." *Regional Studies,* 9 (3); pp. 289-96.

Daniels, P. W. (1985). *Service Industries: A Geographical Appraisal.* London: Methuen.

Davies, R. L. (1970). "Variable Relationships in Central Place and Retail Potential Models." *Regional Studies,* 4 (1); pp. 49-61.

Davies, R. L. (1974). "Comments on the Problems of Calibrating Shopping Models." *Regional Studies,* 8 (3/4); pp. 307-9.

Davies, R. L. (1977). *Marketing Geography: With Special Reference to Retailing.* London: Methuen.

Dickinson, R. A. (1983). "Innovations in Retailing." *Retail Control,* 51 (June-July); pp. 30-54.

Dodd, S. C. (1950). "The Interactance Hypothesis: A Gravity Model Fitting Physical Masses and Human Groups." *American Sociological Review,* 15 (2); pp. 245-56.

Dombey, N. (1975). "Experts at Public Inquiries." *The Planner,* 61(8); pp. 299-301.

Douglas, E. (1948). "Measuring the General Retail Trading Area—A Case Study: 1." *Journal of Marketing,* 13 (4); pp. 481-97.

Douglas, E. (1949). "Measuring the General Retail Trading Area—A Case Study 2." *Journal of Marketing,* 14 (1); pp. 46-60.

Ducca, F.W. and R. H. Wilson. (1976). "A Model of Shopping Centre Location." *Environment and Planning A*, 8 (6); pp. 613-23.

Dunn, E.S. (1956). "The Market Potential Concept and the Analysis of Location." *Papers and Proceedings of the Regional Science Association*, 2: 183-94.

Eagle, T. C. (1988). "Context Effects in Consumer Spatial Behaviour." Pp. 299-324 in *Behavioural Modelling in Geography and Planning*, edited by R.G. Golledge and H. Timmermans. London: Croom Helm.

Eilon, S., R. P. R. Tilley, and T. R. Fowkes. (1969). "Analysis of a Gravity Demand Model." *Regional Studies*, 3 (2); pp. 115-22.

Ellwood, L. W. (1954). "Estimating Potential Volume of Proposed Shopping Centres." *The Appraisal Journal*, 4 (October); pp. 581-9.

Engel, J. F., R. D. Blackwell, and P. W. Miniard. (1986). *Consumer Behaviour*. Hinsdale: Dryden Press.

Ewing, G. O. (1974). "Gravity and Linear Regression Models of Spatial Interaction: A Cautionary Note." *Economic Geography*, 50 (1); pp. 83-8.

Field, B. G. and B. D. MacGregor. (1987). *Forecasting Techniques for Urban and Regional Planning*. London: Hutchinson.

Fik, T. J. and G. F. Mulligan. (1990). "Spatial Flows and Competing Central Places: Towards a General Theory of Hierarchical Interaction." *Environment and Planning A*, 22 (4); pp. 527-49.

Fisch, O. (1981). "Contributions to the General Theory of Movement." *Regional Science and Urban Economics*, 11 (2); pp. 157-73.

Fisk, C. (1985). "Entropy and Information Theory: Are we Missing Something?" *Environment and Planning A*, 17 (5); pp. 679-87.

Fotheringham, A. S. (1981). "Spatial Structure and Distance Decay Parameters." *Annals of the Association of American Geographers*, 71 (3); pp. 425-36.

Fotheringham, A. S. (1983a). "A New Set of Spatial-interaction Models: The Theory of Competing Destinations." *Environment and Planning A*, 15 (1); pp. 15-36.

Fotheringham, A. S. (1983b). "Some Theoretical Aspects of Destination Choice and their Relevance to Production-constrained Gravity Models." *Environment and Planning A*, 15 (8); pp. 1121-32.

Fotheringham, A. S. (1984). "Spatial Flows and Spatial Patterns." *Environment and Planning A*, 16 (4); pp. 529-43.

Fotheringham, A. S. (1985). "Spatial Competition and Agglomeration in Urban Modelling." *Environment and Planning A*, 17 (2); pp. 213-30.

Fotheringham, A. S. (1986). "Modelling Hierarchical Destination Choice." *Environment and Planning A*, 18 (3); pp. 401-18.

Fotheringham, A. S. (1988). "Market Share Analysis Techniques: A Review and Illustration of Current U.S. Practice." Pp. 120-59 in *Store Choice, Store Location and Market Analysis*, edited by N. Wrigley. London: Routledge.

Fotheringham A. S. and D. C. Knudsen. (1985). "Discontinuous Change in the Relative Location of Retail Outlets: Further Results." *Modeling and Simulation*, 16 (1); pp. 111-5.

Fotheringham, A. S. and M. E. O'Kelly. (1989). *Spatial Interaction Models: Formulations and Applications*. Dordrect: Kluwer.

Fotheringham, A. S. and M. J. Webber. (1980). "Spatial Structure and the Parameters of Spatial Interaction Models." *Geographical Analysis*, 12 (1); pp. 33-46.

Garner, B. J. (1970). "Towards a Better Understanding of Shopping Patterns." Pp. 179-86 in *Goegraphical Essays in Honour of K.C. Edwards*, edited by R. H. Osborne, F. A. Barnes, and J. C. Doornkamp. University of Nottingham: Department of Geography.

Garrison, W. L. (1956). "Estimates of the Parameters of Spatial Interaction." *Papers and Proceedings of the Regional Science Association*, 2; pp. 280-88.

Gautschi, D. A. (1981). "Specification of Patronage Models for Retail Centre Choice." *Journal of Marketing Research,* 18 (2); pp.162-74.

Ghosh, A. (1985). "Parameter Nonstationarity in Retail Choice Models." *Journal of Business Research,* 12; pp. 425-36.

Ghosh A. and C. S. Craig. (1986). "An Approach to Determining Optimal Locations for New Services." *Journal of Marketing Research,* 23 (4); pp. 354-62.

Ghosh, A. and S. McLafferty. (1982). "Locating Stores in Uncertain Environments: A Scenario Planning Approach." *Journal of Retailing,* 58 (4); pp. 5-22.

Ghosh, A. and S. L. McLafferty. (1987). *Location Strategies for Retail and Service Firms.* Lexington: D.C. Heath.

Gibson, M. and M. Pullen. (1972). "Retail Turnover in the East Midlands: A Regional Application of a Gravity Model." *Regional Studies,* 6 (2); pp. 183-96.

Gilligan, C. T., P. M. Rainford, and A. R. Thorne. (1974). "The Impact of Out-of-town Shopping, A Test of the Lakshmanan-Hansen Model." *European Journal of Marketing,* 8 (1); pp. 42-56.

Goldstucker, J. L., D. N. Bellenger, T. J. Stanley, and R. L. Otte. (1978). *New Developments in Retail Trading Area Analysis and Site Selection.* Atlanta: Georgia State University, College of Business Administration.

Golledge, R. G. (1983). "Models of Man, Points of View, and Theory in Social Science." *Geographical Analysis,* 15 (1); pp. 57-60.

Golledge, R. G. and H. Timmermans. (1988). *Behavioural Modelling in Geography and Planning.* London: Croom Helm.

Gould, P. (1972). "Pedagogic Review." *Annals of the Association of American Geographers,* 62 (4); pp. 689-700.

Griffith, D. A. and K. G. Jones. (1980). "Explorations into the Relationship Between Spatial Structure and Spatial Interaction." *Environment and Planning A,* 12 (2); pp. 187-201.

Grigg, D. B. (1977). "E.G. Ravenstein and the 'Laws of Migration'." *Journal of Historical Geography,* 3 (1); pp. 41-54.

Guelke, L. (1971). "Problems of Scientific Explanation in Geography." *The Canadian Geographer,* 15 (1); pp. 38-53.

Haines, G. H., L. S. Simon, and M. Alexis. (1972). "Maximum Liklihood Estimation of Central-city Food Trading Areas." *Journal of Marketing Research,* 9 (May); pp. 154-9.

Hallam, B. R., S. E. Warren, and C. Renfrew. (1976). "Obsidian in the Western Mediterranean: Characterisation by Neutron Activation Analysis and Optical Emmision Spectroscopy." *Proceedings of the Prehistoric Society,* 42; pp. 85-110.

Hallefjord, A. and K. Jornsten. (1985). "A Note on Relaxed Gravity Models." *Environment and Planning A,* 17 (5); pp. 597-603.

Hansen, M.H. and C. A. Weinberg. (1979). "Retail Market Share in a Competitive Environment." *Journal of Retailing,* 56 (1); pp. 37-46.

Harris, B. (1964). "A Note on the Probability of Interaction at a Distance." *Journal of Regional Science,* 5 (2); pp. 31-5.

Harris, B. and A. G. Wilson. (1978). "Equilibrium Values and Attractiveness Terms in Production-constrained Spatial-interaction Models." *Environment and Planning A,* 10 (4); pp. 371-88.

Haynes, K. E. and A. S. Fotheringham. (1984). *Gravity and Spatial Interaction Models.* Beverly Hills: Sage.

Herbert, D. T. and C. J. Thomas. (1990). *Cities in Space: City as Place.* London: David Fulton.

Hodges, S. and D. Kennett. (1973). "Practical Problems of Gravity Modelling." *Long Range Planning,* 6 (4); pp. 41-6.

Hollander, S. C. (1960). "The Wheel of Retailing." *Journal of Marketing,* 24 (July); pp. 37-42.

Hollander, S. C. (1981). "Retailing Theory: Some Criticism and Some Admiration." Pp. 84-94 in *Theory in Retailing: Traditional and Non-traditional Sources,* edited by R. W. Stampfl and E. C. Hirschman. Chicago: American Marketing Association.

Howell, R. D. and Rogers, J. D. (1983). "The Estimation of Patronage Models in the Presence of Interindividual Heterogeneity and Nongeneric Attributes." Pp. 307-18 in *Patronage Behaviour and Retail Management,* edited by W. R. Darden and R. F. Lusch. New York: North-Holland.

Hua, C. (1980). "An Exploration of the Nature and Rationale of a Systemic Model." *Environment and Planning A,* 12 (6); pp. 713-26.

Hua, C. and F. Porell. (1979). "A Critical Review of the Development of the Gravity Model." *International 'Regional Science Review,* 4 (2); pp. 97-126.

Hubbard, R. (1979). "Parameter Stability in Cross-sectional Models of Ethnic Shopping Behaviour." *Environment and Planning A,* 11 (9); pp. 977-92.

Hubbard, R. and A. F. Thompson. (1981). "Preference Structures and Consumer Spatial Indifference Behaviour: Some Theoretical Problems." *Tijdschrift voor Economische en Sociale Geografie,* 72 (1); pp. 35-9.

Hudson, R. (1976). "Linking Studies of the Individual with Models of Aggregate Behaviour: An Empirical Example." *Transactions of the Institute of British Geographers,* 1 (2); pp. 159-74.

Huff, D. L. (1962). "A Note on the Limitations of Intraurban Gravity Models." *Land Economics,* 38; pp. 64-6.

Huff, D. L. (1963). "A Probabilistic Analysis of Shopping Centre Trade Areas." *Land Economics,* 39; pp. 81-90.

Huff, D. L. (1964). "Defining and Estimating a Trading Area." *Journal of Marketing,* 28 (July); pp. 34-8.

Huff, D. L. (1966). "A Programmed Solution for Approximating an Optimum Retail Location." *Land Economics,* 42; pp. 293-303.

Huff, D. L. and G. J. Jenks. (1968). "A Graphic Interpretation of the Friction of Distance in Gravity Models." *Annals of the Association of American Geographers,* 58 (4); pp. 813-24.

Huriot, J-M., T. E. Smith, and J-F.Thisse. (1989). "Minimum-cost Distances in Spatial Analysis." *Geographical Analysis,* 21 (4); pp. 294-315.

Hyman, G. M. (1969). "The Calibration of Trip Distribution Models." *Environment and Planning,* 1 (1); pp. 105-12.

Ingene, C. A. (1983). "Consumer Expenditures and Consumer Satisfaction with the Spatial Marketing System." *Journal of Macromarketing,* 3 (Fall); pp. 41-54.

Jain, A. K. and V. Mahajan. (1979). "Evaluating the Competitive Environment in Retailing Using Multiplicative Competitive Interactive Models." Pp. 217-35 in *Research in Marketing,* edited by J. Sheth. Greenwich: JAI Press.

Jayet, H. (1990a). "Spatial Search Processes and Spatial Interation: 1. Sequential Search, Intervening Opportunities and Spatial Search Equilibrium." *Environment and Planning A,* 22 (5); pp. 583-99.

Jayet, H. (1990b). "Spatial Search Processes and Spatial Interaction: 2. Polarization, Concentration, and Spatial Search Equilibrium." *Environment and Planning A,* 22 (6); pp. 719-32.

Jensen-Butler, C. (1972). "Gravity Models as Planning Tools: A Review of Theoretical and Operational Problems." *Geografiska Annaler,* 54B (1); pp. 68-78.

Johnston, R. J. (1973). "On Frictions of Distance and Regression Coefficients." *Area,* 5; pp. 187-91.

Johnston, R. J. (1976). "On Regression Coefficients in Comparative Studies of the 'Frictions of Distance'." *Tijdschrift voor Economische en Sociale Geografie,* 67 (1); pp. 15-28.

Jung, A. F. (1959). "Is Reilly's Law of Retail Gravitation Always True?" *Journal of Marketing*, 14 (2); pp. 62-3.

Kaashoek, J. F. and A. C. F. Vorst. (1984). "The Cusp Catastrophe in the Urban Retail Model." *Environment and Planning A*, 16 (7); pp. 851-62.

Kasakoff, A. B. and J. W. Adams. (1977). "Spatial Location and Social Organisation: An Analysis of Tikopian Patterns." *Man*, 12; pp. 48-64.

Kivell, P. T. and G. Shaw. (1980). "The Study of Retail Location." Pp. 95-155 in *Retail Geography*, edited by J. Dawson. London: Croom Helm.

Knudsen, D. C. and A. S. Fotheringham. (1986). "Matrix Comparison, Goodness-of-fit, and Spatial Interaction Modelling." *International Regional Science Review*, 10 (2); pp. 127-47.

Kohsaka, H. (1989). "A Spatial Search-location Model of Retail Centres." *Geographical Analysis*, 21 (4); pp. 338-49.

Korcelli, P. (1976). "Urban Spatial Interaction Models in a Planned Economy: A Review." *International Regional Science Review*, 1 (2); pp. 74-87.

Lakshmanan, T. R. and W. G. Hansen. (1965). "A Retail Market Potential Model." *Journal of the American Institute of Planners*, 31 (May); pp. 134-43.

Lakshmanan, T. R. and C. Hua. (1983). "A Temporal-spatial Theory of Consumer Behaviour." *Regional Science and Urban Economics*, 13; pp. 341-61.

Landau, U., J. N. Prashker, and B. Alpern. (1982). "Evaluation of Activity Constrained Choice Sets to Shopping Destination Choice Modelling." *Transportation Research A*, 16 (3); pp. 199-207.

Lord, J. D. and D. B. Mesimer. (1982). "Trade Area, Land Use Mix, and Diurnal Shifts in Store Patronage Patterns." *Akron Business and Economic Review*, 13 (3); pp. 17-22.

Lösch, A. (1954). *The Economics of Location*. New Haven: Yale University Press, translated by W. H. Wolgom and W. F. Stolper.

Louviere, J. J. and G. J. Gaeth. (1987). "Decomposing the Determinants of Retail Facility Choice Using the Method of Hierarchical Information Integration: A Supermarket Illustration." *Journal of Retailing*, 63 (1); pp. 25-48.

Louviere, J. J. and H. Timmermans. (1990). "A Review of Recent Advances in Decompositional Preference and Choice Models." *Tijdschrift voor Economische en Sociale Geografie*, 81 (3); pp. 214-24.

Lowry, I. (1964). *A Model of Metropolis*. Santa Monica: Rand Corporation.

Luce, R. (1959). *Individual Choice Behaviour*. New York: John Wiley.

Mackay, D. B. and R. W. Olshavsky. (1975). "Cognitive Maps of Retail Locations: An Investigation of Some Basic Issues." *Journal of Consumer Research*, 2 (3); pp. 197-205.

Mackay, J. R. (1958). "The Interactance Hypothesis and Boundaries in Canada: A Preliminary Study." *Canadian Geographer*, 11 (1); pp. 1-8.

Mahajan, V., S. Sharma, and D. Srinivas. (1985). "An Application of Portfolio Analysis for Identifying Attractive Retail Locations." *Journal of Retailing*, 61 (4); pp. 19-34.

Malhotra, N. K. (1984). "The Use of Linear Logit Models in Marketing Research." *Journal of Marketing Research*, 21 (February); pp. 20-31.

Malhotra, N. K. (1988). "Some Observations on the State of the Art in Marketing Research." *Journal of the Academy of Marketing Science*, 16 (1); pp. 4-24.

Manchester University (1964). *Regional Shopping Centres in the North West*. Manchester University: Department of Town Planning.

Mayer, R. J. and T. C. Eagle. (1982). "Context-induced Parameter Instability in a Disaggregate-stochastic Model of Store Choice." *Journal of Marketing Research*, 19 (1); pp. 62-71.

Mayo, E. J., L. P. Jarvis, and J. A. Xander. (1988). "Beyond the Gravity Model." *Journal of the Academy of Marketing Science*, 16 (Fall); pp. 23-9.

Mazurkiewicz, L. (1985). "A Statistical Model of a Multitrip Spatial-interaction Pattern." *Environment and Planning A,* 17 (11); pp. 1533-39.

McGoldrick, P. J. (1990). *Retail Marketing.* London: McGraw-Hill.

McKinney, W. M. (1968). "Carey, Spencer, and Modern Geography." *The Professional Geographer,* 20 (2); pp. 103-6.

McNair, M. P. (1931). "Trends in Large Scale Retailing." *Harvard Business Review,* 10 (October); pp. 30-9.

McNair, M. P. (1958). "Significant Trends and Developments in the Post-war Period." Pp. 1-25 in *Competitive Distribution in a Free High Level Economy and its Implications for the University,* edited by A. B. Smith. Pittsburg: University of Pittsburg Press.

Miller, E. J. and S. R. Lerman. (1979). "A Model of Retail Location, Scale, and Intensity." *Environment and Planning A,* 11 (2); pp. 177-92.

Miller, H. J. and M. E. O'Kelly. (1991). "Properties and Estimation of a Production-constrained Alonso Model." *Environment and Planning A,* 23 (1); pp. 127-38.

Moore, S. and G. Attewell. (1991). "To Be and Where Not to Be: The Tesco Approach to Locational Analysis." *OR Insight,* 4 (1); pp. 21-4.

Muench, T. J. (1988). "Quantum Agglomeration Formation During Growth in a Combined Economic/Gravity Model." *Journal of Urban Economics,* 23 (2); pp. 199-214.

Murray, W. and M. B. Kennedy. (1971). "Notts/Derbys: A Shopping Model Primer." *Journal of the Royal Town Planning Institute,* 57; pp. 211-15.

Nakanishi, M. and L. G. Cooper. (1974). "Parameter Estimation for a Multiplicative Competitive Interaction Model—Least Squares Approach." *Journal of Marketing Research,* 11 (August); pp. 303-11.

NEDO (1970). *Urban Models in Shopping Studies.* London: National Economic Development Office.

Nevin, J. R. and M. J. Houston. (1980). "Image as a Component of Attraction to Intraurban Shopping Areas." *Journal of Retailing,* 56 (1); pp. 77-93.

Niedercorn, J. H. and V. B. Bechdolt. (1969). "Economic Derivation of the 'Gravity Law' of Spatial Interaction." *Journal of Regional Science,* 9 (2); pp. 273-82.

Niedercorn, J. H. and V. B. Bechdolt. (1972). "An Economic Derivation of the 'Gravity Law' of Spatial Interaction: A Further Reply and a Reformulation." *Journal of Regional Science,* 12 (1); pp. 127-36.

Nijkamp, P. (1975). "Reflections on Gravity and Entropy Models." *Regional Science and Urban Economics,* 5; pp. 203-25.

Nijkamp, P. and J. Poot. (1987). "Dynamics of Generalised Spatial Interaction Models." *Regional Science and Urban Economics,* 17; pp. 367-90.

Nijkamp, P. and A. Reggiani. (1987). "Spatial Interaction and Discrete Choice: Statics and Dynamics." Pp. 625-45 in *Contemporary Developments in Quantitative Geography,* edited by J. Hauer, H. Timmermans, and N. Wrigley. Dordrecht: D. Reidel.

Nijkamp, P. and A. Reggiani. (1990). "Logit Models and Chaotic Behaviour: A New Perspective." *Environment and Planning A,* 22 (11); pp. 1455-67.

O'Brien, L. and F. Harris. (1991). *Retailing: Shopping, Society, Space.* London: David Fulton.

O'Kelly, M. E. (1981). "A Model of the Demand for Retail Facilities Incorporating Multistop, Multipurpose Trips." *Geographical Analysis,* 13 (2); pp. 134-48.

O'Kelly, M. E. and H. J. Miller. (1989). "A Synthesis of Some Market Area Delimitation Models." *Growth and Change,* 20 (Summer); pp. 14-33.

Olsson, G. (1965). *Distance and Human Interaction: A Review and Bibliography.* Philadelphia: Regional Science Research Institute.

Olsson, G. (1966). "Central Place Systems, Spatial Interaction and Stochastic Processes." *Papers of the Regional Science Association,* 18 (1); pp. 13-45.

Olsson, G. (1970). "Explanation, Prediction, and Meaning Variance: An Assessment of Distance Interaction Models." *Economic Geography*, 46; pp. 223-33.

Openshaw, S. (1973). "Insoluble Problems in Shopping Model Calibration when the Trip Pattern is not Known." *Regional Studies*, 7 (4); pp. 367-71.

Openshaw, S. (1975a). *Some Theoretical and Applied Aspects of Spatial Interaction Shopping Models*. Norwich: Geobooks.

Openshaw, S. (1975b). "A Reply to R. L. Davies on the Problem of Calibrating Shopping Models." *Regional Studies*, 9 (3); pp. 279-80.

Openshaw, S. (1976). "An Empirical Study of Some Spatial Interaction Models." *Environment and Planning A*, 8 (1); pp. 23-41.

Openshaw, S. (1977). "Optimal Zoning Systems for Spatial Interaction Models." *Environment and Planning A*, 9 (2); pp. 169-84.

Openshaw, S. (1983). *The Modifiable Area Unit Problem*. Norwich: Geobooks.

Openshaw, S. (1986). "Modelling Relevance." *Environment and Planning A*, 18 (2); pp. 143-50.

Openshaw, S. (1989a). "Computer Modelling in Human Geography." Pp. 70-88 in *Remodelling Geography*, edited B. Macmillan. Oxford: Basil Blackwell.

Openshaw, S. (1989b). "Making Geodemographics More Sophisticated." *Journal of the Market Research Society*, 31 (1); pp. 111-31.

Openshaw, S. and P. J. Taylor. (1979). "A Million or so Correlation Coefficients: Three Experiments on the Modifiable Areal Unit Problem." Pp. 127-44 in *Statistical Applications in the Spatial Sciences*, edited by N. Wrigley. London: Pion.

Oppenheim, N. (1990). "Discontinuous Changes in Equilibrium Retail Activity and Travel Structures." *Papers of the Regional Science Association*, 68; pp. 43-56.

O'Sullivan, P. (1977). "On Gravity and Eruptions." *The Professional Geographer*, 29 (2); pp. 182-5.

Pacione, M. (1974). "Measures of the Attraction Factor: A Possible Alternative." *Area*, 6 (4); pp. 279-82.

Pankhurst, I.C. and P. E. Roe. (1978). "An Empirical Study of Two Shopping Models." *Regional Studies*, 12 (6); pp. 727-48.

Parry Lewis, J. and M. J. Bridges. (1974). "The Two-stage Household Shopping Model used in the Cambridge Sub-region Study." *Regional Studies*, 8 (3/4); pp. 287-97.

Parry Lewis, J. and A. L. Traill. (1968). "The Assessment of Shopping Potential and the Demand for Shops." *Town Planning Review*, 38 (4); pp. 317-26.

Penny, N.J. and D. Broom. (1988). "The Tesco Approach to Store Location." Pp. 106-19 in *Store Choice, Store Location and Market Analysis*, edited by N. Wrigley. London: Routledge.

Pipkin, J. S. (1981). "The Concept of Choice and Cognitive Explanations of Spatial Behaviour." *Economic Geography*, 57 (4); pp. 315-31.

Pooler, J. A. (1977). "The Origins of the Spatial Tradition in Geography: An Interpretation." *Ontario Geography*, 11; pp. 56-83.

Poston, T. and A. G. Wilson. (1977). "Facility Size Versus Distance Travelled: Urban Services and the Fold Catastrophe." *Environment and Planning A*, 9 (6); pp. 681-6.

Ravenstein, E. G. (1885). "The Laws of Migration." *Journal of the Statistical Society*, 48; pp. 167-227.

Ravenstein, E. G. (1889). "The Laws of Migration." *Journal of the Statistical Society*, 52; pp. 214-301.

Recker, W. W. and H. J. Schuler. (1981). "Destination Choice and Processing Spatial Information: Some Empirical Tests with Alternative Constructs." *Economic Geography*, 57 (4); pp. 373-83.

Reilly, W. J. (1929). *Methods for the Study of Retail Relationships*. Austin: University of Texas Bulletin No. 2944.

Reilly, W. J. (1931). *The Law of Retail Gravitation*. New York: William J. Reilly.

Reilly, W. J. (1953).(2nd edition) *The Law of Retail Gravitation.* New York: Pilsbury Publishers.

Reynolds, D. R. (1969). "A 'Friends-and-Neighbours' Voting Model as a Spatial Interaction Model for Electoral Geography." Pp. 81-100 in *Behavioural Problems in Geography: A Symposium,* edited by K. R. Cox and R. G. Golledge. Evanston: Northwestern University Department of Geography.

Reynolds, J. (1990). *"Evaluating the Use of Spatial Marketing Techniques in Retail Decision Making."* Paper presented at British Academy of Management Annual Conference, Glasgow.

Reynolds, R. B. (1953a). "A Test of the Law of Retail Gravitation." *Journal of Marketing,* 28 (3); pp. 273-7.

Reynolds, R. B. (1953b). "A Rejoinder." *Journal of Marketing,* 18 (2); pp. 172-4.

Rhodes, T. and R. Whitaker. (1967). "Forecasting Shopping Demand." *Journal of the Town Planning Institute,* 53 (5); pp. 188-92.

Rijk, F. J. A. and A. C. F. Vorst. (1983). "On the Uniqueness and Existence of Equilibrium Points in an Urban Retail Model." *Environment and Planning A,* 15 (4); pp. 475-82.

Roberts, A. (1982). "Superstore and Hypermarket Impact Analysis." *The Planner,* 68 (1); pp. 8-11.

Roberts, M. (1971). "Shopping [2]." *Official Architecture and Planning,* 34 (July); pp. 539-44.

Rogers, D. S. (1984). "Modern Methods of Sales Forecasting B. Gravity Models." Pp. 319-31 in *Store Location and Store Assessment Research,* edited by R. L. Davies and D. S. Rogers. Chichester: John Wiley.

Rogers, D. S. (1987). "Shop Location Analysis." Pp. 33-40 in *The Changing Face of British Retailing,* edited by E. McFadyen. London: Newman Books.

Rose, G. S. (1987). "Reconstructing a Retail Trade Area: Tucker's General Store, 1850-1860." *The Professional Geographer,* 39 (1); pp. 33-40.

Roy, J. R. (1990). "Spatial Interaction Modelling: Some Interpretations and Challenges." *Environment and Planning A,* 22 (6); pp. 712-6.

Roy, J. R. and B. Johansson. (1984). "On Planning and Forecasting the Location of Retail and Service Activity." *Regional Science and Urban Economics,* 14 (3); pp. 433-52.

Sayer, R. A. (1977). "Gravity Models and Spatial Autocorrelation, or Atrophy in Urban and Regional Modelling." *Area,* 9 (3); pp. 183-9.

Schneider, M. (1959). "Gravity Models and Trip Distribution Theory." *Papers and Proceedings of the Regional Science Association,* 5; pp. 51-6.

Schuler, H. J. (1981). "Grocery Shopping Choices: Individual Preferences Based on Store Attractiveness and Distance." *Environment and Behaviour,* 13 (3); pp. 331-47.

Schwartz, G. (1962). "Laws of Retail Gravitation: An Appraisal." *University of Washington Business Review,* 22 (1); pp. 53-70.

Senior, M. L. (1979). "From Gravity Modelling to Entropy Maximizing: A Pedagogic Guide." *Progress in Human Geography,* 3 (2); pp. 175-210.

Shepherd, I. D. H. and C. J. Thomas. (1980). "Urban Consumer Behaviour." Pp. 18-94 in *Retail Geography,* edited by J.A. Dawson. London: Croom Helm.

Sheppard, E. S. (1978). "Theoretical Underpinnings of the Gravity Hypothesis." *Geographical Analysis,* 10 (4); pp. 386-402.

Sheppard, E. S. (1979). "Gravity Parameter Estimation." *Geographical Analysis,* 11 (2); pp. 120-32.

Sheth, J., D. M. Gardner, and D. E. Garrett. (1988). *Marketing Theory: Evolution and Evaluation.* New York: John Wiley.

Slater, P. B. (1989). "Maximum-entropy Representations in Convex Polytopes: Applications to Spatial Interaction." *Environment and Planning A,* 21 (11); pp. 1541-6.

Sleight, P. and B. Leventhal. (1989). "Applications of Geodemographics to Research and Marketing." *Journal of the Market Research Society,* 31 (1); pp. 75-101.

Spencer, A. H. (1978). "Deriving Measures of Attractivenss for Shopping Centres." *Regional Studies*, 12 (6); pp. 713-26.

Stanley, T. J. and M. A. Sewall. (1976). "Image Inputs to a Probabilistic Model: Predicting Retail Potential." *Journal of Marketing*, 40 (3); pp. 48-53.

Stanley, T. J. and M. A. Sewall. (1978). "Predicting Supermarket Trade: Implications for Marketing Management." *Journal of Retailing*, 54 (2); pp. 13-22, 91-2.

Stetzer, F. (1976). "Parameter Estimation for the Constrained Gravity Model: A Comparison of Six Methods." *Environment and Planning A*, 8 (6); pp. 673-83.

Stewart, J. Q. (1941). "An Inverse Distance Variation for Certain Social Influences." *Science*, 93 (2404); pp. 89-90.

Stouffer, S. A. (1940). "Intervening Opportunities: A Theory Relating Mobility and Distance." *American Sociological Review*, 5 (December); pp. 845-67.

Stouffer, S. A. (1960). "Intervening Opportunities and Competing Migrants." *Journal of Regional Science*, 2 (1); pp. 1-26.

Strohkarck, F. and K. Phelps. (1948). "The Mechanics of Constructing a Market Area Map." *Journal of Marketing*, 13 (April); pp. 493-96.

Sweet, F. H. (1964). "An Error Parameter for the Reilly-Converse Law of Retail Gravitation." *Journal of Regional Science*, 5 (1); pp. 69-72.

Tabuchi, T. (1984). "The Systemic Variables and Elasticities in Alonso's General Theory of Movement." *Regional Science and Urban Economics*, 14; pp. 249-64.

Thorpe, D. (1975). "Assessing the Need for Shops—or, Can Planners Plan." Pp. 43-52 in *Retail Planning and Development*. London: Planning and Transport Research and Computation.

Timmermans, H. (1980). "Consumer Spatial Choice Strategies: A Comparative Study of Some Alternative Behavioural Spatial Shopping Models." *Geoforum*, 11; pp. 123-31.

Timmermans, H. and R. G. Golledge. (1990). "Applications of Behavioural Research on Spatial Problems II: Preference and Choice." *Progress in Human Geography*, 14 (3); pp. 311-54.

Timmermans, H., R. van der Heijden, and H. Westerveld. (1984). "Decisionmaking Between Multiattribute Choice Alternatives: A Model of Spatial Shopping-behaviour Using Conjoint Measurements." *Environment and Planning A*, 16 (3); pp. 377-87.

Timmermans, H. and K. J. Veldhuisen. (1981). "Behavioural Models and Spatial Planning: Some Methodological Considerations and Empirical Tests." *Environment and Planning A*, 13 (12); pp. 1485-98.

Tocalis, T. R. (1978). "Changing Theoretical Foundations of the Gravity Concept of Human Interaction." Pp. 65-124 in *The Nature of Change in Geographical Ideas*, edited by B. J. L. Berry. Dekalb: Northern Illinois University Press.

Turner, R. and H. S. D. Cole. (1980). "An Investigation into the Estimation and Reliability of Urban Shopping Models." *Urban Studies*, 17 (2); pp. 139-57.

van Lierop, W. and P. Nijkamp. (1980). "Spatial Choice and Interaction Models: Criteria and Aggregation." *Urban Studies*, 17 (3); pp. 299-311.

Voorhees, A. M. (1957). "The Geography of Prices and Spatial Interaction." *Papers and Proceedings of the Regional Science Association*, 3; pp. 130-33.

Wade, B. (1983). *Superstore Appeals–Alternative Impact Assessment Methods* Reading: Unit for Retail Planning Information.

Wagner, W. B. (1974). "An Empirical Test of Reilly's Law of Retail Gravitation." *Growth and Change*, 5 (July); pp. 30-5.

Walmsley, D. J. and J. G. Lewis. (1984). *Human Geography: Behavioural Approaches*. London: Longman.

Webber, M. J. (1977). "Pedagogy Again: What is Entropy?." *Annals of the Association of American Geographers*, 67 (2); pp. 254-66.

Weisbrod, G. E., R. J. Parcells, and C. Kern. (1984). "A Disaggregate Model for Predicting Shopping Area Market Attraction." *Journal of Retailing*, 60 (1); pp. 65-83.

Whysall, P. (1981). "Retail Competition and the Planner." *Retail and Distribution Management,* 9 (3); pp. 44-7.

Wilkinson, C. (1980). "Status Quo-ism in Modelling—A Shopping Models Approach." *Planning Outlook,* 23 (1); pp. 30-3.

Williams, H. C. W. L. and K. S. Kim. (1990a). "Location-spatial Interaction Models: 2. Competition Between Independent Firms." *Environment and Planning A,* 22 (9); pp. 1155-68.

Williams, H. C. W. L. and K. S. Kim. (1990b). "Location-spatial Interaction Models: 3. Competition Between Organisations." *Environment and Planning A,* 22 (10); pp. 1281-90.

Williams, H. C. W. L., K. S. Kim, and D. Martin. (1990). "Location-spatial Interaction Models: 1. Benefit-maximizing Configurations of Services." *Environment and Planning A,* 22 (8); pp. 1079-89.

Williams, J. and C. Arnott. (1977). "A New Look at Retail Forecasts." *The Planner,* 63 (11); pp. 170-2

Williams, P. A. (1988). "A Recursive Model of Intraurban Trip-making." *Environment and Planning A,* 20 (4); pp. 535-46.

Wilson, A. G. (1967). "A Statistical Theory of Spatial Distribution Models." *Transportation Research,* 1; pp. 253-69.

Wilson, A. G. (1968). "Notes on Some Concepts in Social Physics." *Papers and Proceedings of the Regional Science Association,* 22; pp. 159-93.

Wilson, A. G. (1971). "A Family of Spatial Interaction Models, and Associated Developments." *Environment and Planning,* 3 (1); pp. 1-32.

Wilson, A. G. (1984). "Making Urban Models More Realistic: Some Strategies for Future Research." *Environment and Planning A,* 16 (11); pp. 1419-32.

Wilson, A. G. (1988). "Store and Shopping-centre Location and Size: A Review of British Research and Practice." Pp. 161-86 in *Store Choice, Store Location and Market Analysis,* edited by N. Wrigley. London: Routledge.

Wilson, A. G. (1989). "Classics, Modelling and Critical Theory: Human Geography as Structured Pluralism." Pp. 61-69 in *Remodelling Geography,* edited by B. Macmillan. Oxford: Basil Blackwell.

Wilson, A. G. and M. J. Oulton. (1983). "The Corner-shop to Supermarket Transition in Retailing: The Beginnings of Empirical Evidence." *Environment and Planning A,* 15 (2); pp. 265-274.

Wrigley, N. and P. A. Longley. (1984). "Discrete Choice modelling in Urban Analysis." Pp. 45-94 in *Geography and the Urban Environment: Progress in Research and Applications Volume IV,* edited by D. T. Herbert and R. J. Johnston. Chichester: John Wiley.

Young, E. C. (1924). *The Movement of Farm Population.* Ithaca: Cornell Agricultural Experiment Station, Bulletin 426.

Young, W. J. (1975). "Distance Decay Values and Shopping Centre Size." *The Professional Geographer,* 27 (3); pp. 304-9.

Yuill, R. S. (1967). "Spatial Behaviour of Retail Customers." *Geografiska Annaler,* 49B; pp. 105-14.

Zipf, G. K. (1949). *Human Behaviour and the Principle of Least Effort: An Introduction to Human Ecology.* Cambridge: Addison-Wesley.

PART III

MARKETING PRACTICE AND CONSUMER BEHAVIOR

GAMES, CONTESTS, SWEEPSTAKES, AND LOTTERIES:

PRIZE PROMOTION AND PUBLIC POLICY

Steven W. Kopp and Charles R. Taylor

ABSTRACT

This paper discusses the history of a promotional practice that is widely used today: the contest, game, or sweepstakes, collectively known as prize promotions. There are many societal and legal factors that have influenced the use of the prize promotion by retailers and manufacturers. These fundamental arguments are the same ones that present-day marketers must consider.

I. INTRODUCTION

Sweepstakes, games, and contests (collectively known as "prize promotions") are now among the most popular forms of promotion used by retailers and manufacturers. Companies sponsor a veritable plethora of games that offer hundreds of millions of dollars in prizes each year. The current resurgence of these games has been attributed to a trend toward state-run lotteries that have

Research in Marketing, Supplement 6, pages 151-166.

increased the awareness of consumers to the appeal of fantastic prizes, and to the fact that prize promotions are more involving to participants than are advertising or other types of promotions and are thus more appealing to sponsors (Govoni, Eng, and Galper 1986; Ward and Hill 1991).

The purpose of this paper is to discuss the history of prize promotions. The use of promotions based on giving away prizes with some element of chance or skill parallels the history of the "lottery." Just as governments and individuals have sponsored many private and public lotteries to raise money, so have businesses conducted prize promotions to increase sales. Often the two practices are indistinguishable. For this reason, the description of early prize promotions traces a thread through two extensive historical discussions of lotteries in England (Ewen's *Lotteries and Sweepstakes* 1932 [1978]) and in the United States (Ezell's *Fortune's Merry Wheel* 1960). The popularity of prize promotions by businesses can be traced to the societal and legal elements that have both encouraged and prohibited lotteries over the course of civilization.

II. A BRIEF HISTORY OF THE LOTTERY

The lottery has existed for several centuries for many purposes, from divination to general entertainment. There are 18 references to drawing by lot in the Old Testament. The Roman emperors Nero (A.D. 37-68) and Hegliogabalus (A.D. 204-222) conducted lotteries that awarded slaves or pieces of gold to the winners (Ezell 1960). Ewen (1972) provides evidence that lotteries were used by the Greeks, Celts, and Teutonic tribes for many purposes.

How the practice spread throughout Europe is unclear. Ezell (1960) attributes the expansion of the lottery to festivals, which carried the custom through to the feudal princes and merchants of northern Europe. He further suggests that Francis I of France saw the popularity of the private lottery and instigated public lotteries in 1539 to raise funds for his government. According to Ewen (1932), the popularity of the lottery in the "Lower Countries" could not have failed to arouse the interest of the English people in the Middle Ages, even though he finds no trace of the lottery there until the Elizabethan Lottery of 1568. Ezell suggests that the practice in England followed a definite pattern, beginning with small raffles similar to those used today followed by "enterprising individuals" who disposed of their merchandise through drawings. This was followed by the adoption of the lottery by the government, which wished to curb deceptive lotteries and also glean a profit from such a popular practice.

A. Governments and Lotteries

Because of the popularity of the lottery, governments on all levels have adopted them in order to raise funds, often as a substitute for taxation. Ezell

(1960) observed without citation that ancient Venetian governments initiated lotteries in order to generate revenue, while Ewen (1932) presented evidence of government-sponsored lotteries in 1445 in several French towns. In many cases over the course of history, in fact, the lottery has been so well integrated into the financial structure of some federal governments (France, for example) that the legal abolition of lotteries on moral grounds has been virtually impossible. Lotteries throughout history have been sponsored or licensed by governments that would at the same time prohibit private lotteries in order to protect the government-authorized lotteries from competition. Therefore, many times merchants have sold government-authorized lottery tickets at a premium in order to increase the number of customers. When lotteries have been prohibited by governments, merchants often have offered their own versions as a means of promotion.

At the same time, the lottery by itself has been the source of passionate controversy as it has always been seen by some as a form of gambling. Government attitudes and actions have ranged from laissez faire to the proscription of unauthorized lotteries to complete prohibition. This aspect of the practice has also been one of the inescapable criticisms of prize promotions. The lottery in at least some form, however, has been virtually impossible to stifle.

III.   EARLY PRIZE PROMOTIONS

Lottery-type games were used to stimulate sales by medieval Italian shopkeepers (Ewen 1972). These merchants kept *lusus ollae*—"urns of fortune"—in which a number of ballots were marked with the names of merchandise from their warehouses. Customers were allowed to pay a fee for the chance to draw from the urn and were then able to collect whatever prize showed on the ballot. It is likely that the popularity of the lottery which spread across Europe during the sixteenth and seventeenth centuries brought with it the practice by businesses of offering prizes along with purchases, but examples are difficult to find until the 1700s.

Many examples existed of prize promotions during the late seventeenth century when lotteries flourished. Ewen (1932) provides advertisements for lotteries conducted by merchants that involved the sale of goods by lottery. Chemists, jewelers, publishers, "tradesmen of every class," found that the use of lotteries "proved of great assistance in attracting custom and disposing of surplus stocks" (Ewen 1932, p. 168), until 1722 when the practice was declared an illegal method of trade. This did not stop the practice. It is noted by Webb (1989) that barbers, snuff makers, tailors, eating houses, and tea merchants in Dublin in 1700s offered their customers the chance to win prizes. This practice was so widespread, in fact, that Parliament passed further laws in 1739 to try to suppress these "private lotteries" because it was considered a practice of unfair trade (Webb 1989).

A. Lotteries and Prize Promotions in Colonial America

The lottery was well-entrenched in colonial society. Private lotteries were used by new immigrants who would raffle their material belongings in order to obtain currency which was often in short supply—articles of property (houses, land) that an individual wished to sell but that were too expensive could not command an acceptable price. As Thomas Jefferson noted, "The lottery is here a salutory instrument for disposing of it, where men run small risks for the chance of obtaining a high prize" (in Lipscomb 1903, p. 405). Private lotteries were criticized by many (including Cotton Mather) for being "a plain cheat upon the people" (Gordon 1833). Indeed, the lottery could be held by anyone who desired to instigate one so it is not surprising that corrupt or deceptive lotteries became quite prevalent. Often prizes were of low quality or never awarded.

It is ironic that one of the primary sources of discontent with the lottery in the American colonies was from the businessmen, who complained that the practice of prize promotions diverted large sums of money from conventional business channels. A merchant of Salem wrote in 1719 that the Massachusetts legislature disliked "the lotteries practiced of late, as differing little from Gaming for Money; and as being really pernicious to Trade" (in Ezell 1960, p. 19). In fact, one of the stated reasons most governments indicated for prohibiting unlicensed lotteries was the fact that the poor and lower classes would indeed neglect their work and instead tarry around taverns where raffles were commonly held, undoubtedly to the unfair profit of the publican. This was labeled a public nuisance: promoters were to be fined and, by the middle of the 1700s, all lotteries in the most populous states were required to be licensed by the state governments.

During the seventeenth and eighteenth centuries, these government-approved lotteries were very widely used to finance the construction of many American universities, including the University of Pennsylvania, Rutgers, and Harvard. Lotteries were also employed at all levels of government to fund the Revolutionary War and to build factories and various public works. Following the Revolutionary War, governments used lotteries to pay for war damages, to expand public facilities in the East, and to develop cities in the new West (Griffin 1981).

Again, merchants involved in other types of retail business would purchase lottery tickets which they would sell to their patrons at a premium. Included in this lot was none other than Phineas T. Barnum, who opened a store in Bethel, Connecticut in 1826. He began selling lottery tickets at a 10 percent commission along with is regular stock of stewed oysters, fruit, confectionery, and toys. The lottery sales proved so lucrative that Barnum approached Yates & McIntyre, a lottery brokerage, with the intent of opening an office in Pittsburgh. He learned that he could make a considerably higher profit from the ticket sales if he bought the tickets directly from the city managers of the lotteries. Barnum did just that, establishing his own lottery distributorships throughout Connecticut (Barnum 1927).

Well into the 1800s, in both England and the United States, the voices of those who disfavored the lottery became stronger. There were several reasons for this. Probably most importantly, lotteries and the governments that authorized them in the early 1800s were very often corrupt. One of the most infamous examples of this was that of the Missouri State Lottery. In 1833, the state government licensed a lottery to raise $15,000 to build a mile-long railroad from New Franklin to the Missouri River. Later, it was decided that a plank road would be built instead. The license was repealed in 1839, as Missouri followed many other states in eliminating lotteries. Three years later, the state legislature passed a law "abolishing all lotteries." In addition, the town of New Franklin was abandoned and most of the plank road collapsed into the river. Amazingly, the "New Franklin Lottery"—to become known as the Missouri State Lottery after the Civil War—was still conducted at a feverish rate, at one point twice daily. In fact, the purveyors of the lottery evaded Missouri officials by holding the lottery in Windsor, Canada, in 1845. In 1855, the agents of the lottery were fined for selling tickets, but their conviction was overturned by the state supreme court. Several other attempts at deterring the lottery agents failed in the legislature. Finally, a constitutional provision by the state and federal law put the scandal-ridden New Franklin Lottery to rest, but not until more than ten years after the Civil War (Gordon 1833). This exemplified many deceitful lotteries of the day, and provided impetus for antilottery laws throughout the country.

Another reason for the decline of the lottery in the mid-1800s was a shift in the values of society. In England, lotteries of all forms had long been viewed as a form of gambling that appealed to the masses and offended Victorian-era values. Lotteries, with a few exceptions, were abolished in England in 1826 (Miers and Dixon 1979). This phenomenon was later repeated in the United States. Public lotteries were frowned upon by Jacksonian reformers who wished to dispose of statutorily-granted privileges to the upper classes. The lottery (along with drink, pawnbrokers, prostitution, and charitable organizations) came to be seen as one of the primary causes of pauperism (Ezell 1960). By 1850, the Supreme Court was to state that the lottery was a "widespread pestilence..." which "infects the whole community...it plunders the ignorant and the simple" (Phalen vs. Virginia 1850, p. 168). By the outbreak of the Civil War, many states had enacted laws to punish any person involved with any form of lottery and had revoked the licenses for ongoing lotteries, but the various states had considerable difficulties in controlling the influx of unauthorized lottery tickets from states that did not outlaw the practice (Delaware in particular) and from England. It was not until after the Civil War that Congress passed laws that would prohibit the use of the postal service for lottery distribution and effectively eradicate the legal lottery from all states for nearly a century. Still, abolitionists took some comfort in the fact that what had once been a flourishing industry was now carried on only covertly (Ezell 1960).

However, as public lotteries became increasingly prohibited, drawings were merely shifted to friendly communities, and the use of the "game" or "sweepstakes" as a retail promotional device became more attractive to both consumers and retailers. This phenomenon was observed in England and the United States. In response to the abolition of public lotteries, private, illegal lotteries proliferated, particularly in taverns (Ezell 1960). In England, drinking establishments would offer sweepstakes on horse racing as a means of attracting customers (Ewen 1932; Miers and Dixon 1979). Ironically, governmental attempts to control lotteries actually increased and reinforced the use of the "game" or "sweepstakes" as a retail promotional device (Ewen 1932).

The Civil War and the resulting damages provided a nearly perfect excuse for reviving government-licensed lotteries. While some states had included antilottery provisions in their first constitutions (West Virginia, Nevada, Nebraska), other states licensed lotteries that became at once very popular including the nefarious Louisiana Lottery. Along with this resurrection came many deceptive schemes that were considered quite illegal prize promotion in the form of "gift companies." These enterprises operated ostensibly as straight merchandise sales organizations, but were in reality lotteries that were set up in such a way as to evade the law. The customer would purchase a sealed ticket that described a prize. Another $1 fee would affect the delivery of that prize ("Gift Enterprises" 1868). Often the prizes were fraudulent or nonexistent, but these gift companies were active in practically all states during the late 1860s.

Rampant deceit in the new lotteries brought the federal government into the picture. In 1868, Congress began curbing lotteries on a national scale by forbidding the use of the postal service for distribution of any letters or circulars concerning any "offering of prizes of any kind under any pretext whatever" (15 Stat. 194). In the following 20 years, because of a massive scandal in the Louisiana Lottery (Buel 1892) and because of strong prohibitionist sentiment by churches and political groups, the lottery took a beating, to the point of complete extermination. In 1894, Congress ended the legal lottery in the United States.

This presented a considerable boon and at the same time, a risk to merchants. On the one hand, some people seemed to have an insatiable desire to take a chance and get something for nothing or next to nothing. On the other hand, many types of prize promotions by retailers would now be illegal in most states. In fact, while formerly sanctioned lotteries were no more, definitions of what constituted a "lottery" determined what retailers could and could not use for promotional purposes.

Under common law, a single but very ambiguous definition of what constituted a lottery had been developed (and still applies today): a *chance* to win a *prize* that was offered for some type of *consideration*. The element of consideration referred to the amount a patron had to pay in order to participate. Each individual state (and each federal government agency) developed its own definition of each of the three components. If a business conducted a prize promotion that was determined to have all three of these elements, the practice was considered to be a lottery. For example, the practice of selling small pieces of candy with a chance to draw a prize of money was held to be a lottery in Pennsylvania (Commonwealth vs. Sheriff 1873), since the purchase of the candy was deemed to be consideration paid for the chance to win the prize.

However, as individual states tried to enforce laws based on their own definitions, discrepancies appeared. Retailers who wished to use any type of game or contest risked legal penalties if they were unable to avoid the three elements that legally comprised a lottery. Courts in different states did indeed come to quite disparate interpretations of the lottery terms. An example of this occurred in the 1890s. A man who called himself "The Great Yellowstone-Kit" conducted a traveling medicine show in the South, ultimately to come to Mobile, Alabama. There, he provided such amusements as greased pole climbing, magic shows, and dancing acts (at no charge) in order to attract patrons for his questionable medical remedies. At his farewell performance, the Great Kit held a "Jubilee Night," where his advertisements proclaimed that at the end of his usual show, he would hold a raffle for prizes for anyone who came to his tent and submitted his or her name. On that particular night, the show charged an admission fee (twenty cents to the sittees, ten cents to the standees, no charge to the people who stayed at home). Yellowstone-Kit was indicted for carrying on a lottery based on Alabama statutes. The state supreme court, however, overturned the conviction asserting that because there was no consideration paid in order to participate, there was no lottery (*Yellowstone-Kit* vs. *State* 1890). This case set a precedent that is recognizable today: "no purchase necessary" offered by prize promoters. It is interesting to note that the attorney general in this case argued that because the shows and drawing increased the sales of medicines, thereby enlarging the income of the proprietor, there was indeed consideration and therefore a lottery. Only four years later, however, the *Minneapolis Times* newspaper was convicted for distributing free calendars that were numbered and those numbers were drawn each day for a cash prize. The judge in this case held that any amount of effort (even checking the newspaper each day for a matching number) constituted consideration, so that the newspaper was indeed conducting a lottery (Williams 1958).

These same questions plagued prize promoters in England, where similar prohibitions were enacted at roughly the same time. In 1892, the publisher of a London publication *Pick-me-up* were charged with publishing a lottery in the form of a missing word competition. The publishers argued that since their contest required both skill and judgment (eliminating the "chance" element) because contestants had to select a word to fill in a blank in a sentence. The magistrate held that the publishers actually selected words at random for the contest and in fact no real skill was involved (Ewen 1932).

A relatively large number of legal cases involving prize promotions occurred following the prohibition of lotteries in the United States in 1894. This may suggest either that there were a large number of prize promotions sponsored or, more likely, that sponsors no longer knew what was legal and what was not. For example, various states found that the use of trading stamps as a promotional device was a lottery (*State* vs. *Hawkins* 1902), while others held the opposite opinion (*State* vs. *Shugart* 1903; *Ex parte West* 1905). This made many potential sponsors reluctant to carry on any prize promotion at all. Further examples are provided in two court decisions involving the same promotion (*U.S.* vs. *Jefferson* 1905; *Sheedy* vs. *District of Columbia* 1902). The game in question had participants collect coupons placed in "Mother Oats" packages in an effort to spell the word "MOTHERS." The Federal court found that since the chance of finding the letter "O" was one in 500, a lottery existed. Thus, in the first decade of this century, the lottery watchdogs of the federal government and highly inconsistent states now discouraged manufacturers and retailers from sponsoring many contests.

Nathaniel Fowler also offered discouraging words on prize promotions without mentioning the legal questions (Fowler 1897). In his comprehensive discussion of advertising and publicity practices, Fowler opposed prize-giving as a method of advertising, asserting that the practice was "at the best unobjectionable uselessness" (p. 505). Fowler recognized that offering prizes was useful only in stimulating "transient, not permanent, custom" and that a large number of participants would likely be disappointed and "think ill of the offerer." While on the whole Fowler disparaged prize promotions, he did concede that "its value lies in the interest it creates," but that the interest in the prize detracted from the image of the advertiser as well as from the product advertised. Prize promotions had indeed seen perhaps their lowest point.

By 1915, however, several manufacturers reported the successful use of contests (Johnson 1916). Several sponsors reported very high response to contests, including those that required a substantial amount of effort to enter. The makers of Bon Ami cleanser, for example, ran a contest in 1915 asking housewives to list all of the uses of the product. A cash prize was offered to the person producing the longest list. Concurrently, another contest was run that required the contestant to write a letter telling whether they liked Bon Ami cake or powder cleanser better and why. The company received over

25,000 entries for the list of uses, about 6,000 letters, and estimated that more than 200,000 women seriously considered how many uses they could find for Bon Ami. The Fleischmann Company also reported unexpectedly high response to a contest that required the collection of large numbers of labels from its yeast products and offered ponies as prizes to boys and girls who collected the most.

Another highly successful and publicized contest was conducted by Fould's milling company in 1918 ("Fould's Conundrum Contest"). The contest which offered one $100 first prize and ten $10 prizes, required entrants to write a conundrum for Fould's spaghetti. Announcements posted in streetcars, subways, and trains in large cities nationwide included the following sample conundrum written by cartoonist Rube Goldberg:

Question: *What is the difference between a man eating Fould's spaghetti and powder on a woman's nose?*
Answer: *One looks for more and the other is more for looks.*

The company was pleased when it received 20,000 conundrums, and was impressed that the entries came from people from all walks of life. The winning entry was received from Mr. Harry S. Southgate of Rochester, New York:

Question: *Why is Fould's Spaghetti like the American flag during war-time?*
Answer: *Because there are many ways of serving it.*

The fact that physicians, lawyers, clergymen, factory workers, carpenters, and others participated is an important one, because it is demonstrative of one of the central themes of this paper: if they are legal, a large group of people from a variety of occupations and social classes will participate in prize promotions. Generally, periods of low popularity of prize promotions are more a result of legislative or judicial response to some form of corruption in state run lotteries, private lotteries, or business sponsored prize promotions.

The Bon Ami and Fould's examples illustrate the beginning of the popularity of contests (as opposed to sweepstakes) just prior to 1920. With most courts adopting a very strict definition of chance, it was necessary for sponsors to introduce some element of skill to the promotion in order to feel confident that it would not be ruled a lottery. Thus, contests involving writing a jingle, writing essays, guessing numbers, or requiring some similar effort became the dominant form of prize promotion in the 1920s, with this dominance persisting until the 1950s. As some have pointed out (e.g. "Sweepstakes, Contests, and Games" 1968), these contests were really somewhat of a substitute for the lotteries or sweepstakes many firms would have preferred but could not legally conduct.

Rather than fret about only being able to run contests, successful promoters began to capitalize on their potential benefits. In the Bon Ami contest described previously, some of the uses of the cleanser sent in by housewives were later used in advertising. Further, the letters received regarding the preference for powder or cake were useful from a market research standpoint and were also considered in portrayals of certain issues of the product in magazine advertisements. The M.C.D. Borden Fabric Company sponsored a dressmaking contest in 1928 and 1929 that also was effective from a marketing research standpoint ("Expanding the Successful Consumer Contest" 1929). The contest was conducted at hundreds of stores nationwide, with thousands of designs being submitted. Not only were an estimated 100,000 dressmaking students in schools or sewing clubs exposed to the contest, but winning designs or modifications of them proved to be good sellers. The contest proved to be an excellent means of researching popular product designs.

By the late 1920s, a few analyses of contest popularity from an academic perspective could be found. Kleppner (1925) listed contest input as one means of making a product distinct from this competitors and commented that much information can be gained from contest entries. In a marketing textbook, White (1927), noted the increasing reliance of some publications on such promotions, and cautioned that they must not concentrate so much on the contest as to lose interest in the quality of the product. In 1928 ("Consumer Contests Come in Cycles"), one writer noted the tendency of contests to come in cycles, stressing their staying power as a promotional tool:

> There is no doubt that the consumer contest is a sales instrument that has been extensively tested and found to possess excellent sales possibilities. It seems destined to continue in use for a considerable time to come.

Even in current times there are peaks and valleys in the use of prize promotions, but as White stated, there always seem to be a demand for the prize promotions.

While contests continued to be popular in the 1930s, they were caught in the center of a bitter controversy and were closely regulated. Several groups that advocated legal, state run lotteries began to form. By 1935, an organized drive led by U.S. Representative Edward A. Kenny to put the federal government back into the lottery business was in place ("Slogans Through the Mails" 1935). Groups of citizens in favor of lotteries began to formed. One impetus behind the creation of these groups was the huge amount of money that was either going to foreign run lotteries or to illegally operated lotteries while the country was mired in depression. Estimates placed the amount of money leaving the country at $3 billion for the period from 1932 to 1934 (Parrish 1934). In 1935, nearly one-half of the money collected by the famous Irish Hospital's Sweepstakes was from the United States (Ellison and Brock 1936). More countries, including France, Russia, Argentina, China, and Italy were entering the lottery business at a time when illegal lotteries were thriving within the United States. For these reasons, it is not surprising that some groups began to advocate the lottery as a potential means of income for both state and federal governments in a time of depression. Indeed, a 1935 national poll conducted by *Fortune* magazine indicated that 55.3 percent of respondents were in favor of a legalized national lottery ("Lotteries" 1935). There were, as before, some religious groups, particularly the leadership of the Methodist and Presbyterian churches, which remained vehemently opposed to the lottery.

One prolottery group established in the 1930s was the National Conference on Legalizing Lotteries. Led by Mrs. Oliver Harriman and three other well-respected Manhattan socialites, the group set up its own slogan contest by requiring a one dollar "membership" fee to join the NCLL ranks ("Lottery Defended by Mrs. Harriman" 1936). Initially, the U.S. Postal Service required only the naming of a closing date and that identical prizes be awarded in case of a tie ("Slogans Through the Mails" 1935). Ironically, when this type of contest was imitated by illegitimate organizations, the Post Office was forced to crack down on them ("Stakes and Sweeps" 1936). When a large number of promotional games under numerous guises sprang up during the Depression, many states made very restrictive rulings as to what constituted a lottery (e.g. *State* vs. McEwan 1938) and again prize promotions were heavily restricted. Enforcement was shared by the Federal Trade Commission, which had become involved in the regulation of lotteries in 1925, the Federal Communications Commission, which was empowered to regulate radio contests that were actually lotteries, and the U.S. Postal Service. The FTC was particularly active in the 1930s, issuing cease and desist orders to hundreds of manufacturers (Lichtenberger 1986). Because of strict state, federal, and postal regulations, marketers were forced to severely limit both the consideration and chance elements of their promotions from the 1930s into the 1950s. As a result, sponsors emphasized contests of skill, which more or less avoided the question of chance.

The controversial nature of prize promotions may have been part of the reason behind some antithetical treatments of the subject. For example, a 1931 edition of *Printer's Ink* contained an article ("Another Radio Contest, No More No Less" 1931) describing a skit put on by the Association of National Advertisers spoofing radio contests. In the skit, it was requested that buyers of "Monday Morning Mouthwash" save 52 bottles of the product—one for each Monday of the year. When all 52 had been collected, the contestant was to inscribe on each, in Chinese characters, in not less than 300 words how he or she washed their mouth with the product. The prize was a papier mache model of the Empire State building, and in the event of a tie, "the other winner will be shot." Another contest that used a different approach deserves note. The Grand Valley Brewing company of Ionia, Michigan ran a contest in which contestants wrote in what they did not like about Friar's Ale ("A Consumer Contest in Reverse" 1935). While 65 percent of the entries actually made positive remarks, prizes were awarded for the best constructive criticism. The company believed that sales rose 30 percent as a direct result of the promotion.

During the 1930s the contests began to attract serious attention from the business press. Some writers, including Larabee (1935), portrayed contests as a poor, short-term substitute for advertising. Larabee was particularly irritated by one contest run by a producer of baked beans that required the collection of ten labels in order to enter a drawing for a luxury car. He stated that:

> There are always enough hopeful souls among the population of this somewhat over-populous country so that any kind of a bribe, though it may be more nebulous than the chance of winning a prize in the Irish Sweepstakes, will get them to rush out and buy a product.

The author went on to caution against having consumers buy for the chance of a prize rather than a brand preference and argued that consumers could become anesthetized to "contest ballyhoo" in the long run. As the quote illustrates, there was also concern within the business community over ethical issues in prize promotion. Textbooks went beyond example and provided instructions for sponsors on how to run a successful contest (Rushmore 1938).

On the other side, many marketers reported success. In 1935, the Mohawk Carpet company reported that it successfully boosted normally slow carpet sales to unprecedented levels via the use of a contest ("Contest Follow-up" 1935). Merchandising Facts, Inc. also ran a highly publicized contest in 1935 in which housewives answered 400 questions in a full page newspaper ad pertaining to brand usage, brand preferences, and purchase cycles. Based on the success of this contest, other research firms began to use similar techniques.

While some contests, again generally requiring skill, were run during the 1940s, the decade saw relatively few prize promotions. This may have been partly because World War II left businesses and the nation at large with concerns more pressing than prize promotions. Prize promotions, just as advertising expenditures, declined during the war. However, games, contests, and sweepstakes became so popular in the late 1940s that a spate of "textbooks" were published that provided secrets for participants to win the games, including such titles as *Prize Contests–How to Win Them* (King 1949), *How to Win Prize Contests* (Sunners 1940), *Premier Contest Course* (Cox 1953), and *How to Win Contest Prizes* Keith 1954). Included were trade secrets that the sponsors used, instructions on how to write better jingles and limericks, and how to write winning slogans. "Professional contestants"—people who would enter as many contests as they could get into—presented a chronic problem to sponsors (Pomerance 1960; Gross 1961).

Prize promotions had once again gained momentum. Many states relaxed their interpretations of the consideration component of a lottery. Thus, sweepstakes involving an element of chance were not automatically considered to be gambling, and regulation on these types of promotions became less restrictive. This was exemplified in *FCC* vs. *American Broadcasting Co., Inc.*

(1954), when the U.S. Supreme Court overturned an FCC ruling stating that the "commercial benefit" of the advertiser or promoter could constitute consideration and thereby create a lottery. The court ruled that since the "only effort required for participation is listening" (p. 294), the giveaway contests broadcast on radio were not lotteries. Within the next ten years it was common for retailers, especially supermarkets and gas stations, to use sweepstakes as a means of building traffic (Gross 1961; Allvine 1969).

From 1950 to 1960, the amount of money businesses spent on contests more than doubled (Meredith 1962). The increased ownership of televisions provided an attractive medium through which sponsors could advertise a contest and reach many potential contestants. The General Cigar Company, for example, received well over one million entries when it offered extravagant prize packages to winners of a drawing who correctly picked the winners of the final four televised NCAA football games in 1962 ("Adding a New Twist to a Contest" 1963). The increased celebrity of sweepstakes was also fueled by the general public's increased tolerance of gambling, as evidenced by the initiation of New Hampshire's state lottery in 1964 and many others that followed.

By the mid-1960s, the transition from the use of contests as the dominant means of prize promotions to sweepstakes or games requiring some type of matching or collecting of game pieces was complete (Marden and Kane 1968). By 1968, an article in the *Incentive Marketing* yearbook commented that, "...few, if any, recent promotions have bothered with the skill elements that used to account for large shares of such promotional events" ("Sweepstakes, Contests, and Games" 1968). Games sponsored by gas stations achieved phenomenal popularity in the 1960s, to the point where many felt they had to sponsor a game to stay in business (Miller 1968). Many such promotional games were mismanaged or corrupt, however, leading to the Federal Trade Commission to step in with new rules that singled out gasoline and food retailers. These rules mandated the disclosure of: the odds of winning; the geographic area in which the contest was to be conducted; the duration of the contest; and the random nature of the contest. Many prior sponsors found that these regulations reduced or eliminated their ability to support a game with television advertising, since a substantial portion of the commercial had to be devoted to stating rules and disclaimers ("Games Are Back, But Less Fun Amid Legalities and Apathy" 1972). State laws were amended to be consistent with this tighter regulation, which led many marketers to avoid prize promotions altogether throughout the early to mid-1970s (Allvine, Teach, and Connelly 1976).

The FTC remained active in regulation, questioning whether phrases like "you may have already won" could be used to get a player to overestimate the chance of winning. In 1971, the FTC subscribed to this view when it found that the Reader's Digest Sweepstakes, for instance, did not present "a reasonable opportunity to win" with odds of 480,00 to 1 ("In the matter of Reader's Digest Assn Inc." 1971).

With the advent of rub-off technology, the idea of the "instant winner" helped to contribute to a resurgence of sweepstakes and games in the late 1970s. The acceptance and popularity of state lotteries and other legalized gambling helped as well (Edmondson 1986). It was difficult for state legislatures to justify strict regulation of games when they were using a similar form of gambling to generate income for themselves (Govoni, Eng, and Galper 1986).

The decline in federal regulation and the continued growth of sweepstakes and games in the 1980s (Fueroghne 1989; Wells, et al. 1989; Govoni, Eng, and Galper 1986; Kleppner, Russell, and Verrill 1983) has brought forth an increase in the number of legal disputes between contest players and contest sponsors (Taylor and Kopp 1991). In 1989, for example, Kraft sponsored its "Ready to Roll" promotion. A printing error in newspaper advertising led 21,000 people to believe they had won the top prize (a minivan) when only one person was supposed to win ("Kraft Snafu Could Cost $4 Million Dollars" 1989). While these disputes have resulted in negative publicity and lawsuits for some sponsors, they do not yet appear to have substantially reduced sponsor enthusiasm for games or sweepstakes (nor is this a new occurrence—see Gross 1961, p. 253).

IV. CONCLUSION

It seems that if the games exist, people will play them. The sponsorship of contests, sweepstakes, and games has ebbed and flowed as a result of complex interactions with societal attitudes, hence governmental restrictions, concerning gambling and lotteries. Indeed, the *types* of prize promotions that are offered seem to be subject, not to demand, but to supply which is determined by the law. It has been argued that the "gambling instinct" exists universally and that the only constraint on prize promotions is that of the laws concerning lotteries.

In this context, it is interesting to note the comments of sociologist Amitai Etzioni on a broadcast of ABC's "Nightline" television program in 1984. Speaking on the effects of sweepstakes on society he said:

> It used to be taught that if you work hard, save, you retire, and then you have fun and games. They (sweepstakes) provide a quickie, a shortcut. You bet, next week, next month you have it, you have a million: you no longer have to work, save, be a good American.

It would be argued here that Mr. Etzioni's comments ignore the history of sweepstakes in the United States and, in fact, the history of the lottery in civilization.

REFERENCES

A Consumer Contest in Reverse. (1935, April 4). *Printer's Ink,* p. 38.

"Adding a New Twist to a Contest." (1963). *Printer's Ink,* (May 24); pp. 41-43.

Allvine, F. C. (1969). "The Future for Trading Stamps and Games." *Journal of Marketing, 33* (1); pp. 1-7.

Allvine, F. C., R. D. Teach, and J. Connelly. (1976). "The Demise of Promotional Games." *Journal of Advertising Research, 16* (5); pp. 79-84.

"Another Radio Contest—No More, No less." (1931). *Printer's Ink,* (November 26); p. 63.

Barnum, P.T. (1927). *Struggles and Triumphs: Forty Years of Life of P.T. Barnum, Written by Himself,* New York: A.A. Knopf.

Buel, C.C. (1892). "Degradation of a State: The Charitable Career of the Louisiana Lottery." *Century, 43* (Fall); pp. 681-632.

Commonwealth vs. *Sheriff.* (1873). 6 Leg. Gaz.; p. 51.

"Consumer Contests Come in Cycles." (1928). *Printer's Ink,* (July 5): p. 56.

"Contest Follow-Up." (1935). *Printer's Ink,* (August 29); pp. 44-46.

Cox, C. R. (1953). *Premier contest course.* American Book Concern.

Edmondson, B. (1986). "The Demographics of Gambling." *American Demographics;* pp. 39-41.

Ellison, E. J. and F. W. Brock. (1936). "Lotteries and the Law." *Reader's Digest,* (June); pp. 78-81.

Ewen, C. L. ([1932] 1978). *Lotteries and Sweepstakes.* New York: Benjamin Blom, Inc.

Exparte West (1905). 82 Pacific, p. 434.

"Expanding the Successful Consumer Contest." (1929). *Printer's Ink,* (August 29); pp. 113-116.

Ezell, J. S. (1960). *Fortune's Merry Wheel: The Lottery in America.* Cambridge: Harvard University Press.

Federal Communications Commission vs. *American Broadcasting Co., Inc.* (1954). 347 U.S.; p. 284.

"Fould's Conundrum Contest." (1918). *Printer's Ink,* (January 10); pp. 122-125.

Fowler, N. C. (1897). *Fowler's Publicity.* New York: Publicity Publishing Company.

Fueroghne, D. K. (1989). *"But the People in Legal Said...": A Guide to Current Legal Issues in Advertising.* Homewood, IL: Dow Jones-Irwin.

"Games are Back, But Less Fun Amid Legalities and Apathy." (1972). *Incentive Marketing Facts;* pp. 232-235.

"Gift Enterprises." (1868). (Vol. 7). *Hours at Home;* pp. 446-450.

Gordon, G. W. (1833). *Lecture on Lotteries Before the Boston Young Men's Society.* Boston, MA:

Govoni, N., R. Eng, and M. Galper. (1986). *Promotional Management.* Englewood Cliffs, NJ: Prentice Hall.

Griffin, G. L. (1981). "Missouri Lottery Law: of Promotional Games and Pyramids." *UMKC Law Review, 49* (3); pp. 321-337.

Gross, A. (1961). *Sales Promotion: Principles and Methods for Intensifying Marketing Effort.* (2nd ed.). New York: The Ronald Press Company.

"In the Matter of Reader's Digest Assn, Inc." (1971). 79 *FTC;* p. 696.

Johnson, R. W. (1916). "When a Consumer Contest is Profitable and When It Isn't." *Printer's Ink,* (August 16); pp. 1-10.

Keith, L. (1954). *How to Win Contest Prizes.* Pochahontas, AR.

King, H. (1949). *Prize Contests–How To Win Them.* Lancaster, PA: Rugby House.

Kleppner, O. (1925), *Advertising Practice.* New York: Prentice Hall.

Kleppner, O., T. Russell, and G. Verrill. (1983). *Advertising Procedure* (8th ed.). Englewood Cliffs, NJ: Prentice Hall.

"Kraft Snafu Could Cost $4 Million." (1989). *Advertising Age,* (July 10); p. 53.

Larabee, C.B. (1935). "Substitutes for Advertising." *Printer's Ink,* (December 12); pp. 6, 108.
Lichtenberger, J. (1986). *Advertising Compliance Law.* Westport, CT: Quorum Books.
Lipscomb, A. A. (1903). *The Writings of Thomas Jefferson.* Washington, D.C.: Thomas Jefferson Memorial Association of the United States.
Lotteries. (1935). *Fortune,* (October); pp. 168-169.
"Lottery Defended by Mrs. Harriman." (1936). *New York Times,* (March 23); p. 23.
Marden, B. A. and Kane, R. (1968). "Sweepstakes." *Incentive Marketing Facts;* pp. 228-230.
Meredith, G. (1962). *Effective Merchandising with Premiums.* New York: McGraw Hill.
Miers, D. and D. Dixon. (1979). "The National Bet: The Re-emergence of the Public Lottery." *Public Law,* (Winter); pp. 372-403.
Miller, W. H. (1968). "The Petroleum Game." *Incentive Marketing Facts;* pp. 231-243.
Oliver, B. (1986). "Sales Promotion: Games People Play." *Marketing,* (September 19); pp. 51-52.
Parrish, W. W. (1934). "A Revival of Interest in Lotteries." *Literary Digest, 117;* pp. 9-10.
Phalen vs. *Virginia.* (1960). "How Many Contest Entries Spell Success?" *Journal of Marketing,* 25 (October); pp. 7-10.
Rushmore, E. M. (1938). "Consumer Contests." Pp. 435-445 in *The Handbook of Advertising,* edited by E.B. Weiss. New York: McGraw Hill.
Sheedy vs. *District of Columbia.* (1902). 19 App. D.C.; p. 280.
"Slogans Through the Mails." (1935). *Literary Digest,* (July 27); p. 200.
"Stakes and Sweeps. (1936). *Time,* (April 20); p. 15.
State vs. *Hawkins.* (1902). 93 Am. St. Rep., p. 328.
State vs. *McEwan.* (1938). 120 S.W. 2d, p. 1098.
State vs. *Shugart.* (1903). 100 Am. St. Rep., p. 17.
Sunners, W. (1950). *How to win Prize Contests.* Arco Publishing Company.
"Sweepstakes, Contests, and Games." (1968). *Incentive Marketing Factbook;* pp. 128-131.
Taylor, C. R. and S. W. Kopp. (1991). "Games, Contests, and Sweepstakes Run Afoul: A State of Legal Disorder." *Journal of Public Policy and Marketing, 10* (Spring); pp. 199-214.
U.S. vs. *Jefferson.* (1905). 134 F.; p. 299.
Ward, J.C. and R.P. Hill. (1991). "Designing Effective Promotional Games: Opportunities and Problems." *Journal of Advertising,* 20 (September); pp. 69-81.
Webb, A. (1989). *The Clean Sweep: The Story of the Irish Hospitals Sweepstakes.* London: George G. Harrap & Co., Inc.
Wells, W., J. Burnett, and S. Moriarity. (1989). *Advertising Principles and Practice.* Englewood Cliffs, NJ: Prentice-Hall.
White, P. (1927). *Advertising Research.* New York: D. Appleton and Company.
Williams, Judge F. E. (1958). *Lotteries, Laws, and Morals.* Chicago: Vantage Press.
Yellow-Stone Kit vs. *State.* (1890). 7 So., p. 338.

DATA SOURCES FOR AMERICAN CONSUMPTION HISTORY:
AN INTRODUCTION, ANALYSIS, AND APPLICATION

Terrence H. Witkowski

ABSTRACT

This paper compares and evaluates two data source categories, written evidence and material artifacts, for conducting primary research in American consumption history. It then discusses early probate records and surviving household furnishings as exemplars of these categories and shows how using them together can reveal insights about past consumer behavior.

I. INTRODUCTION

Much new literature has enriched the field of consumption history within the past ten years. In 1982, the seminal *Birth of a Consumer Society* by McKendrick, Brewer, and Plumb investigated evolving forms of consumption

Research in Marketing, Supplement 6, pages 167-182.

and marketing in eighteenth-century England. That same year, Gloria Main's (1982) *Tobacco Colony* and articles by Carole Shammas (1982a, 1982b) depicted consumer behavior in colonial America, while Rosalind Williams (1982) in *Dream Worlds* studied mass consumption in late nineteenth-century France. In 1983, Chandra Mukerji's *From Graven Images* traced our "materialist culture" back to fifteenth and sixteenth-century Europe and the following year Hollander (1984) analyzed the long history of sumptuary legislation or government control over consumption. The year 1985 witnessed articles on American women and domestic consumption (Gordon and McArthur 1985) and the "primitive" aspects of modern consumption (Hirschman 1985). More recent publications include three books, *The Romantic Ethic and the Spirit of Modern Consumerism* (Campbell 1987), *Consumer Choice in Historical Archaeology* (Spencer-Wood 1987) and *Culture and Consumption* (McCracken 1988), three review articles (Hollander 1988; McCracken 1987; Rassuli and Hollander 1986), and three papers on American consumer behavior before the Revolutionary War (Breen 1986, 1988; Witkowski 1989).

Consumer researchers not only should read and learn from consumption history, but also should consider making a contribution of their own. Analyses of the differences and similarities between the past and present help clarify tacit assumptions about "modern" consumers (Hirschman 1985). Historical findings can suggest new ways of thinking about consumer behavior contructs and their interrelationships. Historical methods can be applied to contemporary problems in consumer research. The writing of this history need not justify itself with a continual search for implications. It is valuable and interesting in its own right. Nevertheless, using the past to instruct the present will make consumer research more exciting intellectually and more appealing to a wider audience. Further work in consumption history requires familiarity with its methods and data sources.

This paper focuses on researching the history of American consumers and consumption before 1870. It begins with a brief description and evaluation of two major data source categories—written evidence and material artifacts. Subsequent sections discuss one example of written data, early probate records, and one type of material artifact, surviving household furnishings, in greater detail and suggest ways in which they can mutually augment each other.

II. WRITTEN AND MATERIAL DATA SOURCES

Written records and material artifacts are the two main categories of data sources available to consumption historians. Virtually endless for contemporary societies, written sources become fewer in number and, hence, increasingly manageable the further back in time one ventures. Typical written sources helpful to historians of American consumption include the following, listed from the most public to the most personal:

1. Public records such as tax lists, probate documents, and court proceedings.
2. Stories and letters in newspapers and magazines.
3. Newspaper advertising, handbills, trade cards, and trade catalogs.
4. Nonfiction travel accounts, cookbooks, and housekeeping manuals.
5. Novels, poetry, and other published fiction.
6. Private business records such as account books and letters.
7. Personal writing in the form of letters and diaries.

Academic historians (those employed by colleges and universities) rely upon written sources almost exclusively (Schlereth 1982), while students of material culture use them as external evidence to validate or deny hypotheses about artifacts (Prown 1982).

As a data source, written documents possess both strengths and weaknesses. Newspapers and magazines were originally mass produced and additional copies have been disseminated widely via microfiche and microfilm. Important personal letters and diaries published in book form are also quite accessible. Furthermore, numerical records can be analyzed statistically and even some writing is quantifiable. Literature can give insights into people's inner thoughts and feelings about buying and using things.

However, literature can be an inefficient data source. As Ames (1978) puts it: "Although occasional passages may be illuminating, finding them is not easy" (p. 23). Moreover, written records of all types are often incomplete, difficult to read if penned by hand, and occasionally contradictory. Researchers should always be on the lookout for possible selective perception and retention on the part of the source. Indeed, the person or persons who wrote an account may have had reason to deliberately distort the truth. Since the dominant classes in a society produce most of its writing, their reports might stress priviledged consumers and luxury consumption. American elites seem likely to have produced biased and incomplete descriptions of the consumption behavior of common people, especially blacks and recent immigrants.

Material artifacts are the second category of data sources. So many different kinds of objects fall into this category that a system of classification is desirable for purposes of discussion. Prown (1982) proposes the following scheme, slightly revised by the present author, based on function and progressing from the more decorative to the more utilitarian:

1. Art (paintings, drawings, prints, sculpture, photography).
2. Diversions (books, toys, games, theatrical props, sporting accessories).

3. Adornment (jewelry, clothing, hairstyles, cosmetics, tattooing, other alterations of the body).
4. Modifications of the landscape (architecture, town planning, agriculture, mining).
5. Applied arts (furniture, furnishings, receptacles).
6. Devices (machines, vehicles, scientific instruments, musical instruments, implements).

Material artifacts can also be classified as *found objects*, the bits and pieces archaeologists excavate at historical sites, or *preserved objects*, the antiques and works of fine art housed in public and private collections. Preserved objects are the primary interest of art and architectural historians, decorative arts scholars, folklorists, and collectors who analyze things for their own sake and to gain insight into a particular culture and its variations at a given time, over time, or in comparison with another society (Kirk 1982). They tend to study single items with qualitative methodologies (Schlereth 1983). Schlereth (1982) contends that material data sources have been largely ignored by academic historians.

Like written sources, material artifacts have their advantages and limitations. Most important, they are graphic evidence and sometimes all that remains of what people actually used in their lives as consumers. "Objects created in the past are the only historical occurrences that continue to exist in the present" (Prown 1982, p. 3). Because many kinds of artifacts were used by a broad cross-section of the population, they are potentially more representative data sources than words. Moreover, with the exception of works of art, objects are generally less self-conscious cultural expressions and, therefore, conceivably more truthful (Prown 1982). Through their style, objects communicate tacit but fundamental values of a society (Prown 1980).

On the other hand, they do not reveal beliefs, attitudes, values, and meanings as directly as do written records. Equally important, material artifacts suffer from their own problems of representativeness. Found objects are generally restricted to certain materials, such as ceramics, glass, or precious metals, that can survive many years of burial on land or under water. Leather, wooden, and base metal consumer goods rarely last under these conditions and textiles hardly at all. Aside from pure chance, preserved objects were saved because they possessed special attributes. They may have been of the highest quality, particularly artistic, or originally owned by distinguished, affluent families. More common and often cruder artifacts tended to have deteriorated more rapidly and were discarded as junk. Their survival rate is much less than that of high-style objects. To make matters worse, preserved objects may have been altered over time, either innocently or with intent to deceive, and no longer are the same evidence as they were when first produced and used. Early twentieth-century antique dealers and collectors sometimes restored furniture overzealously and inaccurately. From time to time major museums discover problems with their pieces, pull them from public view, and restore them correctly or, if they are outright fakes, relegate them to their "study" collections (Kaye 1987; Witkowski 1992). These historical accretions remind us that objects live in the present as well as the past.

Although surviving pictorial representations at times provide accurate information about standards of living, they too can be an unreliable witness. For example, the drawings, paintings, and engravings of William Hogarth, the famous eighteenth-century artist, frequently portrayed domestic artifacts with pronounced eccentricity (Hume 1970). Most American paintings before 1800 were portraits and these naturally depicted a relatively well-to-do clientele, their dress, and their surroundings. Early nineteenth-century genre paintings showing middle-class families contemplating purchases from itinerant peddlers (Hills 1974) may have distorted actual consumption behavior in order to instruct or entertain the viewer.

III. PROBATE RECORDS

Early American probate records, considered here to be an exemplar of written data sources, already have benefited consumption history and still have much to offer. Probate records include wills, inventories, and accounts of administration. According to Main (1975):

> The first directed the disposition of property. The second itemized and evaluated the forms of that property. The third furnished reports to the court on the disposition of property in intestacy cases and also in those cases where the will provided an insufficient guide to the legal settlement of the estate (p. 90).

Inventories constitute the vast majority of all probate records. Only one-third to one-half of all inventoried estates left wills, while accounts of administration survive for less than one-third of the cases (Main 1975).

Appraisers, usually neighbors of the deceased, compiled the estate inventories. They listed items, sometimes on a room-by-room basis, and assigned values expressed in pounds, shillings, and pence. Inventories might range from a short account of the few possessions owned by a common laborer to a long list of personal and business merchandise owned by a wealthy merchant. The number of goods and their value tells us about the decedent's standard of living and, in the assortment of goods, about his consumer lifestyle.

As a data source for consumption history, probate records have much to recommend them. Available in print, on microfilm, and in readily accessible archives, they exist in enormous profusion. Indeed, some researchers have found it expedient to draw probability samples from a larger universe of records (Jones 1977, 1980). Probate inventories cover a broad range of people and describe a great variety of consumer goods. Thus, they lend themselves to quantitative research methods.

On the other hand, so many different colonial currencies prevailed at various times and places that investigators must carefully convert them to a more stable currency. Early Maryland inventories even expressed values in terms of pounds of tobacco (Main 1982). Furthermore, estate inventories did not necessarily typify community consumption patterns because of unavoidable age and nonresponse biases (Shammas 1978). Decedents tended to have been older than living neighbors and, consequently, may have had the time to accumulate greater wealth. Also, not all estates were inventoried, especially those of the mobile young and the very affluent. "As a general rule, coverage declined with time, leveling off to 40 percent in Massachusetts by the Revolution and during the nineteenth century" (Main 1975, p. 98). Finally, appraisers may have deliberately omitted some items to protect surviving widows and children who, in turn, may have hidden articles for their own reasons. The claims of creditors kept such practices within reasonable bounds (Main 1982).

Several studies based upon probate records, have contributed to the history of early American consumption. *American Colonial Wealth* and its companion volume, *Wealth of a Nation to Be*, by Alice Hanson Jones (1977, 1980) comprise an ambitious discussion of colonial living standards. Using a probability sample of inventories, Jones estimates aggregate and per capita wealth for the thirteen colonies in 1774 and then examines wealth distributions among regions and among various socioeconomic groups. She finds, for instance, that Southern households averaged about twenty percent more in total consumer goods than did comparable ones in New England and the middle colonies. Since Jones chose to lump all consumer goods into one data category, her work does not reveal much about styles of living. However, since *American Colonial Wealth* reprints facsimiles of all 919 inventories in the sample, it is a valuable resource for further research.

Society and Economy in Colonial Connecticut by Jackson Turner Main (1985) also aggregates different consumer goods, but conducts separate analyses for books and clothing. Even during the relatively primitive conditions of the seventeenth century, about three out of five Connecticut estate inventories mentioned books. Among the more affluent occupations, ministers owned the most, followed by doctors, lawyers and public officials, and, lastly, men of commerce. Expenditures on clothing varied with wealth and occupation, but not with marital status.

Food and clothing in eighteenth-century Pennsylvania are the topic of a study by Lemon (1967). Since inventories rarely include perishables and probably underrepresent clothing (Main 1982), Lemon turns to an alternative probate record: 159 wills of Lancaster County farmers between 1740 and 1790. Wills are an indicator of consumption because they instructed sons to provide their mothers and siblings with specific amounts of "meat, grain, beverages, other foods, material for cloth, and money" (p. 60). From this data source, Lemon concludes that colonial farmers ate three times as much grain, but smaller amounts of meat and dairy products than do today's consumers.

Two studies of colonial Maryland are of greater interest to consumption historians. *Tobacco Colony* by Gloria L. Main (1982) examines lives of planters and their families between 1650 and 1720. Main presents a good deal of information on the classes of material objects within households and discusses how they defined the physical and attitudinal dimensions of consumer life. For example, at all wealth levels, beds and beddings were the most common and valuable group of household furnishings, usually costing more than horses. In general, consumption differences between poor and more affluent planters were largely of degree, not kind. Although the upper third had the wherewithal to live quite well, they chose to live in a relatively plain and simple manner. According to the probate inventories, "few planters, even among the rich and powerful, cared to introduce any decorative note to the interior furnishings of their homes" (Main 1982, p. 166).

Carr and Walsh (1980), use probate records from St. Mary's County, 1658-1777, to document how and when consumer lifestyles changed over time. They hypothesize that the introduction of nonessentials not only made life more comfortable, but also advertised social status. To operationalize their theories, the authors construct an index of consumption by noting the presence or absence, in each inventory, of twelve different consumer goods. The items include (1) earthenware, (2) bed or table linen, (3) table knives, (4) forks, (5) fine earthenware, (6) spices, (7) religious books, (8) secular books, (9) wigs, (10) watches or clocks, (11) pictures, and (12) silver plate. The findings indicate little improvement until 1716 when standards of living began to rise for all social classes. Carr and Walsh interpret this as a signal change in consumer behavior:

> an attempt on the part of the elite to set themselves off from ordinary colonists by adopting some of the refinements and sophistications then being taken up by similar groups in Europe on one hand, and a growing tendency on the other for the lower orders to incorporate some aspects of the life styles of their betters (p. 91).

If this did take place, then colonial consumers were beginning to resemble those of later, industrialized cultures.

To illustrate an actual probate record and how it might be interpreted, Table 1 reproduces the inventory of John Boyd, schoolmaster, who died in Kent County, Delaware, in 1774 (Jones 1977, p. 362). The inventory lists the items in his estate on the left and their values in pounds (L), shillings (s), and pence (d) on the right. All spelling is original and obviously idiosyncratic. Colonial Americans did not have dictionaries and generally spelled words the way they spoke them. Jones estimates that Boyd was between 25 and 44 when he died.

Table 1. The Inventory of John Boyd, Schoolmaster

An inventory of the goods and Chattels of John Boyd Deceased. appraised by us the Subscribers As Followeth as Witness our hands this 4th Day of November 1774.

	L	s	d
To one Watch @	4	10	—
To one Bed one boulster 2 Coverlids 2 sheets & 1 New Bedstead & 2 pillows	4	—	—
To one Bed one boulster 1 pillow one green Rugg one Coverlid 2 blankets 2 old sheets 1 bedsted.	3	—	—
To one Copper Tea Kittle	—	10	—
To one Saddle & Bridle	1	15	—
To one old Loom 3 Slays 3 pair of Gears 2 Shuttles & one old Quill wheel	2	5	—
To old Iron Potts & 2 pair of Hooks	—	10	—
To a parcel of Old Earthen Ware	—	1	4
To one old Linnen Wheel	—	3	9
To one Case Bottle and a parcel of Viols & 2 snuff Bottles	—	1	3
To a pair of fire Tongs & Shovel	—	10	—
To 2 old pails & Tub & Churn	—	2	—
To one old Bagg	—	1	—
To one Pepper box 2 Tin Cups & one old Coffee pot	—	1	—
To one old frying pan	—	2	6
To all his Wearning Apparel	5	—	—
To 3 chairs	—	6	—
To an old Book case & all the Books that are in it	1	5	—
To one old Chest & what is in it	—	5	—
To a parcell of pewter	—	15	—
To one Cow & Calf	5	10	—
To a parcel of old plank	—	10	—
To one Loom	1	10	—
To 4 pair of Gears & 3 Slays & one Mill	—	15	—
To 2 old Sows & 5 year oldl hoggs	5	—	—
To one pair of Stillards	—	5	—
To 60 Weight of Bacon	1	—	—
	L39	13	10

Stephen Lewis

Returned by W. Lewis Jonathon
Caldwell the other appraiser being
dead Nov. 20th 1782

Source: Alice Hanson Jones (1977), *American Colonial Wealth: Documents and Methods,* Vol. 1, New York: Arno Press, P. 362.

Because more than one bed is listed, Boyd probably had a family. For some unknown reason this inventory was not "returned" until eight years after his death.

Boyd's total wealth of a little over 39 pounds places him in the bottom half of all wealthholders in Jones' sample. Teachers received low salaries in the eighteenth century and usually left the profession for a more profitable one (Main 1985). References to a loom, shuttles, quill and "linnen" wheels, a cow and calf, and sows and hogs indicate that Boyd and his family produced part of their own food, cloth, and clothing. They also may have sold or more probably bartered excess production with their neighbors or local tradesmen. Note, too, that beds and bedding were among the most valuable possessions in the estate. His watch, a handy item for a schoolmaster, was the single most expensive consumer good and the only real luxury in the household. Apparently, the family owned no small items of silver, no porcelain, and no looking glasses. They did not even own a kitchen table. Recall, however, that one or more items may have been purposefully omitted from the inventory. If Boyd did have a wife, she might have brought into the marriage her own possessions. Their contribution to family living standards would not have been recorded in her husband's estate.

IV. HOUSEHOLD FURNISHINGS

John Boyd's inventory tells a lot about his consumer lifestyle, but also leaves much to the imagination. For instance, it mentions "a parcel of Old Earthen Ware" and "a parcell of Pewter" without specifying the kinds of items and where they were made. The presence of specialized implements, such as tea bowls, sauce boats, or pewter pepper casters, would indicate relatively sophisticated dining standards. The existence of imported goods would suggest that Boyd's family participated in a global marketing system. Similarly, the entry, "an old Book case & all the Books that are in it," says that Boyd was literate, but does not describe the nature of his education. To answer these questions, the information supplied by probate records needs to be augmented with other types of data sources such as diaries, letters, account books, and even portraiture.

Material artifacts, exemplified by early American household furnishings, can provide still additional information. Historical archaeologists, in their analyses of objects found on eighteenth-century sites, demonstrate one approach to using material data sources. Baugher and Venables (1987), for example, discuss investigations of seven sites in New York state that were linked to specific families with a documented history. Research teams found evidence, in the form of buried ceramic remnants, that both rural and urban families used bowls, mugs, dishes, and tea sets from around the world. This indicates not only the existence of global marketing, but also the fact that buying power, not proximity to a colonial city, determined what and how much the individual purchased. Furthermore, the discovery on many of the sites of quality table and kitchenwares, such as porcelain and better grades of pottery, suggests that "to the best of its ability, the middle class imitated the fashions of the upper class" (p. 50).

Preserved objects are a second material data source. The sizeable decorative or applied arts literature, especially catalogs of exhibitions and museum collections, frequently describes household furnishings in great detail. Typically written for collectors and curators and often emphasizing esthetics, these studies document when, where, how, and by whom objects were made and, whenever possible, trace histories of ownership. The best of this literature, such as Wendy Cooper's *In Praise of America* (1980) or Jobe and Kaye's *New England Furniture* (1984), serves as a very useful reference for consumption history. Still, it is only a prerequisite for further inquiry.

Research on the leading edge of decorative arts scholarship, in contrast, addresses broader issues including consumption and even marketing (Miller 1984). As Ames (1985) puts it: "the field has been in transition from studying antiques or artistic objects as ends in themselves to studying those objects in order to understand society and culture" (p. 79). For example, Barbara Smith's (1985) *After the Revolution* gathers a variety of written sources to document the lives of some of the people who lived in three "period rooms" installed at the Smithsonian's National Museum of American History. In her ambitious study, *At Home: The American Family 1750-1870*, Elisabeth Garrett (1990) uses diaries, letters, housekeeping manuals, and contemporary paintings and prints to recreate room by room how Americans once lived in their houses and how they purchased and consumed different household furnishings.

Fleming (1974) presents a model for artifact study that uses two conceptual tools—a classification of basic properties and a set of operations performed on these properties. An object's properties are its history, material, construction, design, and functions, either intended and unintended functions. The operations include *identification* (a factual description), *evaluation* (judgments), *cultural analysis* (the relationships of the object to its culture), and *interpretation* (the relationships of the artifact to *our* culture). Whereas identification and evaluation are within the tradition of connoisseurship, cultural analysis and interpretation introduce methods of material culture. Fleming assigns somewhat new meanings to terms familiar to consumer researchers. He defines "product analysis" as the ways in which a culture leaves its mark upon an object and "content analysis" as the ways in which an object reflects its culture. He also reminds us that interpretation varies according to the personal and cultural characteristics of investigators and their audiences.

Another advocate of the material culture approach, Jules Prown, persuasively argues that stylistic changes denote shifts in cultural values. In "Style as Evidence" (1980), he shows how the popularity of neoclassical motifs after the Revolutionary War signified the diffusion of Enlightenment thought in America.

Prown (1982) also proposes an intriguing three-stage method for object analysis. The intent of his method "is the quest for cultural belief systems, the patterns of belief of a particular group of people in a certain time and place"

(p. 6). This approach is deterministic since it assumes that the properties of an artifact (the effect) correspond to the mental patterns (the cause) of the producer and of his culture. Prown also contends that the methodology of material culture rests on premises shared by theories of linguistic structuralism and semiotics. That is, people structure their world through forms as well as through language. In turn, these forms "transmit signals which elucidate mental patterns or structures" (p. 6).

In the first stage of object analysis, *description*, the investigator records what can be observed in the object itself, the internal evidence. This includes physical measurement, description of materials, and an analysis of content and configuration or style. The second stage, *deduction*, entails an interaction between the object and the perceiver. Here, the investigator experiences the object with the physical senses, apprehends it intellectually, and perhaps responds emotionally. In the third stage, *speculation*, the analyst reviews information gathered in prior stages and then formulates hypotheses. External evidence in the form of written sources, is then located and analyzed to verify the questions posed by the material artifacts.

I tested Prown's method with antiques from my personal collection in order to learn how consumer behavior might have been affected by early lighting devices. Four eighteenth-century candlesticks, illustrated in Figure 1, were first subjected to internal analysis, an observation of the objects themselves. The candlesticks show wear and minor old repairs, but are otherwise completely authentic. They are fashioned in a simple but pleasing rococo or "Queen Anne" style. The candlesticks range between 7 and 8 1/4 inches in height, 4 1/4 to 5 inches in base width, and weigh, on average, about one pound. They are all made of brass, an alloy of copper and zinc. A barely visible seam indicates that the stems and sockets were cast in two halves, soldered together, and then joined to the bases.

Three of the candlesticks show evidence of once having had a twist-up mechanism for ejecting candle stubs. These devices, operated by grasping the stem and rotating the base, were apparently rather delicate. No maker's marks are present, but, based on external evidence (Burks 1986), they were probably manufactured in Birmingham, England, circa 1760. The provenance of these particular objects is unknown, but Birmingham brass candlesticks were exported to colonial America in great quantities.

In the next stage, deduction, I experimented with candlelight in order to link myself, both intellectually and emotionally, with the eighteenth-century user. Candles were inserted and the candlesticks were placed in different locations, one or two to a room. Although the candles produced far less light than do modern lamps, they did illuminate the house reasonably well and were used as the light source for editing preliminary drafts of this paper. The overall effect was one of tranquility, but also of dancing shadows and mystery. The candles dripped and smoked a bit, particularly when they were moved from

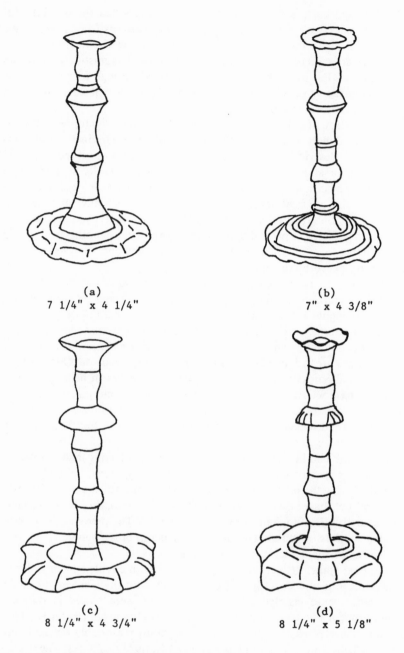

(a)
7 1/4" x 4 1/4"

(b)
7" x 4 3/8"

(c)
8 1/4" x 4 3/4"

(d)
8 1/4" x 5 1/8"

Source: The author's collection. Line drawings by the author.

Figure 1. Eighteenth-century Brass Candlesticks

room to room. Would they have performed much worse had they been made from period ingredients? Finally, all four candles were consumed within about six hours.

Based on these observations, three hypotheses were formulated: (1) The low light levels led colonial consumers to prefer very shiny, reflective surfaces and objects. (2) The dripping and smoking required frequent maintenance activities, both during and after use. (3) Rapid product consumption necessitated the purchase or home production of large supplies of candles.

External evidence in the form of books, diaries, and letters reported in Garrett (1983, 1990) confirms all three hypotheses. If they could afford such objects, eighteenth-century households favored highly polished mahogany furniture with shining brass hardware, numerous reflectors and mirrors, glossy fabrics, bright gold trim, and glittering jewelry. Depending on their ingredients, those made from tallow having the poorest quality, candles ran, smoked, dripped on clothing, smelled awful, and required snuffing the charred end of the wick as often as 40 times an hour to prevent the flame from guttering. Brass candlesticks needed regular cleaning and polishing, a task some families allotted to their younger daughters or nieces. Finally, many consumers dipped or molded their own candles, a messy task saved for the cooler months. "The Reverend Edward Holyoke, president of Harvard College, recorded in his diary on March 22, 1743, 'Made 112 Baybery Candles,' and the following day, 'Made 62 lbs. tallow candles'" (Garrett 1983, p.410).

Although Prown believes the analyst should carry out each stage in sequence, my prior knowledge of candlesticks, candles, and their uses made this difficult. Consequently, the hypotheses stemmed as much from dimly remembered external evidence as they did from my own creative powers. However, further interaction with candles and candlesticks, as well as with other forms of early American lighting such as rushes or oil lamps, might result in new hypotheses and theories. This research procedure also could be extended to old or carefully reproduced furniture, eating utensils, and diversions. Conducting the analysis in a group setting might generate even more, and more insightful, hypotheses.

V. CONCLUSION

This paper has evaluated and compared written and material data sources and their scholarly literature. Early American probate records are accessible and susceptible to quantitative analysis, but do omit some valuable information. Household furnishings found by archaeologists are tangible facts, subject to quantification, but contain limited information and are probably too inaccessible for most scholars. Preserved objects require imagination to pose hypotheses about consumption that then could be validated by external written sources. These artifacts are reasonably accessible, lend themselves to qualitative analysis, and can be used to generate hypotheses. In sum, written evidence and material objects are most effective when used as complementary data sources. They comprise a very promising methodology for deducing past consumer preferences and activities. Further use of these primary sources by consumer researchers will enhance the writing of American consumption history.

NOTES

1. Oral histories collected through long or depth interviews can also be a useful data source, albeit for relatively recent times. For an interesting proposal to recapture the situational effects influencing the adoption of cigarette smoking, see the essay by Meyer in this volume.

REFERENCES

Ames, K. L. (1978). "Meaning in Artifacts: Hall Furnishings in Victorian America." *Journal of Interdisciplinary History,* 9; pp. 19-46.
Ames, K. L. (1985). "The Stuff of Everyday Life: American Decorative Arts and Household Furnishings." Pp. 79-112 in *Material Culture: A Research Guide,* edited by T. J. Schlereth. Lawrence: The University Press of Kansas.
Baugher, S. and R. W. Venables. (1987). "Ceramics as Indicators of Status and Class in Eighteenth-century New York." Pp. 31-53 in *Consumer Choice in Historical Archaeology,* edited by S. M. Spencer-Wood. New York: Plenum Press.
Breen, T. H. (1986). "An Empire of Goods: The Anglicization of Colonial America, 1690-1776." *Journal of British Studies,* 25; pp. 467-499.
Breen, T. H. (1988). " 'Baubles of Britain': The American and Consumer Revolutions of the Eighteenth Century." *Past and Present,* 19; pp. 73-105.
Burks, J. M. (1986). *Birmingham Brass Candlesticks.* Charlottesville: University of Virginia Press.
Campbell, C. (1987). *The Romantic Ethic and the Spirit of Modern Consumption.* New York: Basil Blackwell.
Carr, L. G. and L. S. Walsh. (1980). "Inventories and the Analysis of Wealth and Consumption Patterns in St. Mary's County, Maryland, 1658-1777." *Historical Methods,* 13; pp. 81-104.
Cooper, W. A. (1980). *In Praise of America: American Decorative Arts, 1650-1830.* New York: Alfred A. Knopf.
Fleming, E. M. (1974). "Artifact Study: A Proposed Model." *Winterthur Portfolio,* 9; pp. 153-161.
Garrett, E. D. (1983). "The American Home, Part II: Lighting Devices and Practices." *Antiques,* (February); pp. 408-417.
Garrett, E. D. (1990). *At Home: The American Family 1750-1870.* New York: Harry N. Abrams.
Gordon, J. and J. McArthur. (1985). "American Women and Domestic Consumption, 1800-1920: Four Interpretive Themes." *Journal of American Culture,* 8; pp. 35-46.
Hills, P. (1974). *The Painters' America: Rural and Urban Life, 1810-1910.* New York: Praeger Publishers.
Hirschman, E. C. (1985). "Primitive Aspects of Consumption in Modern Society." *Journal of Consumer Research,* 12; pp. 142-154.
Hollander, S. C. (1984). "Sumptuary Legislation: Demarketing by Edict." *Journal of Macromarketing,* 4; pp. 3-16.

Hollander, S. C. (1988). *Where is Consumption History going?*. Paper presented at the thirteenth annual macromarketing conference, August,San Jose, CA.

Hume, I. N. (1970). *A Guide to Artifacts of Colonial America*. New York: Alfred A. Knopf.

Jobe, B. and M. Kaye. (1984). *New England Furniture: The Colonial Era*. Boston: Houghton Mifflin.

Jones, A. H. (1977). *American Colonial Wealth: Documents and Methods*. New York: Arno Press.

Jones, A. H. (1980). *Wealth of a Nation to be: The American Colonies on the Eve of the Revolution*. New York: Columbia University Press.

Kaye, M. (1987). *Fake, Fraud, or Genuine? Identifying Authentic American Antique Furniture*. Boston: Little, Brown and Company.

Kirk, J. T. (1982). *American Furniture and the British Tradition to 1830*. New York: Alfred A. Knopf.

Lemon, J. T. (1967). "Household Consumption in Eighteenth-century America and its Relationship to Production and Trade: The Situation Among Farmers in Southeastern Pennsylvania." *Agricultural History*,41; pp. 59-70.

Main, G. L. (1975). "Probate Records as a Source for Early American History." *William and Mary Quarterly*, 22; pp. 89-99.

Main, G. L. (1982). *Tobacco Colony: Life in Early Maryland, 1650-1720*. Princeton: Princeton University Press.

Main, J. T. (1985). *Society and Economy in Colonial Connecticut*. Princeton: Princeton University Press.

McCracken, G. (1987). "The History of Consumption: A Literature Review and Consumers' Guide." *Journal of Consumer Policy*, 10; pp. 139-166.

McCracken, G. (1988). *Culture and Consumption: New Approaches to the Symbolic Character of Consumer Goods and Activities*. Bloomington: Indiana University Press.

McKendrick, N., J. Brewer and J. H. Plumb. (1982). *The Birth of a Consumer Society: The Commercialization of Eighteenth-century England*. Bloomington: Indiana University Press.

Miller, G. L. (1984). "Marketing Ceramics in North America." *Winterthur Portfolio*, 19; pp. 1-5.

Mukerji, C. (1983). *From Graven Images: Patterns of Modern Materialism*. New York: Columbia University Press.

Prown, J. D. (1980). "Style as Evidence." *Winterthur Portfolio*, 15; pp. 197-210.

Prown, J. D. (1982). "Mind in Matter: An Introduction to Material Culture Theory and Method." *Winterthur Portfolio*, 17; pp. 1-19.

Rassuli, K. and S. C. Hollander. (1986). "Desire: Induced, Innate, Insatiable? Historians' Views of Consumer Behavior." *Journal of Macromarketing*, 6; pp. 4-24.

Schlereth, T. J. (1982). "Material Culture Studies in America, 1876-1976." Pp. 1-75 in *Material Culture Studies in America*, edited by T. J. Schlereth. Nashville: The American Association for State and Local History.

Schlereth, T. J. (1983). "Material Culture Studies and Social History Research." *Journal of Social History*, 16; pp. 111-143.

Shammas, C. (1978). "Constructing a Wealth Distribution from Probate Records." *Journal of Interdisciplinary History*, 9; pp. 297-307.

Shammas, C. (1982a). "How Self-sufficient was Early America?" *Journal of Interdisciplinary History*, 13; pp. 247-272.

Shammas, C. (1982b). "Consumer Behavior in Colonial America." *Social Science History*, 6; pp. 67-86.

Smith, B. C. (1985). *After the Revolution: The Smithsonian History of Everyday Life in the Eighteenth Century*. New York: Pantheon Books.

Spencer-Wood, S. M. (Ed.). (1987). *Consumer Choice in Historical Archaeology*. New York: Plenum Press.

Williams, R. (1982). *Dream Worlds: Mass Consumption in Late Nineteenth-century France*. Berkeley: University of California Press.

Witkowski, T. H. (1989). "Colonial Consumers in Revolt: Buyer Values and Behavior During the Nonimportation Movement, 1764-1776." *Journal of Consumer Research*, 16; pp. 216-226.

Witkowski, T. H. (1992). *Early American Reproductions: The Manufacture, Marketing, and Consumption of Authenticity*. Paper presented at the American marketing association winter educators' conference, February, San Antonio, TX.

JOCKEY INTERNATIONAL:
A BRIEF HISTORY OF MARKETING INNOVATION

Richard H. Keehn

ABSTRACT

1985 marked the fiftieth anniversary of the introduction of the Jockey brief but the history of Jockey International, Inc. can be traced back more than 100 years. The company has combined distinctive and quality products with innovative marketing to maintain an important place in top-of-the-line underwear. New product development, direct selling to retail dealers, national and local advertising, active dealer support, and avoidance of low price lines and off-price outlets have been major parts of the Jockey strategy.

I. INTRODUCTION AND BACKGROUND

Nineteen-eighty-five marked the fiftieth anniversary of the introduction of the Jockey brief but the history of the founders of the company goes back more than fifty years before that new product introduction. For eighty years what is now Jockey International, Inc. combined distinctive and quality products with innovative marketing to acquire and maintain an important place in

Research in Marketing, Supplement 6, pages 183-202.
ISBN: 1-55938-187-6

top-of-the-line underwear. Ongoing product development, direct selling through quality retail outlets, national and local advertising, active dealer support, and avoidance of off-price outlets and private label goods were major elements in the company's strategy through 1983. Jockey International remained closely held and committed to the apparel industry. This approach differed from many of its competitors who moved into new areas, sold out to larger firms, or went public. The history of Jockey International, Inc. has been the story of one firm's efforts to perform successfully in the highly competitive men's apparel industry.

The beginnings of what is now Jockey International, Inc. date from 1876 when Samuel Cooper began producing and selling high quality woolen stockings from a small rented facility in St. Joseph, Michigan. Between 1835 and 1871 Cooper was a minister of the Methodist Episcopal church serving various congregations in Indiana and there was little in his background to suggest that he would later launch a successful career as a manufacturer of men's hosiery. In 1871 he accepted a semiretired position with the church and spent part of the next few years working as a traveling salesman.[1]

Wool was abundant in southern Michigan in the 1870s, and firms were springing up to provide woolen yarn to the household trade as well as to small manufacturers of woolen goods (Crockett 1972; Niemi 1974). The introduction of the sewing machine led to some factory production of clothing by the 1850s, but the most rapid growth came in the post-1870 period when information on human body measurements allowed for the development of appropriate and standardized sizes (Robertson 1964). Factory produced clothing, including coats, trousers, hosiery, and underwear, gradually replaced home production and custom tailoring for an increasing share of the population (Faulkner 1968). The income elasticity demand for ready-made clothing was high and sales increased with rising family income (Puth 1988). Power operated knitting machines were replacing the older hand operated machines and a growing number of the older semi-obsolete but still usable hand operated machines were available (Corbin 1970).

A friend of Cooper's, A. W. Wells, visited Morris, Minnesota each year where he observed local storekeepers buying crude but durable handmade heavy-duty woolen stockings from area housewives for resale to area lumbermen who had found that factory made stockings were of poor quality. Wells suggested to Cooper that there was a market for high quality factory made all wool stockings.[2]

In 1876, Samuel Cooper moved his family from Indiana to St. Joseph, Michigan and established S. R. Cooper and Sons. He purchased six used hand operated knitting machines, rented some second floor space, hired several young girls as machine operators, and commenced production of heavy duty wool stockings. His sons, Willis and Henry assisted in the business. Cooper's wool socks met with market acceptance and earned the mill a reputation for quality. In 1878 Cooper expanded by acquiring more knitting machines and by integrating backward into yarn spinning. The additional investment strained finances so A. W. Wells invested in the firm and the name was changed to Cooper Wells Company.[3]

Cooper Wells Company, following the traditional method of marketing apparel goods, worked through commission merchants in Chicago who sold the firm's output on a best efforts basis, then remitted the proceeds less costs and selling fee. Samuel Cooper disliked this approach because he had little control over volume and price and was unable to demonstrate to retailers the advantages of his product. He experimented by calling directly on nearby retail stores. The initial response was favorable as the retailers liked dealing with a manufacturer and product they knew. In the early 1880s, sales through the commission merchants were phased out and direct selling to retailers over a growing area became the primary method of marketing the firm's output.[4] Cooper was one of the first apparel manufacturers to integrate forward by selling a small-ticket consumer item direct to retail stores (Porter and Livesay 1971).

A. W. Wells handled finances and served as president after incorporation in 1889. Cooper acted as the firm's chief salesman, traveling throughout the Midwest and West. Until the late 1880s he acted as general manager, subsequently his role in day-to-day activities decreased but he continued an active interest in the company. Samuel Cooper's sons gained experience working for the company; Willis ran the office while Henry was responsible for mill operations. The youngest son, Charles, started his career with the firm in the late 1880s.[5]

By 1892, Cooper Wells was offering a full line of hosiery for men, women, and boys in both cotton and wool. The mill employed 260 hands and daily output was about 500-600 dozen hose. The trade names Cooper Wells and Iron Clad were well-known and respected by a growing number of retail establishments throughout the country.[6]

II. FROM HOSIERY TO UNDERWEAR

Samuel Cooper died unexpectedly in 1892 at the age of 67 and shortly afterward his sons sold the family interest in Cooper Wells Company to Abel Wells, citing policy disagreements with the other owners. At the time, Willis was 38, Henry 35, and Charles 25. Willis and Henry had 16 years of experience in all phases of the hosiery business. Willis moved to Kenosha, Wisconsin to accept a position with the Chicago-Rockford Hosiery Company, then completing a new mill in that city. Charles Cooper joined his brother in Kenosha later in 1892, while Henry Cooper moved to Midland, Michigan to accept a position with Dow Chemical Company. During the 1890s, Chicago-Rockford Hosiery (later

Chicago-Kenosha Hosiery Company) produced a line of hosiery for men, women, and children under the trade name Black Cat, selling direct to retail dealers through more than two dozen traveling company salesmen, the same direct selling approach used by Cooper Wells. Willis became general manager and Charles general superintendent of the mill.[7]

In 1900, while still working for Chicago-Rockford Hosiery Company, Willis and Charles Cooper established a new partnership, Cooper Underwear Company, to produce men's underwear that could be sold by the Black Cat hosiery sales force. Henry Cooper left Dow Chemical to work full time for the underwear firm. The new underwear company produced two types of men's underwear, shirts and drawers, and union suits.[8] Shirts and drawers were the typical men's undergarments at the turn of the century. They provided warmth and some degree of comfort but were somewhat bulky because of the difficulty of holding up the lowers in an era before elastic waistbands. The one piece union suit solved the problem of holding up the drawers by uniting it with the shirt in one garment supported from the shoulders but led to obvious design problems. A drop seat or an open crotch, an opening directly down the rear of the suit, were alternative designs and Cooper Underwear made both versions. Cooper Underwear, marketed under the name White Cat, was similar to that of its competitors, but high quality and direct selling through the Chicago-Rockford sales force enabled the new partnership to increase volume.[9]

The initial success of the underwear business influenced the Cooper's to construct a new mill just east of the Chicago-Rockford facility and this new plant began production in 1903. They incorporated the company in September 1902 with an authorized capital of $100,000, increased shortly to $150,000, with the three Cooper brothers owning the majority of the outstanding stock. Henry became general manager and Willis served as president while continuing as general manager of the hosiery firm. After incorporation, the hosiery and underwear firms continued to share management, office staff, and sales force but were separate corporations with separate production facilities. Chicago-Rockford marketed hosiery under the name Black Cat while Cooper's registered the trademark White Cat for its underwear in 1901.[10]

Cooper Underwear Company was doing well when, in December 1903, Willis and Charles Cooper died in the Iroquois Theater fire in Chicago, a tragedy that claimed almost 600 lives (Jensen 1981). Less than four years after the establishment of the underwear firm, Henry Cooper was forced to assume his brothers' duties at the hosiery firm and take over management of the underwear business. His response to the challenge is indicated by the firm's performance during its first ten years. Sales, which were $182,000 in 1903, increased to over $400,000 in 1910. While profits fluctuated, they were never negative and net worth approximated $240,000 by 1910, reflecting the retention of earnings in the business.[11]

The traditional drop seat union suit was unsatisfactory because the seat was bulky and the necessary buttons tended to break. The open seat model eliminated the drop seat, but the vertical rear opening put two folds of fabric directly in the rear of the wearer where they tended to bunch up. By the early 1900s many individuals were working to improve the product. One of these was Horace Johnson, superintendent of the Cooper mill since 1901. Johnson and Henry Cooper had experimented with several variations prior to 1909 but none worked well. In 1909 Johnson hit upon the idea for the closed crotch union suit. Supposedly the idea came to him in the middle of the night and, afraid he might forget his inspiration, he woke his wife to make a pilot model from scraps and discarded material. His midnight idea was a major improvement in union suit design (Jensen 1983). Instead of a vertical rear opening, the new model had a diagonal opening starting above the hip and ending just above the right knee. The two pieces of body fabric lapped over like an X and could be drawn apart as needed. The diagonal opening removed the edge of the flaps from the center lines of the body, making it impossible for the material to get into the crotch and between the legs. Only a single thickness of cloth covered the wearer in the sensitive areas.[12]

The new design, marketed under the names Kenosha Klosed Krotch and KKK, quickly became the preferred style. Cooper Underwear licensed the design to other producers and collected royalties. Horace "Klosed Krotch" Johnson spent an increasing amount of time in subsequent years trying to prevent infringement on the patent (Lyman 1916). Cooper Underwear annual sales increased from about $400,000 in 1910 to over $1 million in 1916 and peaked at over $3 million in 1920. Profits also increased and were above $100,000 between 1916 and 1919 before a loss was sustained in 1920.[13]

Up to 1912, Cooper Underwear Company and Chicago-Kenosha Hosiery worked closely together. The majority owners of the hosiery mill sold out in 1912 and the close relationship between the two firms was broken shortly thereafter. In early 1913, Henry Cooper sold the Cooper interest in the hosiery mill, resigned as general manager, and thereafter the Cooper family concentrated its efforts on the underwear company. The break forced Cooper Underwear to develop its own sales force and office staff for the first time.[14]

In the post-1913 period, Cooper Underwear produced union suits for men, women, and boys in various knit and woven fabrics including cotton, mercerized lisle, silk and wool, and in a variety of gauges from light to heavy. By 1915 Coopers claimed to be the largest union suit maker in the world. Hosiery and sportswear were added to the line although those products were a small part of total sales. Sales were made direct to retail merchants through a growing number of company salesmen. Stocks were maintained at service branches in New York, Dallas, Los Angeles, and Seattle.[15] A second plant, opened in Manistee, Michigan in 1919, was originally planned to handle war-related production but was converted to underwear in the postwar period

(*Manistee News Advocate* 1918-1919). By 1918 the Kenosha mill employed about 1,000 persons, almost all female.[16]

Cooper Underwear Company became one of the first underwear producers to use national advertising to promote its product when it placed an ad in *The Saturday Evening Post* in 1911. In 1912 J. C. Leyendecker, best known for his Arrow shirt and Kuppenheimer suit ads, was commissioned to do illustrations for Coopers (Schau 1984). A picture of a man in a union suit with one foot on a kit bag was registered as a Cooper trademark in 1912. Another drawing, featuring a mother and children in Cooper products, was also used extensively in national and local promotions. Dealer aids, including booklets, window displays, and local advertising, supplemented national advertising of the brand names Cooper, White Cat, and Kenosha Klosed Krotch. The company did not produce private label apparel and tried to limit distribution to quality retailers.[17]

III. DRIFT, DECLINE, AND REORGANIZATION

Despite the success of Cooper Underwear Company during its first 20 years, there were some disturbing signs. The most important was a change in consumer tastes that weakened Cooper's dominant position in underwear. Increased use of central heating and more frequent bathing reduced the need for heavy underwear, while changes in fashion increased the desire for lighter, more comfortable, undergarments. In the second decade of the twentieth century the Bradley, Voorhus and Day Corporation pioneered a new union suit that was woven, not knit, of a lightweight muslin or nainsook fabric, and was sleeveless with quarter length legs. The lighter fabric and less coverage appealed to an increasing number of men. Other firms, including Coopers, were soon making similar models. Unfortunately, Cooper's did not have a dominant position in this new product area and this had weakened their position in men's underwear by 1920.[18]

Another change in consumer tastes that impacted on the underwear business and Cooper Underwear developed after World War I. The U.S. armed forces issued two-piece underwear consisting of a knitted undershirt and woven, boxer style shorts. During the war millions of men were exposed (no pun intended) to these and wanted to wear them upon return to civilian life. In the 1920s more and more men were switching to nainsook union suits or shirts and drawers. While Coopers produced both new styles, the change in tastes undermined its dominant position based on the traditional union suit.[19]

Additional problems complicated postwar adjustment. The 1920s were not good years for cotton textile and apparel firms in general. Firms located in the North found it increasingly difficult to compete as wage differentials between North and South widened. Clothing and related items became a smaller fraction of the average family's budget and only specialty apparel items with a high-income elasticity of demand fared better than average during the period. A growing number of mills entered the underwear business, increasing price competition in that market. Between 1919 and 1929, knit underwear was one of only three textile industries to experience a decline in output (Fabracant 1940). These developments adversely affected Cooper Underwear in the 1920s and the pressures became more intense during the Great Depression.

In the early 1920s, Cooper was marketing knitted and woven union suits in KKK and nainsook models, woven shorts, knitted shirts, and a full line of hosiery. Pajamas were added in 1923. While the products were touted as superior to the competition, they were not viewed in the marketplace as distinctive enough to provide the firm an edge in the increasingly price competitive underwear market.[20] New products and increased emphasis on hosiery did result in a significant change in product mix. Between 1920 and 1928, knit goods, mainly men's underwear, declined from 72.7 to 37.6 percent of sales, nainsook products held steady at 16 to 18 percent, while hosiery increased in importance from 1.2 to 29.5 percent. Nightwear accounted for about 9 percent of sales in 1928, up from none in 1920.[21]

Cooper Underwear maintained the direct selling approach first adopted by Samuel Cooper years before. Company salesmen called on retail merchants and the company continued to work more closely with these dealers than did their competition. Advertisements in national magazines like *Liberty*, *Colliers*, *American Legion Monthly*, and *College Humor* were designed to create a demand for Cooper products. Advertising copy for use in local papers by dealers was an important part of the marketing effort.[22]

The product and marketing efforts did little to improve performance. Sales were almost $3 million in 1920 but fell to less than $2 million the following year. Volume then increased to $2.7 million in 1922 and to almost $3.8 million in 1923. Sales then leveled off and ran between $3.4 and $3.8 million annually between 1924 and 1928. Losses in 1921 and 1922 were followed by record profits of $214,727 and $267,000 in 1923 and 1924. Despite continuing high volume, profits in the succeeding years fell well below these totals. A loss was reported in the relatively good business year of 1928. The firm continued as a family business with little professional management or organization. Henry Cooper relinquished the presidency to his son Robert in 1913 but remained active in management almost up to his death in 1924.[23]

By 1928 company management and directors were concerned with the lackluster performance and lack of distinctive product. Recognizing the need for new blood, Robert Cooper hired Arthur R. Kneibler to conduct a detailed marketing survey. Kneibler was to play a leading role in the development and marketing of Jockey brand underwear. He had experience in several phases of marketing and direct selling. When his study was completed he was appointed assistant to the president in charge of marketing, advertising and sales promotion. He set to work to improve these areas but did not achieve success for several years. In May 1929, partly because of a recommendation by Kneibler, the company name was changed to Coopers, Incorporated (without an apostrophe) to more clearly reflect the broadened product line.[24]

By 1929, Coopers, Incorporated was in a vulnerable position. The firm no longer had a distinctive product, competition in all lines was increasing, while sales stagnation and low profits after 1924 weakened the financial position. The national business downturn beginning in the middle of 1929 added to the firm's problems. Debts of over $400,000 were due in July 1930 with no visible means of generating the necessary funds.[25]

Ralph Cooper, treasurer and assistant secretary, became convinced that his cousin Robert, as president, was unwilling and unable to resolve the situation. His sister Carlotta was married to Gilbert Simmons Lance, the grandson of Zalmon Simmons, the founder of the Simmons Company, the nation's largest maker of bedding. Ralph Cooper, Art Kneibler, and Lance devised a reorganization plan that resolved the immediate financial crisis and laid the groundwork for future development. Lance sold his interest in the Simmons Company and purchased 76 percent of the outstanding stock of Coopers from members of the Cooper family.[26]

After the reorganization was approved in July 1930, Ralph Cooper oversaw manufacturing, Kneibler took charge of product development and marketing, while Lance concentrated on management and finance.[27] In the fall of 1930, Lance approached the Continental Illinois National Bank in Chicago for assistance. The bank thought that the firm would benefit from the services of a consultant with expertise in finance and engineering and recommended Harry Wolf, the senior partner in Wolf and Company, a Chicago accounting and consulting firm. After Wolf had completed an intensive study of Coopers, Incorporated in early 1931, he agreed to provide ongoing consulting. Wolf reviewed all activities, provided advice and council, and was given full authority for all external financial arrangements but held no official position and had no stock interest until the 1940s.[28]

Between 1929 and 1934 Art Kneibler worked to improve marketing and packaging, experimented with pricing policies, and was responsible for the introduction of an impressive list of improved or new products. These actions were helpful but only marginally successful in increasing volume and market share. Two of his product introductions were successful, but low cost mills quickly began producing imitations so that Cooper's initial advantage was quickly lost. This convinced Kneibler of the importance of developing patentable branded apparel goods.[29]

The seriousness of the problem facing management is graphically illustrated by operating results. Net sales, in excess of $3.2 million in 1929, declined to under $1.3 million in 1931 and had increased to only $1.6 million by 1934. Losses were sustained in 1930-1932 and reached $220,000 in the latter year.

A small profit was earned in 1933 suggesting that the activities of the new management were finally beginning to have some impact.[30]

IV. THE FIRST YEARS OF JOCKEY

The major product breakthrough that Coopers, Incorporated was looking for came in 1934 with the development of the Jockey brief. There are several versions of the inspiration for the Jockey idea. The most colorful is that Kneibler was inspired by a picture in a French magazine of a young man attired in a scanty bikini style swim suit. Work began on a swim garment and then developed into the new brief.[31]

The first Jockey brief was made of rib-knit cotton fabric with double fabric in the crotch to provide a support feature. Lastex was used in the waistband and on the outside of the leg openings to provide comfort and support and these features were subsequently patented. Considerable testing resulted in several design modifications before the original Jockey Model 1001 design was finalized. Kneibler realized that a new undershirt was needed to wear with the new brief so a contoured athletic shirt was developed. The name Jockey was selected after extended discussion of possible names that would create name recognition without negative connotations. Kneibler was mindful of the need to protect the new name and promptly registered the trademark Jockey. He mounted the new brief on cardboard that was bonded and wrapped in cellophane. A retail price of 50 cents was established, well above the discounted prices then prevalent for woven shorts. Kneibler offered retail dealers a 40 percent margin, counting on the product's unique features to attract customer interest at the higher price.[32]

A brief review of the history of men's underwear indicates just how different the new Jockey brief was. Up to and after 1900, knit underwear was popular because it was warm and absorbed perspiration well. The one piece union suit solved the problem of holding up underwear bottoms in an era prior to elastic waistbands. In the post-1915 period the use of interior heating and running hot water increased, allowing men to wear less clothing, bathe more frequently, and develop a greater concern with personal hygiene. In addition, changing styles in men's outerwear led to a desire for lighter and less bulky undergarments. In response to these developments two new underwear previously discussed, the nainsook or woven union suit and woven shorts and knitted shirts, became increasingly popular in the 1920s. By the 1930s men's underwear had changed but was still less functional than women's undergarments. Women wore slips and panties to protect clothing, combining absorbency with less bulk. In addition, women wore bras because the support feature provided additional comfort. The Jockey brief revolutionized men's underwear by offering a minimum of bulk and bind, absorbency through knitted cotton fabric, and light masculine support.[33]

The original Jockey brief and shirt were introduced in a limited way in the fall of 1934. Local stores reported a brisk business but volume elsewhere was limited to a few dozen at each retail outlet. The major marketing breakthrough came during the week of January 19, 1935 when the Davis Store in Chicago, an affiliate of Marshall Field's, agreed to a Jockey promotion assisted by Coopers. The Davis store put in a Jockey window display on State Street and in-store displays of the new brief and shirt. A severe snowstorm hit Chicago the night before the scheduled start of the promotion and Davis store management ordered the window display changed since it seemed pointless to promote skimpy underwear during a blizzard. Fortunately, the orders were not carried out. People stopped to look at the window display and, more importantly, entered the store to buy the new Jockey underwear. The original shipment of 50 dozen was sold out in a few hours and additional shipments had to be rushed from Kenosha. Accompanying newspaper ads helped build customer interest. A retail clothiers association was meeting in Chicago at the time and news of the Davis promotion quickly passed through the meeting since retailers were interested in any item with a solid markup. The Davis Store sold more than 1,000 dozen in one week, far exceeding previous underwear volume. Similar promotions were held in other stores with similar results.[34] The immediate result of the success of the new product was a flood of orders that soon exceeded the Kenosha mill's ability to produce so Coopers contracted with other mills to produce Jockey underwear (*Milwaukee Journal* 1935; *Printers Ink* 1935; *Daily News Record* 1935).

The success of the Jockey brand brief brought a flood of imitations. Kneibler was concerned about the tendency to make Jockey a generic term so Coopers mounted an advertising campaign in *The Saturday Evening Post* and *Colliers* stressing that Jockey was a Coopers, Incorporated trademark, that they were the originators and that there was only one genuine Jockey. In the 1980s Jockey International continued to battle the use of Jockey as a generic term for men's briefs.[35]

About the middle of 1935, the imitations and increased competition began to have an impact and sales began to fall. Retail stores did not realize that the initial sales surge was too good to last and began cutting back on promotion, further hurting sales. The backlog of orders was eliminated and inventories built up rapidly, necessitating drastic cuts in production.[36]

This sales slump was fought in several ways. Kneibler decided that the firm would not engage in price cutting to reduce inventory, thus keeping Jockey a top-of-the-line product. While this decision hurt in the short run, it was crucial to long-run success. In June of 1935, the company learned that Tommy Armour, a well-known professional golfer, wore Jockey underwear. A promotional program was developed around Armour, utilizing national and local newspaper ads. Armour thus became the first of many famous athletes to be featured in Jockey advertising programs. Continuing product development was also used to combat the sales decline. Throughout 1935 the design and marketing staff worked to add a fly front to the Jockey brief but it was difficult to make an opening that would not gap and that would permit longer leg lengths without losing masculine support. The new design, with frontal tapes in the form of a diagonal opening was introduced to the sales force in August 1935. It initially came in longer lengths only and was not added to a brief until Model 1007 was introduced in early 1936. The new brief was not marketed under the Jockey label until later that year.[37]

The marketing and product development work had the desired impact as sales began to pick up near the end of 1935. Reorders began coming in as original users told their friends and as new stores added promotions backed by Jockey national and local advertising.

Aggressive advertising support for the Jockey brand was expanded in the post-1935 period. Ads appeared in *Esquire, Life, Colliers, The Saturday Evening Post,* and *Rotogravure.* Athletes Sammy Baugh and Ellsworth Vines were featured in new national promotions. A marketing study determined that the majority of men's underwear was purchased by women so an increasing share of Jockey advertising was directed toward women. Kneibler refined his strategy of selling through, not to, retail outlets. To work, the retailer had to be provided with support materials and salesperson training to supplement the brand name product.[38]

Store mannequins were not appropriate for demonstrating the support feature, so a "stride" display form with a masculine contour was developed. In the first 18 months after introduction, 7,800 half strides, 1,900 long strides, and 300 full strides were sold to dealers. In 1938 a hosiery display form was introduced in an effort to increase hosiery volume. In 1939 Coopers, Incorporated innovated a counter or tabletop dispenser to hold and display Jockey merchandise, enabling the customer to select the style and size desired. The cellophane package used for Jockey was well suited to this new way to retail men's underwear. Prior to the introduction of the Jockey dispenser, underwear was kept behind the counter and the customer had to ask the clerk for a specific style and size. In an effort to increase stock turns, Coopers developed a model stock control program that helped prevent lost sales because of missing sizes and styles. Another development in Jockey promotion came in 1940 when the Jockey boy statue was introduced for the first time. A live model made promotional appearances for several years, reinforcing the image of the original statue, replicas of which were supplied to each dealer.[39]

Coopers concentrated on selling through department, menswear, dry goods, and general stores and tried to work with the best store(s) in each area but avoided exclusive dealerships in cities of over 5,000 residents. Distribution through large national chains was avoided although some smaller regional menswear chains were customers. Coopers acted quickly to take advantage of Wisconsin and federal resale price maintenance provisions (Wilcox 1955).

This enabled the company to offer dealers a 40 percent markup, protection from price competition, and a brand name quality product.[40]

Another major marketing change was the development of licensing agreements whereby overseas manufacturers were authorized to produce and sell Jockey products in their countries. Prior to World War II, licensee agreements were established in Canada, Great Britain, Australia, and New Zealand. This approach provided overseas market penetration with minimal investment.[41]

The success of the Jockey brand was reflected in performance. Volume in 1934, the last pre-Jockey year, was $1.7 million and led to a small loss on operations. Sales increased to $2.4 million in 1935, topped $3 million in 1937, $4 million in 1939 and $7 million in 1941. A net profit of $27,000 was earned in 1935, exceeded $300,000 in 1938 and topped $400,000 in 1941. Increased volume after the introduction of Jockey products permitted the operation of the Kenosha mill for 50 weeks each year with substantial economies over the previous short production schedules.[42]

On the eve of World War II, Coopers, Incorporated was in sound condition. The Jockey brand was well established with retailers and consumers throughout the country, the product line was highly regarded and expanding, the sales force well trained and productive, the financial position sound, and management experienced. World War II slowed but did not stop the firm's progress. An increasing amount of production went to fill government orders and it was increasingly difficult to maintain an experienced labor force. Materials shortages and government controls complicated operations. Coopers tried to keep the sales force intact despite drastically reduced civilian sales. Jockey ads continued in an effort to maintain consumer brand awareness, something Kneibler felt was essential for postwar success.

V.   POSTWAR DEVELOPMENTS: 1945-1960

Civilian production resumed quickly with relatively few problems. Jockey menswear continued to be distributed primarily to department stores and men's specialty shops. Coopers did not sell through wholesalers, jobbers, or distributors and their products were not available through mail order, chain, discount, or variety stores. Kneibler's strategy called for concentrating on the top end of the underwear business with higher prices and higher margins for producer and dealer. Munsingwear and Carter's competed with Coopers in top-of-the-line underwear while Hanes, BVD, and Fruit-of-the-Loom aimed at the lower quality market. Sears and Penneys became important sellers of men's underwear in the postwar period but neither aimed at the high-priced quality market where Jockey was positioned.[43]

New products in the 1940s included a Jockey sportshort swim trunk with a heavyweight brief liner, a lightweight union suit with the Kenosha Klosed

Krotch and a new brief and T-shirt in a broad knit fabric. In the 1950s the popular V-neck shirt, red Jockey longs and a sleeveless Jockey shirt were introduced. In 1954 the Jockey short became the Jockey brief. The Jockey name was added to the woven short line the same year to capitalize on name recognition. Coopers remained in the hosiery and sportswear business but company offerings met with only marginal success in the marketplace. The women's underwear market was entered in 1952 with Jockette briefs for women. The women who tried the all-cotton briefs liked them but the attempt to sell the product primarily through men's underwear departments was a failure and the line was dropped in 1954.[44]

The major product news in the 1950s was the development of what is now called fashion underwear. Zodiac fancy pants and animal print briefs were first introduced in 1949, adding color to the previously predominantly white briefs and shirt line. Jockey briefs and shirts in mesh fabric and nylon were brought out in 1952, and valentine shorts and Jockey briefs in pastel shades of Celanese in 1955. These developments introduced new fabrics and colors but the design remained the basic Jockey brief.[45]

In 1960 Coopers/Jockey was second to Arrow shirts in advertising expenditures in men's apparel. A 1956 study listed the Jockey brand as one of the eight best known in the world along with Coca Cola, Kodak, and Shell (Riemer 1956). Athletes Byron Nelson, Ned Day, Willie Hoppe, Bill Tilden, and Don Hutson were featured in Jockey promotions.[46]

At the end of World War II there were five Jockey licensees manufacturing and selling Jockey products outside the United States. Art Kneibler spent an increasing amount of time working on the international organization and a standardized licensee contract was developed under his direction. By 1959 the number of overseas licensees had increased to 22 and 40 percent of Jockey sales (including exports) were outside the United States.[47]

Increased sales induced Coopers to improve existing facilities and add new ones. The Kenosha mill was modernized and expanded shortly after the war when it was integrated from knitting through shipping. In 1948 Coopers entered into a contract with Giffen Manufacturing Company in Carlisle, Kentucky to produce woven shorts and other products for sale by Coopers. This relationship expanded as Lance and Wolf became stockholders in Giffen. Three southern mills were opened in the 1950s. Distribution centers were established in Lambertville, New Jersey, Cedartown, Georgia, and Los Angeles, as well as Kenosha and shipments were made from the centers instead of the mills.[48]

Gilbert Lance was the major shareholder in Coopers, Incorporated from 1935 until the mid-1950s when he sold half of his shares to the company with the remainder to be retired after his death. This arrangement gave the Wolf interests control of the company. Cooper, Kneibler, Lance, and Wolf were the main decision makers at Coopers from 1930 until the mid-1950s when they began to reduce their role in day-to-day management. Cooper and Kneibler died in 1958 and Lance in 1960. A new management team and organizational structure was being developed but it was at least 1962 before the problems surrounding the change in ownership and management were overcome. Harry Wolf and his son began to play an increasing role in day-to-day operations although the elder Wolf remained primarily occupied with his consulting and accounting business.[49]

VI. THE ERA OF HIGH FASHION 1960-1983

The post-1960 period has been a difficult one for domestic textile and apparel firms. The men's apparel industry has always been characterized by a large number of relatively small firms with no firm having a large share of the total market. The movement of production facilities to the Sunbelt was only partially successful as foreign textiles and clothing captured an increasing share of the domestic market. These problems were magnified by the business downturns of the mid-1970s and 1980-1982. Several firms dropped out of the men's underwear business including BVD, Manhattan, Ainsbrook, Paris, Carter, Van Heusen and Arrow, although some of the brand names were taken over by other firms. One major Jockey competitor, Munsingwear, came close to bankruptcy (*Business Week* 1983; James 1983). Men's apparel faced another problem. The average expenditure for men's and boy's clothing was about the same in constant dollars in 1970 as in 1917. Much of the growth in reported sales of apparel firms came from population increase and inflation (Krooss 1974). While no one or several firms dominated the industry, the more successful ones carved out significant market positions in specific areas through heavy brand promotion to build retailer support and customer loyalty (Mestre and Lubell 1975).

In 1960, the Coopers product line consisted of four major catagories: woven shorts, knit underwear, men's and boy's hosiery, and men's sportswear with the last two being purchased from outside suppliers. Knitted underwear accounted for about 70 percent of sales while the others accounted for about 10 percent each.[50]

The major change in the underwear business in the 1960-1985 period was the development of high-fashion underwear and Coopers/Jockey was a leader in this new and growing market segment (*Forbes* 1982). The first major Coopers product development in high-fashion underwear came in 1958 with the introduction of Skants briefs. The Skants were cut high on the sides and low at the waist and the stretch nylon fabric was designed to mould to the body. Skants were different in two respects. First, the new brief was made in one of the new synthetic fabrics rather than cotton or a cotton blend. Second, Skants provided less coverage than the traditional brief while still providing masculine support. By its very nature, underwear is not visible but Skants introduced high fashion into men's underwear and opened up new markets.[51] The significant break with the past represented by Skants is illustrated by a comment from *The History of Underclothes*, by C. Willett and Phyllis Cunninton published in 1952,..."man has never used provocative underclothing; its plain prose has been in singular contrast to the poetic allurements worn by women..."(p. 16). The colorful stretch nylon Skants were too daring for the 1950s but paved the way for high-fashion underwear when consumer acceptance of the new product increased in the 1970s.

Colored underwear in the basic lines made some inroads by the 1960s, but by 1965 high-fashion underwear represented only two percent of total underwear sales. Shirts with a tapered body began to increase in popularity in the 1960s. The Life line of fashion colored underwear was introduced under the Jockey name in 1964-65. The briefs were cut slimmer than the standard Jockey brief but were not as extreme as the Skants brief. Later additions were tapered boxers and Bo'sn, Deck, and A-Shirts. Polyester/cotton blends were added to the underwear line in the 1960s.[52]

High-fashion underwear sales increased substantially in the 1970s. Skants was reintroduced as International Skants and other bikini-style briefs added to the line included Elance, Poco, and Micro-3. The Jeans-Brief was added in 1980. The Life underwear line was expanded with Life DP's (dual purpose) underwear-sportswear series. By 1982 fashion underwear accounted for 20 percent of industry sales but over 50 percent of Jockey underwear volume. Coopers remained in the hosiery and sportswear business and a push to increase sales was initiated in the 1980s.[53]

Coopers/Jockey continued the same basic marketing strategy in the post-1960 period. Company salesmen sold direct to 14,000 retail dealers, primarily men's stores and department stores. Despite increasing industry sales through national chains and discounters, Coopers management maintained the policy of selling through traditional retail dealers and, until late in the period, the company did not make private label merchandise.[54]

In 1960, in response to the Textile Fibers Products Identification Act, Coopers revised its package designs rather than trying to fit the required information on the old package. The Coopers name was virtually eliminated from all packaging and the Jockey name appeared more prominently on the face of each package. The former realistic full-length Jockey figure was replaced by a bold outline drawing in stylized technique, most often as a half figure (*Modern Packaging* 1960). In 1971, the company name was changed to Jockey International, Inc. reflecting the importance of the brand name to the company.

Jockey advertising is directed principally to the user of Jockey products so that the merchandise will move to and through retail outlets. The first Jockey TV commercials appeared on the Jack Paar show in 1960. National TV ads continued through the 1960s despite codes that prohibited the showing of underwear on live models. Jockey print ads ran in *Life, Ladies Home Journal,*

Good Housekeeping, Playboy, and *Esquire*. In the early 1970s, a new TV and print campaign featured sports and entertainment celebrities stressing that it was proper to build a wardrobe of colored underwear. In 1977, a new campaign "Take away their uniforms and who are they," featured baseball players Jim Palmer, Steve Carlton, and Pete Rose, football players Jim Hart and Ken Anderson, basketball players JoJo White and Jamaal Wilkes, and hockey player Denis Potvin. Jim Palmer of the Baltimore Orioles emerged as the clear favorite and became an extremely popular symbol of the Jockey brand.[55] In the late 1970s and early 1980s Jockey print ads, some featuring Jim Palmer, appeared in *Time, Playboy, Newsweek, Sports Illustrated, Gentlemen's Quarterly, Esquire, People*, and *Cosmopolitan* (*Forbes* 1982).

By the mid-1980s the International Division oversaw licensees in 35 countries who distributed Jockey products in more than 100 countries throughout the world. The division provided technical information, quality standards and overall marketing assistance and direction to its foreign licensees. All products made with the Jockey label had to have approval from corporate headquarters in Kenosha. For most licensees, Jockey products made up more than 30 percent of their total output. Jockey licensees in the United Kingdom, Germany, and the Scandinavian countries were the largest contributors to royalty income. Jockey became a leading sportswear name in Europe with substantial market share in those areas where licensees operated.[56]

In 1960 company mills were located in Kenosha, Wisconsin, Millen, Georgia, and Belzoni, Mississippi. Harry Wolf acquired Giffen Manufacturing Company in 1964 and changed the name to Blue Grass Industries. Blue Grass, which did a substantial part of the Jockey underwear cut, sew, and package operations, was acquired by Jockey International in the early 1980s. A wholly owned subsidiary, Blue Grass Knitting, was established to provide knit cloth for the Blue Grass plants. When Jockey acquired the Cedar Falls Manufacturing Company, a yarn spinning mill, in August 1982 it became integrated from yarn spinning forward through direct selling to retail outlets.[57]

The Wolf interests acquired majority control of Coopers, Incorporated in 1961 but a Cooper remained as president until 1971. Harry Wolf served as chairman of the board until 1976. H. E. Sommer, a long time associate of Harry Wolf Sr., played an increasing role in Jockey management. Wolf's daughter, Donna Wolf Steigerwaldt, joined the board in April 1978 and assumed the chairmanship the next year. She worked to provide the company with a new philosophy, organization and management style (King 1982).

A year later Steigerwaldt announced that Howard Cooley, with considerable experience in men's apparel, manufacturing, and marketing, had been hired as president and general manager. Cooley moved quickly to initiate changes including updating production equipment, adding computers in production control, inventory management and pattern drawing, and renovating the firm's offices and original Kenosha factory. With extensive sportswear experience,

Cooley acted to improve products and marketing in that area. The advertising budget was increased substantially and product quality and distribution were improved (Morris 1984). In recognition of new developments in retailing, the company brought out the Yves St. Laurent line of higher priced men's high fashion underwear and sportswear. In 1981 Jockey International licensed Silver Knit Industries, Inc. to produce and sell men's hosiery under the Jockey label (Keaton 1982).

One of Cooley's important product decisions was the introduction of Jockey for Her women's briefs. Extensive comparison shopping and testing led to the development of a brief that fit and laundered well and took advantage of the comfort and health advantages of cotton. Introduced around the country in 1983, Jockey For Her met with immediate success and rapidly rose to 18 percent of Jockey volume (Wright 1984).

Unlike many other companies in the apparel and other industries, Jockey International, Inc. by 1985 had not gone public, merged with larger firms, or diversified into unrelated areas. The firm remained closely held, committed to the apparel industry, and continued to follow the marketing strategy first developed by Samuel Cooper and refined and extended by Arthur Kneibler and Harry Wolf after the introduction of the Jockey brief. While growth was somewhat uneven in the post-1960 period, the company rode out the depressed conditions of the mid-1970s and early 1980s better than most of its competitors.

The 1980s saw significant changes in the apparel industry. Many producers dropped out, were acquired by other firms, diversified into other lines, or moved to production of private label goods. An increasing share of clothing is sold through chains, discounters, and off-price outlets, challenging those firms like Jockey International that continued to resist using the new channels of distribution. Imports, which accounted for about 12 percent of U.S. apparel sales in 1973, accounted for over 25 percent by 1983 (*Business Week* 1983; James 1983).

These developments have represented a direct challenge to Jockey International's traditional marketing approach. After 1983 Jockey moved to change some of its longstanding marketing methods. Time will tell how successful management will be in dealing with rapidly changing conditions.

NOTES

1. Information in this paragraph was developed primarily from Anna Cooper, "Samuel Thrall Cooper 1824-1892," undated manuscript in possession of Carlotta Cooper Lance (widow of Gilbert Lance); and Donald F. Walker, "Cooper Family History," manuscript, July 17, 1945, Archives of DePauw University, Greencastle, Indiana.

2. The story is reported in Cooper Underwear Company, "The Story of Cooper Quality Since 1876," (Kenosha, 1912).

3.   Information in this paragraph was reported in *The Cooperator* (published by and for the employees of Coopers, Inc., Kenosha, 1943- 1958), February 1949, pp.1-3.

4.   Ibid.

5.   Information developed from "The Story of Cooper Quality Since 1876."

6.   Ibid.

7.   *The Cooperator*, February, 1949, pp.1-3.

8.   An important source for this study was Robert Menn, "Reflections on Jockey," a manuscript drafted in 1976 and retyped at later dates. Menn was a long-time Jockey employee. The manuscript consists of several chapters but usable page numbers were not assigned to most chapters. Hereafter cited as "Menn 1976" with chapter title following. Information in this paragraph is from, "Years 1876 to 1917." Also "The Story of Coopers Quality Since 1876;"*The Cooperator*, February 1948, pp. 1-3.

9.   Menn 1976, "Years 1876 to 1917."

10.   Cooper Underwear Company Articles of Incorporation, September 13, 1902; Cooper Underwear Company, Directors Minute Books, 1902- 1904; Cooper Underwear Company, *Sales Bulletin*, January 4, 1929; Menn 1976, "Years 1876 to 1917."

11.   Directors Minute Books, 1903-1910; Cooper Underwear Company financial records 1903-1910 in company files; *The Cooperator*, February 1949, pp.1-3./

12.   Coopers, Inc., *Sales Training Manual: Data and Doctrine for All Coopermen* (Kenosha 1952), Chapter 1, hearafter *Sales Training Manual*; Menn 1976, "Years 1876 to 1917."

13.   Cooper Underwear Company financial records for 1902-1920 in Jockey International files.

14.   Menn 1976, "Years 1876 to 1917;" *Sales Training Manual*, p. 8; *The Cooperator*, February 1949, pp. 1-3; "The Story of Cooper Quality Since 1876."

15.   Menn 1976, "Years 1876 to 1917."

16.   Directors Minute Books 1918-1919.

17.   Menn 1976, "Years 1876 to 1917."

18.   *Sales Training Manual*, Chapter 1.

19.   Ibid.

20.   *Sales Bulletins* 1922-1927.

21.   Calculated from miscellaneous documents in company archives.

22.   Information from *Sales Bulletins* and files on company advertisements.

23.   Information from company financial records and Directors Minute Books for the indicated years.

24.   *The Cooperator* February 1949, pp.1-3.

25.   Ibid., March 1949; Directors Minute Books, special shareholders meeting, July 26, 1930.

26.   *The Cooperator*, March 1949; Directors Minute Books, special shareholders meeting July 26, 1930 and special directors meeting July 30- August 1, 1930.

27.   Ibid.

28.   Ibid.

29.   *Sales Bulletin*, 1930-1932 passim; "Sales history," typed manuscript based on *Sales Bulletin*, 1910-1982, no author and no date, p. 2; Menn 1976, "Years 1930-1933: Trimming Our Sails to Go Somewhere."

30.   Developed from financial information for 1930-1933 in company files.

31.   The development of the Jockey brief is discussed in several company documents. See *The Cooperator*, April 1949; *Sales Bulletin*, November 1934; Menn 1976, "Year 1934: At Last Jockey;" *Sales Training Manual*, p.12; "Data Conference of the J. Walter Thomson Company with Coopers, Inc.," September 2, 1938, copy in company files.

32.   *Sales Training Manual*, pp.13-14; Menn 1976, "Year 1934: At Last Jockey," and "Year 1935: Patents and Trademarks."

33.   *Sales Training Manual*, chapter on the history of men's underwear.

34. Several company documents offer slightly different accounts of the Davis Store promotion. Arthur K. Kneibler, Jr. (son of Arthur Kneibler) interview, September 1, 1982; *Sales Training Manual*, p. 14; *The Cooperator* April 1949, p. 2; Menn 1965, "Year 1934: At Last Jockey."

35. *Sales Training Manual*, p.17.

36. Ibid.; *The Cooperator* May 1949, pp. 2-3.

37. *Sales Training Manual*, pp.17-18; *The Cooperator* May 1949, pp. 2-3; Menn 1976, "Years 1935-39: National Advertising." Copies of old advertisements featuring sports figures were in unmarked company files.

38. Ibid.

39. *The Cooperator* June 1949, p. 2; *Sales Bulletin* 1937-1940; "Sales History," pp. 4-6; Kneibler, Jr. interview; Menn 1976, "February 1938: Jockey Cellophane Couple," and "Year 1939: The First Jockey Dispenser."

40. Menn 1976, "Fair Trade Prices."

41. Information on international operations was provided by Jockey International staff. Also *The Cooperator* May 1949, p. 2; Kneibler, Jr. interview; Menn 1976, "Years 1936-1972: International."

42. Information developed from financial and other documents for 1933- 1940 in Jockey International files.

43. Robert F. Cooper, "General policy on Distribution," January 3, 1962 statement to Coopers, Inc. Sales Convention; J.H. Wyss, "How We Sell Underwear in the U.S.A," Jockey International European Licensee Conference, Zurich, September 5-8, 1965.

44. "Sales History," pp.14-21 and 24-33; *Sales Bulletin* 1954. Arthur Millholland (son-n-law of Gilbert Lance) provided details on the Jockette promotion. Additional information came from a "Jockette" file in the company advertising department.

45. "Sales History," pp. 28-33; Menn 1976, "Years 1953-1955-1958: Prints and Colors."

46. Menn 1976, "Years 1938-1954: Sports Champions;" copies of advertisements featuring athletes in company flies.

47. The staff of the International Division supplied information on international operations. Also Menn 1976, "Years 1936-1972: International."

48. Information in this paragraph was developed in conversations with company officers and in several documents provided for review.

49. Jockey International Directors Mintue Books; discussions with company officers and employees; interview with Carlotta Cooper Lance (widow of Gilbert Lance), July 15, 1983; Millholland discussions.

50. A summary of the product line in the 1960s is in Wyss, "How We Sell underwear in the U.S.A," (1965).

51. *Sales Bulletins* 1958-1970.

52. Ibid.

53. Ibid.

54. Robert Cooper, "General Policy on Distribution," (1962).

55. "Sales History," pp. 113-161; discussions with William Hermann, Jockey International vice president, advertising and promotion.

56. Discussions with company officers; Menn 1976, "Years 1936-1972: International."

57. Information taken from several undated and unsigned documents in company files and discussions with company officers.

REFERENCES

Business Week. (1983) . "Imports are Still Ripping into the Textile Industry." (September 5); pp. 56-57.

Business Week. (1984). "Munsingwear: Stitching Together a Comeback." May 28); p. 88.

Clark, V. S. (1929, 1949). *History of Manufacturers in the United States* (Vol. II, 1860-1893). New York: Carnegie Institution of Washington.

Corbin, H. A. (1970). *The Men's Clothing Industry: Colonial Through Modern Times*. New York: Fairchild Publications.

Crockett, N. L. (1972). *The Woolen Industry of the Midwest*. Lexington, KY: University Press of Kentucky.

Cropley, C. (1958). *Kenosha: From Pioneer Village to Modern City,1835-1935*. Kenosha, WI: Kenosha County Historical Society.

Cunnington, C. W. and P. Cunnington. (1951). *The History of Underclothes*. London: Michael Joseph.

Daily News Record. (1935, March 25).

Fabricant, S. (1940). *The Output of Manufacturing Industries, 1899- 1937*. New York: National Bureau of Economic Research.

Faulkner, H. U. (1968). *The Decline of Laissez-faire 1897-1917*. New York: Harper Torchbooks.

Forbes. (1982, June 21). "Understatements."

James, F. E. (1983). "Munsingwear Regains Order and Discipline but Faces a Tough Battle to Restore Profits." *Wall Street Journal* (August 6).

Jensen, D. (1981). "Fire Kills Prominent Kenoshans." *Kenosha Sunday News*(December 27).

Jenson, D. (1983). "Midnight Idea Revolutionized World's Underwear." *Kenosha Sunday News*(June 26).

Keaton, A. (1982). "Jockeying for Position." *Daily News Record*(December 1).

King, C. (1982). "An Interview with Donna Wolf Steigerwaldt." *Memo*(Summer).

Krooss, H. E. (1974). *American Economic Development* (3rd ed.). Englewood Cliffs, NJ: Prentice-Hall.

Lyman, F. H. (1916). *The City of Kenosha and Kenosha County Wisconsin* (Vols. 1-2). Chicago: S. J. Clarke.

Manistee(Michigan)*News Advocate*. (1918-1919). July 1, 1918, April 3, 7, May 22, 1919.

Mestre, E. R., and A. M. Lubell. (1975). "Mergers and Technological Change in the Garment Industry." *The Antitrust Bulletin*; pp. 521-542.

Milwaukee Journal. (1935). "Orders Deluge Kenosha Firm." (March 17).

Modern Packaging. (1960). "The New Cooper's." (September).

Morris, P. A. (1984). "Determined to Succeed." *Florida Engineer*, (September); pp. 4-7.

Niemi, A. W. (1974). *State and Regional Patterns in American Manufacturing 1860-1900*. Westport, CT: Greenwood Press.

Porter, G., and H. C. Livesay. (1971). *Merchants and Manufacturers: Studies in the Changing Structure of Nineteenth Century Marketing*. Baltimore: Johns Hopkins Press.

Printers Ink. (1935). "Jockey Shorts."

Puth, R. C. (1988). *American Economic History*(2nd ed.). Chicago: The Dryden Press.

Reed, S. K. (1983). "How do You Market Unmentionables: You Put Them on Jim Palmer and Call them Fashion." *Savvy*, (July); pp. 34-39.

Riemer, H. (1956). *The World is Catching Up*. New York: Fairchild Publications.

Robertson, R. M. (1964). *History of the American Economy* (2nd ed.). New York: Harcourt, Brace & World.

Schau, M. (1974). *J.C. Leyendecker*. New York: Watson-Guptill.

Time. (1983). "Calvin's New Gender Benders," (September 5); p. 56.

Wilcox, C. (1955). *Public Policy Toward Business*. Chicago: Richard D. Irwin.

Wright, M. E. (1984). "Jockey: The Company that Covered the Gender Gap." *Wisconsin Business Journal*, 3(March); pp. 8-17.

PART IV

HISTORICAL APPROACHES TO MACROMARKETING ISSUES

TOBACCO ADVERTISING ON TRIAL:

AN ASSESSMENT OF RECENT ATTEMPTS TO RECONSTRUCT THE PAST AND AN AGENDA TO IMPROVE THE QUALITY OF EVIDENCE PRESENTED

Timothy P. Meyer

I. BACKGROUND

Over the past decade, U. S. tobacco companies have been attacked on several different fronts. Anti-smoking forces, government regulators, private industry, and other health-oriented groups have worked singly or have joined forces to take on the tobacco industry in the legislative and policy-making arenas and in the courts. The last session of Congress adjourning in late 1990 just prior to the elections once again considered several pieces of legislation aimed at restricting tobacco advertising and promotion. While none of the legislation was put to a full vote in either the House or Senate, the newly elected Congress (returning nearly all incumbents to office) will almost certainly revive the legislation and continue to push for regulatory changes. On the litigation front,

Research in Marketing, Supplement 6, pages 205-220.

ISBN: 1-55938-187-6

cases continue their orderly march to trial. In September of 1990, the case of *Horton* vs. *American Tobacco, et al.*, went to jury and produced a verdict with no monetary damages being assessed against the defendants. The *Cipollone* vs. *Liggett Group, et al.*, case of 1988 was cleared for a new trial in 1991. More than fifty cases against tobacco companies remain on file around the country, most awaiting the outcome of one key case or another.

Efforts on the regulatory front differ significantly from those being made in litigation. The regulatory and policy issues hinge on current concerns— current practices for advertising, promoting and marketing tobacco products in the United States and abroad. Of particular concern is the issue of smoking and youth and the effects of tobacco use on people's health. In court cases, however, there is a necessary and distinct historical focus.

Smokers pursuing litigation have made claims against tobacco companies that stem from the advertising and promotion of cigarettes *prior* to the mandatory labeling of cigarette packages and advertising with the warning from the U.S. Surgeon General. Thus, the court cases revolve around a particular individual's initiation and maintenance of smoking and the alleged liability of cigarette companies who sold a product that was supposed to be inherently dangerous to consumers. Juries are asked to evaluate the environment in which a specific individual lived during a time forty or more years ago and one in which the tobacco companies marketed cigarettes despite questions being raised regarding the health risks of smoking. Since advertising and promotion were different 40 years ago in comparison to today's practices and since the social and cultural milieu in which the plaintiffs lived back then were also substantially different from the world of today, the major problem facing plaintiffs, defendants, juries, and judges becomes one of trying to fairly reconstruct and understand the past—the environments in which tobacco companies operated and those of individual consumers. Compounding this difficult challenge for all parties concerned is the perhaps futile attempt to fairly assess the past in an adversarial proceeding where lawyers rightfully try to win by convincing the jury of their position and discrediting the position of their opponents. Admissability of evidence can also be a difficult problem, blocking the entry of potentially informative data.

The purpose of this paper is (a) to describe the current situation surrounding litigation of tobacco cases requiring reconstruction of past events in which advertising and promotion practices are entered as key issues; (b) to identify major problem areas brought about by insufficient evidence to fairly evaluate the social and cultural environment in which individuals lived 35-40 or more years ago; and (c) to suggest a number of qualitative research procedures that would increase the probability that more reasonable deliberations could be made about those factors deemed responsible for a specific individual's decision to start smoking and to continue to smoke.

II. CURRENT CASES: THE HISTORICAL CONTEXT OF CIGARETTE ADVERTISING EFFECTS

In filing suits against the tobacco companies in the United States, plaintiffs have argued that tobacco companies should be held liable for deaths caused by cigarette smoking because the companies knew about the health risks of smoking but failed to inform consumers of this situation; moreover, tobacco companies continued to advertise and promote their products allegedly addressing consumer health concerns and inferring that their brand of cigarettes was healthier or safer than other brands. In their attempts to prove the case, plaintiffs inevitably engage in a reconstruction of the social environment in which the plaintiff began to smoke and continued to smoke. Included in this reconstruction of course is the cigarette advertising and promotion that was made available through the mass media (broadcast and print) and promotional channels. The impact of the advertising on the individual is thus a critical issue for debate in these cases.

In both the *Cipollone* vs. *Liggett Group, et al.* (1988) case and the recently decided *Horton* vs. *American Tobacco, et al.* (1990), historical reconstruction of the social context of the individual (plaintiff) and the supposed advertising influence formed one of the key issues deliberated by the juries. With cases similar to *Cipollone* scheduled for trial in early 1995, the same issues will once again be in the spotlight. Evidence in both of these cases consisted primarily of expert witness testimony. Experts for the plaintiff argued that advertising was one of several major factors that would likely have influenced the plaintiff to start and to continue smoking. They also argue that smokers from the early 1950s on became concerned about the effects of smoking on their health. Some tobacco companies responded to these concerns by referring to them in their advertising. The plaintiffs' lawyers thus argued that the advertising helped to reassure concerned smokers that their continuing to smoke was not dangerous to their health.

In both *Cipollone* and *Horton*, how cigarettes were advertised back in the early 1950s became a focus for the court. The ads of the specific brands smoked by the plaintiffs came under nearly microscopic examination. Experts on both sides argued about the likely consumer interpretations of some of the ads run in magazines by the cigarette companies. While no one could be sure of how the plaintiffs interpreted the ads at the time they were exposed to them (or even if they were in fact exposed to them), how the average person would interpret the content of the ads was in dispute. In *Cipollone*, the plaintiff introduced empirical research (a content analysis commissioned by the plaintiff's attorneys for this case) by one expert in an attempt to show that ads with supposed health claims were a regular feature up to the middle 1950s (at which point tobacco companies were forbidden to make health-related claims) and that exposure to such ads would likely have influenced the plaintiff to continue to smoke, having been reassured that smoking a particular brand would be safe or at least safer than other brands. Some of these health-oriented ads became relevant to the case because they appeared in magazines that the plaintiff remembered reading occasionally.

In *Horton*, experts for the plaintiff argued along similar lines, contending that the particular brand in question (Pall Mall Reds) was advertised to reassure smokers that this brand was "safer," thus reducing the perceived risks attached to continued smoking. One of the experts spoke to Mr. Horton before he died (he was not living at the time of trial) in a telephone conversation of only fifteen minutes (Mr. Horton's health had seriously deteriorated by that point). Horton was asked if he could recall advertising for Pall Mall and also to what extent he might have been influenced by those ads or by cigarette advertising generally. Since Nathan Horton and Rose Cipollone (the plaintiffs in these cases) both began smoking 40 or more years prior to their deaths, the social/cultural environment during these times also became crucial in deciding the likely influence of cigarette advertising.

The defense in both cases argued that advertising was only one part of the total information environment in which the plaintiffs lived. The decision to smoke was influenced in large part by the fact that many others (peers) also started smoking and continued to smoke; that smoking was socially acceptable and a culturally embedded behavior during these times; and, that common knowledge (prevailing conventional wisdom) clearly recognized the health risks that came with smoking (e.g., routinely calling cigarettes "coffin nails" or "cancer sticks"). Despite this knowledge, the plaintiff made a free choice to smoke.

The *Cipollone* case marked the first time that a jury had awarded a plaintiff monetary damages ($400,000 to the family of Rose Cipollone) in a suit against U.S. tobacco companies. But this award was later overturned by the 3rd U.S. Circuit Court of Appeals. The *Horton* case resulted in a jury verdict that found shared responsibility for Horton's death to reside with Horton, himself, and with the defendants (*American Tobacco Co., et al.*), but no monetary damages were assessed against the tobacco companies. As new cases come to trial, once again, the historical context—the social/cultural milieu—in which the plaintiff lived will be the focus in the retrial; and, once again, the influence of advertising on the plaintiff will be one crucial issue in the spotlight.

III.   HISTORICAL RECONSTRUCTION IN TOBACCO AD CASES: EMERGING PROBLEMS

When cases come to trial, both sides naturally select those arguments and evidence that they feel will be instrumental in determining the jury's verdict. Moreover, the legal discovery process allows attorneys on both sides to know the opposing witnesses, evidence, and arguments in advance of the trial itself. Once the case goes to trial, the case plays out more or less according to this predetermined agenda. The greatest uncertainties occur in the cross examination of witnesses; in the tobacco ad cases, the influence of advertising is the province of expert witnesses on both sides. An examination of trial transcripts of direct and cross examinations of the advertising experts reveals a number of serious problems stemming from the limited evidence available for interpretation by these experts.

A. Absence of Context: Social and Historical

The first problem centers on the absence of context, both social and historical. Experts talk about advertising as it appeared in the years before the plaintiff started smoking and continued to smoke. While references are made to the general social/cultural milieu, little visible evidence is offered of what it was like "back then" and "back there" (where the plaintiff lived). What is introduced as evidence for the jury to consider? A series of tobacco ads drawn essentially from magazines and a few selected TV cigarette commercials. The jury is thus put in a most difficult situation where it will likely focus on an almost incredibly narrow range of evidence that is visible and objectively present and, therefore, not focus much if at all on the context in which the individual plaintiff lived.

What is excluded from the deliberations is the social/cultural environment of the plaintiff. What was it like to live in New York City and in New Jersey (Cipollone) or in Mississippi (Horton) when the plaintiffs were growing up? How did people go about the ordinary, mundane rituals of day-to-day living? What did they talk about? What did they know? Where did such general knowledge come from? What media were available? What media were the plaintiffs specifically exposed to? How was the content of the various media interpreted? What ads were they exposed to? Which cigarette ads? How were they interpreted by the plaintiff (not by the experts looking back at the ad with the advantage of expertise and 40-plus years of hindsight and experience)? What were their peers doing, how were they living? What was important to them? How were they raised and treated by their parents? How about siblings? Neighbors? The answers to these types of questions represent essential information to understanding the world of the individual (plaintiff), yet no serious attempt is made to present this to the court for consideration.

Also missing is the appropriate context for evaluating and interpreting the advertising. First of all, how were the ads interpreted by consumers generally and the plaintiff specifically when the ads were available some 40 or more years ago? Secondly, specific tobacco ads were presented in the midst of many other tobacco ads; tobacco ads in turn were presented among ads for a multitude of other products and services; the many ads for products and services were also presented in an environment filled with other media advertising, most notably via radio, newspapers, the movies, and as the 1950s rolled on, television; all of advertising was of course embedded within the predominant content forms of these media (news, information, editorial content, and entertainment fare in the print and broadcast media). Interpersonal influence was also a significant factor during these times; in the case of smoking initiation, peer influence was as strong or stronger then than it is now. Social forces affecting a given individual would also include schools and teachers, parents, peers, churches and religious upbringing, government, and the mass media.

When experts testify on the historical development of advertising and describe trends in how cigarettes (and other tobacco products) were advertised, the historical focus is on how the advertising was developed and ultimately manifested itself to consumers, but then, only a very small part of how smoking and cigarettes were observable in the social environment. There is little or no attempt made to provide a historical focus on the social/cultural environment of the plaintiff and then to see how (or even if) the advertising of cigarettes or a particular brand fit into this specific environment. The critical evidence in dispute inevitably revolves around several specific ads selected by the plaintiff's attorneys and experts because they are perceived to be the ones best suited to winning the issue. And, since these ads are greatly enlarged for easy viewing by the judge and jury, they possess a magnified visual impact dimension not applicable to other evidence. The jury does not even get a chance to see the actual ads in the context of their actual sizes in the magazines in which they appeared. Thus, even the consideration of the ads themselves is not even remotely faithful to their natural context of presentation.

Devoid of appropriate contexts, the evidence presented, how it is presented, and the myriad of important factors presented cursorily, if at all, all point to a process where unfairness is virtually guaranteed. Such unfairness benefits neither side, the court, or society (which expects the courts to fairly deliberate and resolve interpretive issues on its behalf based on the goal of an objective examination of the relevant facts).

B.   Content Analysis of Tobacco Ads: Severe Limitations

The second problem in assessing the impact of tobacco advertising on plaintiffs centers on the research tool of content analysis and its attendant limitations. While few scholars would question the utility of content analysis as a research tool in some circumstances, appropriate use and interpretation of such analyses need to be examined and considered when evaluating its use in tobacco ad cases.

Berelson (1952) described content analysis as a tool suitable "...for the objective, systematic, and quantitative description of the manifest content of communication" (p. 15). Content analysis is objective in the sense that the procedures used are uniformly applied in the analysis while producing the same (or very similar) results among different analysts. Content analysis also is systematic in that it is supposed to draw a representative sample of content from a supposedly representative range of sources of such content. In the case of cigarette advertising, a representative sample of such advertising between 1950 and 1955 would be drawn from all advertising media and from within each of the media. Categories of content (what the specific ads contain that were selected for study) would thus be established and counts made across the ads within each of the categories. Coders who assign specified attributes to the categories would have to be in near total agreement in their assignments to give the analysis reliability (ergo, its objectivity). Other analysts who examined the same ads and coded them according to the categories as specified in the original investigation should also arrive at the same results (or close).

As a research tool, content analysis is intended to limit itself to only those characteristics of manifest content that are obvious to coders. This limitation is necessary to enable analysts to agree on the coding decisions. As Holsti's (1961) seminal text on content analysis points out: when coding units of content, "...one is limited to recording only those items which actually appear in the document" (p. 12). Inferring "hidden meanings" or arbitrarily instructing coders to place certain types of content in categories that have multiple and perhaps diverse interpretations of meaning is an inappropriate and misleading procedure. "There should be no 'reading between the lines'; ideally the account should be limited to what is apparent to everyone" (Leiss, Kline, and Jhally 1990, p. 219).

Applying these principles to the use of content analyses in the tobacco ad cases to date, a cigarette ad that claims to have a smoother, milder taste (those words in the text or copy of the ad) could present problems beyond the simple category of claims made about the smoothness or mildness of the cigarette's taste. Instructing coders to include terms like smoother and milder in a category designating health-related claims would represent a difficult problem of interpretation. Coders would all agree because of the researcher's instructions for deciding what kinds of word and phrases go into which of the predetermined categories. But, whether such an inclusion is objective and reasonable is certainly debatable. How consumers, themselves, (or the plaintiff, ideally) interpreted these words would thus be far more important in correctly assessing the accuracy of the content assignment than the actions of the coders. Therefore, content analysis of tobacco ads should be limited to frequencies for attributes actually presented in the ads (not inferred or arbitrarily defined). What these patterns of repetition mean to consumers can only be determined by consumers. Leiss, Kline, and Jhally, (1990) emphasize that content analysis "...cannot tell us anything about how audiences may be 'reading' messages..." and that it must never be used to represent the audience's interpretation of that content nor to "...demonstrate the effect on the audience" (p. 224).

Content analysis of past cigarette advertising is also limited in that it asks coders in the late 1980s to judge the content of ads dating back to the 1930s or even earlier. No one knows the degree to which meanings of ad content would be different or where these differences would occur. Coders today have the enormous benefit of hindsight which would almost certainly affect their interpretations. And, using college students as coders has also precluded the use of people in their late 60s or early 70s who at least would have been alive when the ads actually appeared; at least they would have lived through some experiences comparable to that of the plaintiffs.

The way content analysis has been used to date in tobacco ad cases is also inherently unfair in that only selected magazines are analyzed, only the tobacco ads are analyzed (as opposed to all the other types of ads running in the same magazines), ad content from other media and nonadvertising content from all media (magazines included) are *not* content analyzed; finally, no systematic attempts are made to include the influence of other salient factors in the plaintiffs' environments. The thrust of this criticism is simple: because content analysis is represented as a reliable, systematic and objective research tool, the findings take on a scientific aura in comparison to everything else that is *not* analyzed in the same way and, therefore, does not carry the same credibility nor is it likely to be as heavily weighed by the jury in its deliberations.

C.   Level of Abstraction

A third and final problem for discussion revolves around the concept of level of abstraction. Experts are called upon to present their opinions on how advertising works and how tobacco advertising was likely to have worked in the past. Their expertise, however, is dependent on the level of abstraction. Experts will readily talk about how advertising has effects on consumers in an aggregate sense. For example, consider some of the possible effects of cigarette ads on teenage males; there are some who think that smoking is a socially desirable "merit badge" that signifies maturity and adulthood and will undoubtedly be influenced by others around them who also smoke. As smokers, they in turn will be more likely to be influenced by cigarette ads that appeal to them as a segment of the smoking market; Marlboro ads would be far more likely to have a positive effect on these males than Virginia Slims ads (which are obviously directed at women). Not all teenage males will be affected in the same ways by various cigarette ads; not even all teenage males who want to appear older and more mature will be influenced in the same way or to the same degree by the cigarette ads.

So, how does cigarette advertising affect teenage males? Well, the answer from an expert point of view would depend on the level of abstraction—how specific do you want to be when describing the likely effects. Moreover, how certain do you want to be in accurately specifying the effects? In a general sense, teenage males who would want to appear older and more mature than they really are would, as a group, be likely candidates to become smokers; and for those who start smoking, some cigarette ads might be influential. How about the effect of cigarette ads on a certain individual? Here the level of abstraction moves from the aggregate to the individual, and with this move, so goes the ability of the expert to say with any substantial amount of certainty what the effects of some cigarette ads are likely to be. Experts can talk about how groups of smokers tended to switch brands and where the switches took place; but not everyone in the designated group (usually defined by demographics held in common by group members—a facilitator of marketing research) behaved in the same way. Standard behaviorist research methods to date are rendered useless in predicting individual behavior; these methods have some success in predicting group or aggregate tendencies under certain measurement conditions, but cannot be used for individual behavior predictions or explanations.

Level of abstraction matters a great deal in the tobacco ad cases to date. How the individual plaintiff was affected is the central interest, but experts are forced to speculate based on aggregate behaviors. How a plaintiff was affected by cigarette advertising and promotion remains highly speculative because the research tools used most often to study advertising effects are not designed to measure effects on specific individuals. Ironically, an entire arsenal of qualitative research procedures ideally suited to studying individuals and individual behavior is readily available and could have, indeed should have been put to use in trying to come to grips with those factors most responsible for an individual's decision to start and continue to smoke. Some of these basic tools are described in the third major section of this paper; how these tools could be meaningfully applied to tobacco ad cases is also addressed.

IV. RECONSTRUCTING THE PAST: USING QUALITATIVE PROCEDURES TO ENHANCE THE QUALITY OF EVIDENCE PRESENTED

By now it should be clear that attempts to date in tobacco ad cases to reconstruct the past have been generally inadequate; previous cases have relied on biased and insufficient evidence and information to enable jurors to fairly evaluate the merits of the opposing cases. Given the availability of qualitative research procedures that have been developed to study "situated individuals"— individuals as they have existed or continue to exist in a particular environment—it would seem most desirable to consider some of these tools and to apply them in the information/evidence gathering processes and to introduce appropriate findings for the court's consideration. The introduction of such findings represents the opportunity for a marked improvement over the quality of evidence relied upon in past cases (as likely to be relied upon in rapidly upcoming cases). Each of several basic qualitative procedures is briefly described and some of its potential applications to tobacco ad cases are discussed.

Qualitative research has a long and time-honored tradition in many academic disciplines, including cultural anthropology, sociology, psychology, political science, and communication. Qualitative research is referred to by many different labels, including ethnography, naturalistic inquiry, case studies, and others. Anderson (1987) and Anderson and Meyer (1988) have described the dominant characteristics of qualitative research in the field of communication (including mass communication and advertising). These characteristics include: (a) *inductive* (logical positivism in traditional social science is of course deductive), moving from specific examples studied intensely over time to generalizations where warranted; (b) *eidetic*, directed at the goal of understanding the totality of meaning before the meaning of any of the parts becomes apparent; (c) *subjective*, viewing the world from the point of view of the individual being studied (e.g., seeing the world from the plaintiff's point of view and understanding his or her frame of reference for interpreting the world); (d) *contextual*, seeking to understand not only the various social and cultural settings in which an individual lives (or lived) but also the interpretation of those settings by the individual; (e) *mundane*, describing the ordinary actions of ordinary individuals in ordinary settings but studying the individual in a highly systematic and explicit manner; (f) *preservationistic*, always trying to preserve the individual within the context of social actions (in opposition to traditional social science research methods that aggregate individual data for units of analysis); and (g) *interactive*, looking at all of the factors, large and small, that play a role in shaping the meanings of the world of the individual. Not included in this list is the apparent distinction between so-called qualitative and so-called quantitative research. As Kirk and Miller (1986) have observed, such a distinction is false and misleading in that qualitative research is often concerned with quantitative measures and that quantitative records are often kept or secured for analysis by qualitative researchers. The particular characteristics of qualitative research just listed help to provide clearer distinctions (true distinctions?) between qualitative procedures and hypothetico-deductive models and methods of social science. These characteristics thus seem far better suited to analyzing the effects of tobacco advertising and promotion on a specific individual than the traditional aggregate data analysis procedures employed in the social sciences.

Qualitative procedures also present a comfortable fit with the traditional tools of historical analysis (Marshall and Rossman 1989; Schudson 1984). Historical analysis of course is a method for discovering what happened in the past through the examination of records and accounts. Traditional primary and secondary sources are used; primary sources would include oral testimony of the individual(s) involved, recollections and observations of friends, personal documents and records, and so forth; secondary sources would include an analysis of items or objects generally available while the individual lived and at specified critical times (e.g., just before the plaintiff began smoking or when the plaintiff thought about quitting). Specific qualitative procedures could be meaningfully applied to the plaintiffs in tobacco ad cases. These techniques and examples follow.

A. Life Histories

In both the *Horton* and *Cipollone* cases, the plaintiffs were deposed by defense attorneys to allow them an opportunity to learn more about them; the plaintiffs were obviously interviewed at length by their attorneys. Attorneys, however, are not trained as historians nor as qualitative researchers skilled at interviewing and interpreting the world from another's frame of reference (although many attorneys could cultivate such expertise with some training and experience). Trained researchers could be used to interview the plaintiff, the family, friends, neighbors, coworkers, acquaintances, and so forth of the plaintiff; the researcher would also examine any writing done by the plaintiff, correspondence directed to him or her or written by him or her; also of interest would be specific books, newspapers, and magazines read, the radio programs listened to, the television programs watched, the consumer habits across a variety of products and services as inventoried, and so forth.

Schwartz and Jacobs (1979) identify four features of competent life histories: they should be *autobiographical* but corroborated by others to gauge accuracy, completeness, selective memory or perceptions, and so forth; they should be as *detailed* as possible; the account should *cover* as much of the individual's life as possible; accounts should be *dated* as accurately as possible to enable the researcher to look at units of life experience as sequential units with preceding units affecting consequential ones. Life histories compiled for the plaintiffs or for others with comparable life histories would have provided a solid baseline from which specific influences on smoking could be closely analyzed and interpreted. If the plaintiff is unwilling or unable to provide the information for compiling a life history, other individuals who are (were) much like the plaintiff could be substituted as long as those researched were representative along key dimensions (age, communities and neighborhoods lived in, occupation, education, marital status, smoking history, etc.).

B. Depth or Long Interviews

Before describing the research procedures of the long (or depth) interview, McCracken (1988) laments the reticence of consumer behavior researchers to use qualitative procedures generally: "Caught up in the preoccupations of positivism, consumer research has been unprepared, until recently, to credit any but the most limited range of qualitative methods as useful. Even here, in the development of the focus group, there has been substantially more concern with practice than theory. Recently, a broader range of qualitative methods has been developed and applied" (p. 15). McCracken's conclusions refer to the field of consumer behavior's preoccupation with studying consumers in the aggregate while disdaining the intensive examination of the individual. Recent research does show definite movement toward a broader acceptance and application of some qualitative procedures beyond focus groups, including the long interview with individual consumers. Examples of this recent trend include: Barnett (1985), Belk (1986, 1987), Durgee (1986a, 1986b), Hirschman (1985), Hirschman and Holbrook (1986), Holbrook (1987a, 1987b), Sherry (1987), Wallendorf (1987), and O'Guinn and Faber (1989).

The long or depth interview is also known in qualitative circles as "informant" interviews. The notion of informant is perhaps a useful one in that the informant is a person who has the knowledge and experiences of interest to the researcher but also has the potential for communicating this knowledge and experience. In this sense, not all individuals who have the requisite knowledge and experience qualify as desirable informants; only those who are able and willing to share their knowledge and experiences with the researcher will be useful informants.

Regardless of what they are called, long interviews have the potential to produce enormous benefits. Their goal is to elicit depth information from respondents who are in a position to describe a range of experiences and accumulated knowledge with the researcher. Ordinarily, long interviews are carefully planned, have an overall structure or organizational scheme, attend to and elicit as much detail as possible, and are time consuming for the respondent (and the researcher, too). The overriding objective is to see things from the respondent's point of view.

McCracken (1988) suggests four basic steps in implementing long interviews. The first step is to review analytic categories and to begin the design of the interview. This step demands that the researcher thoroughly review the available literature in the particular areas of interest. Analytic categories that accurately represent the dimensions of experience sought after by the researcher will likely result from highly knowledgeable interviewers; in short, long interviews are *not* open-ended fishing expeditions that hope to hit on something of interest and value.

The second step is to review the cultural categories and add to the interview's design. The interviewer/researcher must have a solid foundation of the cultural context in which the individual lives (or has lived). If you wanted to know more about what it was like to grow up in rural Mississippi during the late 1940s and early 1950s, you would have to immerse yourself in historical analysis of what was going on generally during these times, and if possible, in areas of rural Mississippi. A review of books, newspapers, magazines, and films would be one way of getting a feel for the cultural context. An examination of the individual's possessions, households in which he or she lived, collections of memorabilia, and so on. would also be part of this stage of the inquiry. All of this study helps to prepare the interviewer.

The third step includes the discovery of cultural categories. At this point the general questionnaire is prepared and the interview process is initiated. As the interview unfolds, answers to questions will undoubtedly trigger many additional questions and/or lines of inquiry that will be pursued by the researcher. The interviewer looks for distinctive key words, labels, or phrases as signals to seek out additional explanations. The interviewer will eventually cover all the basic categories, but which categories emerge as more important than others is usually only determined as the interview itself emerges.

The fourth and final step is to discover the analytic categories. In short, all of the interview data must be analyzed by the researcher. As mentioned in step three, predetermined analytic categories may not hold up when the interview is completed. Some areas may emerge that require more study by the interviewer and a return to the individual for clarification or additional information. Interviews, thus, require researcher access over the entire period of analysis.

The product of long interviews is a richly descriptive narrative that has probed in depth key areas of interest. Some of these key areas may have emerged from a respondent's life history; others may have been suggested by the examination of the individuals possessions, collections of memorabilia, and so on. Other topics will of course have been elicited by the interviews.

As applied to plaintiffs in tobacco ad cases, long interviews could be used profitably in several ways. It would obviously be useful to conduct a long interview with the plaintiff; in addition it would be of immense value to interview family members, friends, acquaintances, coworkers, or even strangers who have apparently lived a life similar to the plaintiff. (Perhaps a necessity to account for biases introduced by plaintiffs, their families, and friends, etc. who may provide unreliable information in an attempt to mask potentially damaging information.) These interviews should be done by experienced, trained researchers who have no vested interest one way or the other in the particulars of the court case—a disinterested third party. The narrative should be carefully examined by the attorneys and experts on both sides but should be introduced and shared with the judge and jury. Such interviews, coupled with a comprehensive life history, can provide baseline information that enables all participants in the trial to better and more fully understand the plaintiff.

C. Content Analyses

A previous section of this paper was critical of content analysis as it has been used to date in tobacco ad cases. Therefore, it may seem strange to see it listed as a useful qualitative procedure. This apparent contradiction is easily resolved.

The previously stated criticism of content analysis is *not* with the research tool itself, but rather the way in which it has been applied and its highly selective applications. Content analysis is an extremely useful tool to aid understanding in historical reconstruction. This procedure not only identifies the occurrence (or nonoccurrence) of specific events or aspects of these events; it allows us to evaluate the frequency with which these things occur; and, it allows us to compare the relative frequencies of occurrence from one thing (category) to another.

To be an objective and informative source of evidence, content analysis must be applied appropriately and uniformly. The use of so-called denotative categories is essential, avoiding the assignment of meaning and inferences about what units of content mean (and to whom). Objective categories systematically establish basic categories that can be compared for frequency of occurrence.

When the only content analysis introduced into evidence is of cigarette advertising, the tool has an unfair and misleading impact on the litigation process. Cigarette ads as compared to what? becomes the relevant question. Other ads in the same magazines should also be content analyzed to provide a reasonable frame of reference; all the nonadvertising content in the magazines should also be content analyzed. After all, all media content contributes to the individual's information environment which is in turn embedded in the individual's social and cultural environment. Other media available at the time need to be included. While transcripts of radio or television broadcasts may not be available, local newspapers almost always are. Advertising and nonadvertising content needs to be content analyzed.

Films that were shown in the plaintiff's community should also be content analyzed. Films in the late 1940s and early 1950s provided the dominant visual communication form (television doesn't really take off until the mid-1950s). Films also reflected many social and cultural mores in operation at the time. How did people dress, talk, express themselves, and so on? Directly relevant to the tobacco cases, it should be noted that films with contemporary characters in contemporary settings frequently showed smoking as a routine activity. Barry Levinson's film, "Avalon," takes place in the late 1940s and the early 1950s and reflects what it was like for him to grow up in Baltimore (and the suburbs) during that particular period. People are shown smoking, often heavily, in the film; that's what a lot of people did back then. Suffice to say, films of the time should be included in the content analyses.

V. SUMMARY AND CONCLUSIONS

This paper has described the current situation surrounding litigation of tobacco cases that have included the historical reconstruction of past events of which cigarette advertising and promotion have supposedly been a part. Historical reconstruction has been a necessary, vital ingredient in these cases, but it has not been done with sufficient depth, breadth, or uniformity. This paper has also identified major problem areas brought about in part by this insufficiency of quality evidence that has precluded a fair, comprehensive evaluation of the plaintiffs' social and cultural milieus in which they grew up and lived. These problems included the absence of social and historical context consideration, failures of content analyses as they have been used to date, and the failure to utilize the appropriate level of abstraction when attempting to specify the impact of tobacco ads on the individual plaintiffs. Qualitative procedures were offered as having the potential to markedly improve the fairness and accuracy of tobacco ad cases. These procedures included the basic tools of historical analysis, life histories, long or depth interviews, and content analyses (applied appropriately and uniformly).

Qualitative research procedures have been developed to study individuals. They are also designed to provide a wealth of descriptive data that reconstructs the individual's perceptions or sense of reality from the individual's point of view. These tools enable others to see the world as the individual sees it or saw it and reveal this perspective through the application of these tools by skilled and experienced qualitative researchers. The quality of information presented in tobacco ad cases would be enhanced considerably by the application of qualitative research procedures. Also enhanced, presumably, would be the quality of the deliberations, the evaluation of more comprehensive evidence, and the resulting verdicts.

REFERENCES

Anderson, J.A. (1987). *Communication Research: Issues and Methods.* New York: McGraw-Hill.

Anderson, J. A. and T. P. Meyer. (1988). *Mediated Communication: A Social Action Perspective.* Newbury Park, CA: Sage.

Barnett, S. (1985). "Everyday Life Ethnography: Case Studies of Dishwashing and Diapering." In *On Beyond Interviewing: Observational Studies of Consumer Behavior,* edited by J. Clar. Chicago, IL: Conference Proceedings, October 10.

Belk, R. W. (1986). "Art Versus Science as Ways of Generating Knowledge about Materialism." In *Perspectives on Methodology in Consumer Research,* edited by D. Brinberg and R. Lutz. New York: Springer-Verlag.

Belk, R. W. (1987). "The Role of the Odyssey in Consumer Behavior and in Consumer Research." In *Advances in Consumer Research,* edited by M. Wallendorf and P. Anderson. Provo, UT: Association for Consumer Research.

Berelson, B. (1952). *Content Analysis in Communication Research*. New York: Free Press.

Cipollone vs. *Liggett Group, et al.* (1988). Federal District Court, NJ.

Durgee, J.F. (1986a). "Depth-interviewing Techniques for Creative Advertising." *Journal of Advertising Research*, 25 (6); pp. 29-37.

Durgee, J.F. (1986b). "Richer Findings from Qualitative Research." *Journal of Advertising Research*, 26 (4); pp. 36-44.

Hirschman, E.C. (1985). "Scientific Style and the Conduct of Consumer Research." *Journal of Consumer Research*, 12 (2); pp. 225-239.

Hirschman, E.C. and M. B. Holbrook. (1986). "Expanding the Ontology and Methodology of Research on the Consumption Experience." In *Perspectives on Methodology in Consumer Research*, edited by D. Brinberg and R. Lutz. New York: Springer-Verlag.

Holbrook, M.B. (1987a). "From the Log of a Consumer Researcher." In *Advances in Consumer Research*, edited by M. Wallendorf and P. Anderson. Provo, UT: Associaton for Consumer Research.

Holbrook, M.B. (1987b). "What is Consumer Research?" *Journal of Consumer Research*, 14 (1); pp. 128-132.

Holsti, O. (1969). *Content Analysis for the Social Sciences and Humanities*. Reading, MA: Addison-Wesley.

Horton vs. *American Tobacco, et al.* (1990). Circuit Court, MS.

Kirk, J. and M. L. Miller. (1986). *Reliability and Validity in Qualitative Research*. Newbury Park, CA: Sage.

Leiss, W., S. Kline, and S. Jhally. (1990). *Social Communication in Advertising*. New York: Routledge.

Marshall, C. and G. B. Rossman. (1989). *Designing Qualitative Research*. Newbury Park, CA: Sage.

McCracken, G. (1988). *The Long Interview*. Newbury Park, CA: Sage.

O'Guinn, T.C. and R. J. (1989). "Compulsive Shopping: A Phenomenological Exploration." *Journal of Consumer Research*, 16 (2); pp. 147-157.

Schwartz, H. and J. Jacobs. (1979). *Qualitative Sociology: A Method to the Madness*. New York: Free Press.

Sherry, J.F. (1987). "Keeping the Monkeys Away from the Typewriters: An Anthropologist's View of the Consumer Odyssey." In *Advances in Consumer Research*, edited by M. Wallendorf and P. Anderson. Provo, UT: Association for Consumer Research.

Spradley, J.P. (1979). *The Ethnographic Interview*. New York: Holt, Rinehart & Winston.

Wallendorf, M. (1987). "On the Road again: the Nature of Qualitative Research on the Consumer Behavior Odyssey." In *Advances in Consumer Research*, edited by M.Wallendorf and P. Anderson. Provo, UT: Association for Consumer Research.

THANK THE EDITORS FOR THE BUY-OLOGICAL URGE!
AMERICAN MAGAZINES, ADVERTISING, AND THE PROMOTION OF THE CONSUMER CULTURE, 1920-1980.

Richard W. Pollay

ABSTRACT

Throughout the twentieth century America's largest-selling magazines have courted potential advertisers in the professional advertising media. These advertisements to advertisers were studied for information regarding the audiences reached by the magazines, the editorial and promotional tactics used, and evidence of credibility, influence, and impact upon their audiences. The study concludes that magazines worked hand in glove with the advertisers. Far from being reluctant partners to the purveyors of progress, the magazines were enthusiastic merchandisers of materialism and its manners.

Research in Marketing, Supplement 6, pages 221-235.
Copyright © 1994 by JAI Press Inc.
All rights of reproduction in any form reserved.
ISBN: 1-55938-187-6

I. INTRODUCTION

American magazines underwent a dramatic transformation during the late nineteenth century Progressive Era, as Wilson (1983) argues very convincingly. This is perhaps not surprising, as much of the social fabric was changing with the emergence of greater literacy, urbanization, advertising agencies, the craft of copywriting, and a host of new consumer goods. But the character of the magazine in the earlier Gilded Age as a literary communication from elites to other "gentle readers" seems quite removed, nay aloof, from the more pedestrian domestic and commercial functions adopted in the emergent consumer culture. The nature of the contrast is summarized in Table 1.

It is clear that at least some publishers and editors redirected their attention and intentions to the advertisers' interests at an early stage. For example, Curtis Publishing, later to become known for pioneering market research techniques, was promising its readers in 1886 that they could have confidence in its advertisers. Curtis refused ads from the more notorious of the patent medicine promoters to give this claim credibility. By the 1890s the Curtis publications, most notably the *Ladies' Home Journal*, were "stripping" the editorial matter, running the continuations of stories in single columns on back pages, thus forcing readers through the bulk of the advertising. During this decade they were also designing ads and selling them to manufacturers, predating the copywriting and art direction function to be exercised later by agencies. Wilson's study of four different kinds of magazines suggests that Curtis was not alone in seeing the merits of serving potential advertisers.

But it seems unlikely that the evolution of magazines was completed by 1920, even though by that time magazines were providing audited circulation data and other market research information to advertisers. They were also spending money on advertisements for themselves to potential advertisers within the pages of *Advertising Age, Advertising Agency, Advertising and Selling*, and *Printer' Ink*. This paper reports the results of a study of such advertisements in order to explore the evolution of the partnership between publishers and their advertisers since the Progressive Era.

The character of these advertisements as evidence deserves some comment. Clearly these documents, like all advertising, are subject to hyperbole and puffery. Grandiose claims on subjective matters made by these magazines must be taken with a grain of salt at the least. But more specific information can be accepted as credible. Audience statistics, information about merchandising programs, dealer support, new editorial formats, and so forth, must have been verifiable to satisfy the media buyers of both advertising agencies and clients. Data regarding audiences could have been validated with information from independent services like the Audit Bureau of Circulations.

The need for hard information to sell the expensive advertising space of the largest magazines was clearly felt early in the century. *American Weekly*, a

Table 1. The Transformation of American Magazines, 1880-1920

	Gilded Age	Progressive Era
Editors:	Elite, Ivy League	Immigrants, Midwesterners
Edirorial Policy:	Passive, Accepting	Aggressive, Soliciting
Content:	Liberal Arts	Domestic Arts
Style:	Literary	Colloquial
"Heroes":	Intellectual Leaders, Politicians	Celebrities, Producers, and Consumers
Audience:	Class Regional Elites "Gentle Readers"	"Mass" National Middle Class Consumers
Circulation:	Private, controlled Privileged	Public, open Exaggerated
Income Sources:	Subscriptions Modest	Advertising Generous

Source: Wilson (1983).

Sunday supplement magazine distributed to over five million families a week in the 1920s, asserted that it offered advertisers a "transcontinental steamroller that crushes market resistance." Nonetheless, its price of $15,000 per page required it to battle its way onto every media list for advertisers:

> It secures no contracts through 'fair haired' influence or kindly favor. $15,000 a page puts it out of the "let's-help-old-Bill's-boy" and "we-might-as-well-throw-a-little-business-to-Charlie's" class. The third assistant space buyer and the sales manager's stenographer can't influence its selection. It's a think-before-you-look rate, a stop-look-and-listen rate—a rate that provokes verification and invokes comparisons. Every order must submit to an inquisition of facts and figures; every contract first runs a gamut of quizzes and questions.[1]

II. PROGRAMS OF PARTNERSHIP

A. Serving Up Segments

Home and family service magazines dominated the industry for decades. Their focus on domestic affairs is exemplified by the best known of them: *Better Homes and Gardens, Good Housekeeping, Ladies' Home Journal, McCall's,* and *Woman's Home Companion.* These magazines touched upon all of the myriad aspects of everyday life. *Better Homes and Gardens,* in a contest challenging advertising and agency people to articulate the magazine's character, noted that it was a mass circulation magazine, but could also be perceived as a building, home furnishings, or food magazine. It could have also called attention to the editorial and advertising material providing instruction regarding fashion, parenting, marital relations, entertaining, holiday customs, and social climbing. Even the apparently obvious perception of the magazine as primarily a woman's magazine might be naive, for it claimed in the 1950s that nearly half of its readers were men, presumably husbands.[2]

Because they represent both purchasing power and potential style leaders, the affluent have always been a target for advertisers and thus magazines promised delivery of affluent audiences. *Cosmopolitan*, which during the 1920s was a fiction magazine with a million and a half circulation, ran campaigns in several trade journals then identifying itself as a "class" magazine. These ads presented an abundance of information as to the prosperity and property of its audience, and admitted that "*Cosmopolitan* has found it mighty profitable to cultivate these free spenders."[3]

The trend towards greater specificity of demographic information regarding magazine audiences is not the only way in which magazines meet the needs of marketers. Large magazines, meeting the competition of special interest magazines, worked increasingly to deliver specific audience segments to advertisers. *Look* pioneered the regional edition concept for these large magazines in 1959 and by 1963 offered 52 different geographic zones that could be purchased independently. These regional editions provided advertisers with even greater flexibility in planning local promotions, permitting sales campaigns in key-prospect areas, facilitating new product introductions with regional sequential roll-outs and product copy testing in locally confined zones. During this same decade, publishers organized their printing and distribution, with the assistance of computers, so that they could offer advertisers not only regions but particular groupings of customers. *Reader's Digest*, for example, offered a special educational edition that would reach 400,000 teenagers and 18,000 high-school faculty members.[4]

This development of special editions during the 1960s was by no means the first or an isolated instance of the magazines working hand in glove with advertisers to increase advertising effectiveness. Through a variety of programs, magazines have assembled and distributed data, created and placed point-of-purchase displays enlisting the cooperation of dealers and distributors, and generally assumed a significant responsibility for merchandizing efforts. The sale of their audiences to advertisers seems to have been far more than the delivery of an incidental by-product of their editorial efforts.

B. Market Research

Throughout the century, publishers have been providing advertisers with a wealth of information about their circulation and the marketplace in general. This effort was also pioneered by the Curtis Publishing Company, with its creation in 1914 of a statistical bureau for commercial research, an effort that helped father the modern field of market research. This department estimated market potentials for various regions in the country and informed advertisers of the characteristics of the two million weekly subscribers to *The Saturday Evening Post* and the 1.65 million *Ladies' Home Journal* subscribers. Many magazines followed suit. For example, *Cosmopolitan* offered to help advertisers reach the national consumer market adequately, systematically, and at a reasonable cost by their accumulated data on the "favored class" which "in social life, sets the standards of complete living," and from whom the advertiser could expect "intelligent reading."[5]

In the 1930s *True Story*, already acknowledged in advertising circles as a source of authentic economic information on working class wage earners, began to report some sociological data. Based upon a mail survey of their subscribers, they published the book "How to Get People Excited." It had already been requested by more than 2,500 advertising men while the campaign was still in effect.

The supplying by magazines of information for marketers probably pinnacled in the *Farm Journal's* 1944 publication of a 48 volume set of information on each and every one of the 3,072 counties in the United States. Published cooperatively with the U.S. Department of Commerce and using forms supplied by them, this compendium provided information not only on the population and its occupation, age, and ethnic background, but also detailed information on housing, manufacturing, agriculture, and wholesale and retail trade. Although magazines can today supply media buyers with data tapes dense with information, this publication presented an awesome amount of effort without the assistance of computers.[6]

Magazines also supplied manufacturers with other kinds of publications that condensed information about consumer interests or successful strategies. For example, in the 1950s *McCall's* organized at least two conventions which led to such publications. A "Soft Goods Supermarket Clinic" assembled manufacturers and advertising people and led to a digest available free for the asking to this professional audience. In another effort, 100 women selected for their demonstrated interest in remodeling and redecorating, their ability to communicate, and balanced by state and income characteristics to provide a good national cross-section, were assembled in Washington, D.C. for the first annual Congress on Better Living. Stenographers recorded the three-day event, including the roundtable discussions of these participants, and these transcripts together with completed questionnaires were analyzed and a final report made available to members of the home furnishings industry for guidance in manufacturing and marketing.[7]

C. Magazine Merchandising

Throughout the century, magazines have engaged in a diverse set of activities that seem quite tangential to their editorial mission, but highly relevant to their function as advertising vehicles, and indicative of their perception of being what *Colliers* once called "partners in progress" with marketers. Early in the century the Curtis Publishing Company, publishers of *Ladies' Home Journal* and *The Saturday Evening Post* among other titles, proudly proclaimed its censorship of advertisements. This practice, imitated by other magazines who could afford the luxury, involved primarily the rejection of ads by fly-by-night operators and other scoundrels, the rejection of ads for certain unappealing products, and the screening of ad copy for unfair tactics. With the elimination of ads for potato bug eradicators (a mail order con of rural subscribers at the turn of the century), chewing tobacco, and ads of notorious and outrageous exaggeration, the publisher strove to "protect each reader, thus securing his confidence...(and) protecting everybody against unfair tactics, knocking, untruth, or exaggeration."[8] This strategy permitted magazines to offer advertisers not only a placement where they would be freer from competition, but also a magazine that would have the increased goodwill and trust of its readership.

Occasionally, extraordinary efforts were expended toward establishing credibility. For example, *McCall's* initiated a laundry project in 1934 that involved, in 14 months of study by over 5,000 workers, researching the kinds of soap, equipment and problems of shrinking, ironing, fading, wrinkling, bleaching, and drying of laundry materials. All of this effort was to make *McCall's* a homemaking authority by providing housewives with a volume of information far in excess of what they could acquire in a lifetime of trial and error. During the same time *McCall's* was attempting to establish itself as a style authority with a traveling theater. This truck-trailer traveled from department store to department store across the country, showing a 40-minute film and providing an environment to host prospective subscribers. This, the magazine felt, was a "fresh, original approach to the selling of style and circulation, a better way to merchandise a great magazine to readers and retailers throughout the country." This reach for the credibility of excellence and authority is most recently manifested by the 1970s sponsorship by the *Ladies' Home Journal* of Teacher of the Year awards given at the White House, a Women's Superstar Sports Championships on television, and a nationally televised honoring of eight "Women of the Year."[9]

In the 1950s magazine publishers initiated much merchandising activity, largely through provision of point-of-purchase advertising materials supplied to cooperating dealers. One of the best known of these efforts was the "As advertised in *Life*" campaign. For example in 1951, 933 drug stores ran storewide promotions of this type, and advertisers bought nearly two million pieces of point-of-purchase material for use in other drug stores. At the same time, the promotion department of *Woman's Home Companion* offered food marketers a merchandising kit that would provide dealers with four different display cards suggesting complete meals, "take-one" recipe booklets, shopping lists to complete the recipes and shelf markers to call consumers' attention to specific ingredients throughout the store. In 1957, *The Saturday Evening Post* ran a food store spectacular for 35 participating products. This effort involved distribution of 115,000 display kits to 68,000 members of the National Association of Retail Grocers, 1,500,000 newspaper lines and 500 million radio and television impressions in an all-out tie-in advertising campaign that produced a reported $50 million increase in store sales.[10]

By the 1970s consumer magazines had executives with focused responsibility for this type of marketing and merchandising. The drug and toiletries manager of *Women's Day* magazine created a "spring bouquet of beauty promotion" in 1975 that attracted 3,221 stores and 51 drug store chains. These participating dealers received point-of-sale materials, display idea sheets, and ad mats to aid in advertising the products in local newspapers. Also offered were similar promotions run cooperatively with other associations such as an annual "Dream Kitchen Contest" with the American institute of Kitchen Dealers and the National Appliance Dealers Association.[11]

Not to be outdone, *Family Circle* offered a "Good Looks/Good Health Ideas" program annually. It promised not only its audience of over 17 million women who shop in supermarkets for health and beauty aids, but a special editorial and advertising section and editorial support consisting of in-depth articles on health, beauty, and grooming. The magazine also provided personalized shelf-talkers, displays, and posters for some 8,000 supermarkets, all at no extra cost to the advertiser. In addition, advertisers would be featured in *Advanced News,* a *Family Circle* merchandising paper circulated to 2,200 store managers, chain executives, and toiletries merchandisers.[12]

Perhaps the most famous of all of the efforts of magazines to assist advertisers in their merchandising is the series of public labels provided by *Good Housekeeping.* Starting in the early 1920s, the magazine created a testing laboratory, apparently unbiased, scientific, and practical. After being tested with varying degrees of thoroughness, products could acquire the now-obscure Bureau or Institute seals, or the more well-known and persistent "Guaranteed as Advertised" emblem. This guarantee offered replacement or refund of money for products that were defective or not as advertised. Since the cost of most consumer goods is modest, this guarantee could be offered with little worry of financial consequences; little testing was required. Advertisers adhering to a minimum of honesty, willing to provide replacements or underwrite refunds and, of course, willing to advertise in *Good Housekeeping,* could easily obtain this endorsement. Thus, this guarantee was simultaneously insubstantial and meaningful: insubstantial in monetary terms, but meaningful in its reassurance to consumers. The endorsement by the magazine, lending its own credibility to that of the manufacturer, produced a totally unambiguous identification of certain products, and their attendant consumer behaviors, as elements of "good housekeeping."

In the late 1930s, when all three public labels were still in use, *Good Housekeeping* asserted that "they are American 'buy-words'—signposts that guide millions of women to satisfying purchases."[13]

III. ASSESSING MAGAZINE MARKETING

This sampling of merchandising programs, coupled with the obvious solicitation of advertisers to their pages, amply demonstrates that the editors were far from reluctant sharers of space with the advertising community. This is perhaps not surprising when we recognize that advertising revenue typically makes up the vast majority of the total revenue for the magazine enterprise. It does suggest, however, that magazines must be viewed as propagandists with a purpose more pedestrian than might otherwise seem. It is simplistic and naive to view magazines as merely a commercial literary form, supplying editorial content as its product to attract readers, the apparent consumers. Such a view sees advertising as simply a by-product endured out of economic necessity to subsidize the editorial intention, however noble or humble.

It seems much more appropriate to recognize magazine publishing as a business that delivers the audience as its product to advertisers as its consumers. The editorial process is merely the mechanism by which the product, the audience, is produced. The essential editorial objective is the capturing of a particular audience, ideally one that is large, affluent, and which shares a common interest as consumers. Subscription revenue is almost incidental income. The point of much magazine subscription pricing is to "qualify" readers as genuine and seriously interested so that they can be more convincingly sold to potential advertisers. Even that necessity is now disappearing, as more and more magazines are given away through controlled distribution methods that also qualify the readership.

A. The Power of Print

If market influence in congruence with its advertisers is the magazine's function in the twentieth century, we need to ask about its prospects for effectiveness. What are the characteristics of this media that might make it effective in today's noisy communication environment or in yesterday's less electrified one? According to an ad which *Good Housekeeping* ran in a trade publication some years ago:

> Magazines are surely the most selective focussing instruments in the whole world of communications. They select definite areas of concern and interest. Therefore, they select audiences... Magazines reach particular levels of education, lifestyle, and responsiveness. They reach eyes that are searching out their content—inquisitively. Contemplative minds, motivated enough to purchase the medium. They present ideas that can be discussed, passed

along. Reviewed and re-reviewed. At leisure. At the pace of comprehension. At the depth of curiosity's demand.[14]

A year later (1981) *Good Housekeeping*, in a widely reprinted campaign, offered these thoughts about a magazine's tremendous audience of one:

> The act of reading is essentially a process of thinking... It is a concentratively individual act. An involvement. The reader makes the printed communication happen... releases the magic that causes words on a page to leap into living thoughts, ideas, emotions... It is addressed to and received by individuals, one at a time—each in the splendid solitude of his or her own mind. There, the silent language of print can whisper, rage, implore, accuse, burst into song, explode into revelation, stab the conscience, or work—a healing faith.[15]

With the technical capacity for high resolution color photography and other items of graphic excellence, and with the freedom to make the verbal message as brief or as long as felt appropriate, the magazine has often been a favorite medium for copywriters. As expressed by the senior vice president and executive creative director of N.W. Ayer:

> A magazine gives you the freedom to tell your story the way it needs to be told. With one picture or with a thousand words. You can startle without the fear of being too loud. You can educate without having to speak at high speed. You can whisper without the fear of not being heard. Because the only limit is your taste, your insight, your imagination.[16]

Small wonder, then, that magazine advertising has continued to grow over time, and grow on a per capita basis, even if not as a percentage of total advertising, despite the additions of new electronic media. Clearly, radio and television did earn audiences and advertising revenue of their own, but competing against radio was relatively easy. For example, of the 128 minor features one maker felt might potentially determine the selection decision of an automobile, only one of those is best presented by radio—the tone of the horn. Television networks attracted a mass market and as a result caused the most grief to these magazines with a lack of demographic focus. Magazines serving special interests have continued to flourish and proliferate in the 1970s. While television tempted a viewing audience heavy in high-school dropouts, magazines sold to the better educated, the higher incomed, and the more influential.

Audiences of this character were of course of great interest to advertisers. In 1925 *Good Housekeeping* sold nearly 1,700 pages to 723 different advertisers, 286 of which used *Good Housekeeping* exclusively. By 1923 the readers of *McCall's* alone would buy 300,000 new automobiles, and spend over $1 million per week on sugar. Over 20 million meals a day were served on "*McCall's* Street" that year. By 1955 *Life* was able to deliver a total audience of 26,450,000 peoples from a circulation of slightly over 5.6 million copies. This attracted 4,398 pages of advertising at a cost to advertisers of over $121 million dollars. That year the ten largest national magazines sold a total of over 22,000 pages to advertisers for an average of almost $18,000 a page and a total revenue of approximately $390 million. With *Reader's Digest* beginning to accept advertising space that year, it quickly took over as the largest circulation advertising medium. By 1963 it had a circulation of over 13,750,000 copies per issue and each advertising page was looked at more than 60 million times, according to Politz, reaching one out of every four families in America. The 1964 Politz magazine study showed that *McCall's, Good Housekeeping,* and *Ladies' Home Journal* reached a collective audience of over 48 million women and teenagers.

In 1963 a campaign by General Electric using only 4 Curtis magazines with *The Saturday Evening Post* as the "spearhead," produced over 475 million actual ads in print, and more than 1,350,000,000 adult impressions on an audience that included over 63 percent of all college educated breadwinners.[17]

The backbone of this advertising has been the persistent and patient presence of America's blue chip companies. In 1946, *The Saturday Evening Post* was able to list 349 such companies who had advertised consistently along the "Post Road" from 10 to 47 years. The success of the firms listed in Table 2 suggests the rewards accruing to those with the greatest persistence. These advertisers are in these pages only because it works, or as the *Post* says, "It gets to the heart of America."[18]

B.   Involvement and Impact

Even given the persuasive intent of editors and advertisers, and the mass market that they reach, the magazines might be poorly read or disbelieved, although this would be strange for both loyal subscribers and those buying single issues. The primary evidence that the audience has been involved is, of course, the sales success of the advertisers. American Motors, for example, testified to the *Readers' Digest* delivery of over a half a million prospects to their showrooms in 1964. Publishers also noted the extent to which their articles were reprinted, quoted, discussed, preached in pulpits, and even occasionally written into the *Congressional Record*. The world's largest investment house, Merrill Lynch, was "struck by an unexpected avalanche of letters, wires, and phone calls from bank presidents, corporation executives, educators, and thousands of others," as a consequence of a two-part article in *The Saturday Evening Post*. The normally sagacious firm was amazed at the response for they had "no idea the *Post* was so widely read and so well respected."[19]

Cards and letters from readers have long been used by magazine editors as evidence of the responsiveness and involvement of their readers. Without any

Table 2. Great American Business
Leaders Who Have Consistently Used
The *Saturday Evening Post* (1946)

Firm	Years Used by 1946
Eastman Kodak	47
The Mennen Company	46
Parker Pen Company	46
Pro-phy-lac-tic Brush Company	46
Remington Rand	46
Colgate-Palmolive-Peet	45
North Brothers Manufacturing Co.	45
Florsheim Shoe Company	44
General Mills	44
Goodyear Tire & Rubber Company	44
Procter & Gamble	44
RCA (Radio Corporation of America)	44
American Safety Razor Company	43
Cadillac Motor Car Division, GM	43
General Foods Corporation	43
Nash-Kelvinator Corporation	43
Oldsmobile Division, GM	43
Packard Motor Car Co.	43
Quaker Oats Company	43
Elgin National Watch Company	42
B.F. Goodrich Company	42
Prudential Insurance Company	42
Socony-Vacuum Oil Company	42
United States Playing Card Company	42
Cluett, Peabody & Company	41
Swift & Company	41
Bristol-Meyers Company	40

Source: The *Saturday Evening Post* advertisement in *Printer's Ink,* 3/
1/46.

advertising inducement at all, *Women's Day* readers wrote more than 600,000 letters to the editorial offices in 1947. At the same time, women were sending in nickels and dimes for 283,000 pamphlets and leaflets from the *Woman's Home Companion.* The *Companion's* packaged program of materials for women's clubs was subscribed to by 1,288 such clubs. A series of public service articles over a two year period attracted some 795,000 reprint requests. More recently *Family Circle*, with an average audience of over 13 million readers per issue, received over 2 million letters in 1972. A notice of less than two inches of space in the March 1973 issue of *Family Circle* led to 500,000 requests to the American Petroleum Institute for their booklet on efficient energy use. Two years later, an article on free samples and booklets led to almost 2 million mailed responses.[20]

IV. THE HISTORICAL EVOLUTION

In order to clearly see the maturation process of magazines and their increasing participation in the propaganda for products, we can recapitulate and, while so doing, let the editors speak for themselves. In the early part of the century, the essential problem for publishers was the establishment of credibility of their advertisers, that they attempted by means of a selectivity which at least pruned out the most obvious rascals and scoundrels. In addition, these editors explicitly instructed their readership to trust and heed the advertisers. As the editors of *Home Life* boasted, "Our readers have been educated to ask for advertised articles and to believe in the responsibility of our advertisers!"[21]

The publishers soon realized that they were, at least in some cases, selling both the homes of today and tomorrow. In 1926, for example, *Better Homes and Gardens* noted that their teen audience was already deciding how to build, landscape, and furnish their future homes, and the editors volunteered to "make a place in those homes for your products." This was accomplished in part by establishing research organizations or other feedback mechanisms that would permit the publisher to more precisely understand the consuming public. The editors then adapted and coordinated the editorial and advertising materials to channel this interest. "Never were editorial pages so closely allied with industry in feeding women's material wants," proclaimed a 1937 ad for the *Woman's Home Companion*. Supportive copy for this statement included the following:

> Sixteen hundred enthusiastic "reader-editors" are helping us determine the *Companion's* editorial contents and service...Sixteen hundred typical homemakers in as many American communities—telling us what foods they eat, what shoes and corsets they wear, what home equipment they own, or want to own...exchanging experience for advice.

Never has a magazine discussed feminine interests so intimately over the national back fence. This type of information was then utilized to offer manufacturers a:

> Line of least resistance—an equipment article clears the way for an improved refrigerator...a fashion page breaks down opposition to a current style...a single recipe opens up the field for a new food—a brand selling makes gain on gain! Such things are accomplished by women's magazines all the time.[22]

With World War II involving so many men on battle fronts, women's roles as the planner, purchaser, and manager of the purse strings increased substantially. So too did the importance of women's magazines. Testimonials to *Better Homes and Gardens* from readers thanked them for the many ways in which the magazine helped them anticipate the changes that wartime living made necessary. This training apparently made even traditional husbands confident that they were:

Leaving the purse strings in able hands. They know that years of training have prepared the American woman for the biggest, toughest buying job of this, or any other generation. She is aware that the jungle is getting thicker, and that she needs more help. But she is also assured that such advice and guidance will be forthcoming from her women's service magazines.

With the extra demands of war work, with growing shortages of help and equipment, homemaking must be carefully studied, planned and simplified. Fortunately for your hurried, harried wife, women's service magazines like the *Companion* shortcut her tasks, organize her day, give her the very homemaking information she needs.[23]

As the end of the war approached, magazines and advertisers joined in the general concern of how to realign the economy to peacetime without reversion to the Depression experience. The specific mission of advertisers, expressed with fighting fervor by the editors of *True Story*, was to make customers, for customers make jobs for servicemen:

This is no community chest, give-the-boys-a-break proposition. It is a serious problem of survival. Ten million servicemen must be absorbed back into industry. The specific job of your advertising is to so burn your brand name into their minds and hearts so that after the war they will buy new jobs into being.[24]

By the early 1950s, this process was so complete it could be taken for granted. It seemed to be so much a part of human nature that magazines vied to claim credit for having created this "Buy-ological urge." The millions of entranced consumers were an answer to an advertiser's dream:

They immediately slip into the kind of buying mood that advertisers dream about. This buying mood is created by the very nature of *Better Homes and Gardens*. Every page of every issue features practical suggestions on how readers can make their homes and their lives better and more enjoyable.[25]

V. CONCLUSION

Magazines have enthusiastically joined the persuasion effort of advertisers. They have instructed readers to believe and heed advertisers, given their own endorsements, engineered editorial material to increase advertising effectiveness, and designed and executed supplemental merchandising programs of substantial magnitude. This needs, however, to be interpreted carefully. It is not accurate to take these magazines to task for having betrayed the trust given them by their enormous audiences. The interesting fact is not that the largest selling magazines turned mercenary, but that the magazines most replete with propaganda on behalf of materialism and its manners were the largest sellers. Thus it is more accurate to perceive the magazines, however mercenary their motivation, as meeting some interest of the public. There was truth to such famous magazine claims as these:

- To put it simply, people have faith in the [*Reader's*] *Digest*...[and] this faith...over and over again leads people to action.
- Never underestimate the power of a woman! Nor the power of a magazine women believe in!

It remains for us now to identify those values that have been reinforced by the magazine advertising discussed here. Clearly advertising presents persuasive images that define "good housekeeping" and "the good life." To the extent they are successful, we are seduced and emulate this ideal. But the question of whether business, through its persuasion apparatus of advertising, is leading Americans down the primrose path, is behind us. Pushing it is a moot point. More serious than this question of causality is the question of quo vadis—where are we heading? What are the values most prevalent in the purposefully persuasive portion of our communication—our commercial culture's propaganda to itself.

There is nothing so powerful as an idea, especially if persuasively presented to a wide audience. Magazine advertising does this and "the right idea can change the everyday living habits of millions of families. And that's the kind of ideas *Better Homes and Gardens* (and similar magazines) specializes in."[26]

Given the potential social impact of these ideas, which touch all aspects of home and family life, it behooves us to ask what social behaviors and roles are displayed and what norms and values are characteristic of magazine advertising.

NOTES

These notes specify the locations of the advertisements discussed, identifying the trade journals, dates, and pages of their publication, with the magazine-advertiser shown parenthetically. No authors or titles appear because these are ads, not conventional articles. The trade journals are fully identified when first noted, with abbreviations used thereafter: *Advertising Age* [*AA*]; *Advertising and Selling* [*A&S*]; and *Printers' Ink* [*PI*].

1. *Printer's Ink* [*PI*]. 10/13/27, pp. 102-103. (*American Weekly*).

2. *PI*. 3/23/56, pp. 54-55. (*Better Homes and Gardens*).

3. *Advertising & Selling* [*A&S*], 10/21/25, p. 18. (*Cosmopolitan*).

4. *PI*, 1/4/63, pp. 34-35 (*Look*); *PI*, 7/8/66, p. 5 (*Reader's Digest*).

5. *PI*, 2/26/14 (Curtis); *PI*, 1/25/23; 10/13/27 (*Cosmopolitan*).

6. *AA*, 11/15/42, p.. 7; 11/22/37, p. 43 (*True Story*); *AA*, 11/4/46, pp. 30-31 *The Farm Journal*).

7. *PI*, 2/5/54 (*McCall's*).

8. *PI*, 2/26/14 (Curtis, *The Saturday Evening Post*).

9. *AA*, 6/16/34, p. 25 (*McCall's*); *AA*, 4/21/75, p. 30 (*Ladies' Home Journal*).

10. *PI*, 2/20/53, p. 32 (*Life*); *PI*, 1/9/53 (*Woman's Home Companion*); *PI Monthly*, 11/57 (*The Saturday Evening Post*).

11. *AA*, 4/21/75, p. 51 (*Woman's Day*).

12. *AA*, 5/12/75, p. 11 (*Family Circle*).

13. *AA*, 11/29/37, p. 8 (*Good Housekeeping*); *PI*, 3/19/43, pp. 12-13 (*Good Housekeeping*).

14. *AA*, 5/26/80 (*Good Housekeeping*).

15. *AA*, 10/19/81, p. S13 (*Good Housekeeping*).

16. *AA*, 10/26/81 (Magazine Publisher's Association).

17. *A&S*, 4/21/26, p. 65 (*Good Housekeeping*); *PI* 1/25/23, pp. 162-163 (*McCall's*); *AA*, 2/20/56, p. 79 (*Life*); *AA*, 3/63; 1/65 (*McCall's*); *PI*, 3/1/63, pp. 2-3 (Curtis-GE).

18. *PI*, 3/1/46 (*The Saturday Evening Post*).

19. *PI*, 10/2/64, pp. 2-3 (*Reader's Digest*); *A&S*, 8/48, p. 9 (*The Saturday Evening Post*).

20. *PI*, 10/17/47, p. 86 (*Woman's Day*); *A&S*, 7/48;   10/48-12/48 (*Woman's Home Companion*); *AA*, 3/26/73, p. 3; 5/19/75, p. 13; 6/16/75, p. 13 (*Family Circle*).

21. *PI*, 11/22/14 (*Home Life*).

22. *A&S*, 5/26/26, P. 57 (*Better Homes and Gardens*); *PI*, 11/18/37, pp. 58-59 (*Woman's Home Companion*); *PI*, 10/21/37, pp. 58-59 (*Woman's Home Companion*).

23. *PI*, 3/19/43, p. 39 (*Woman's Home Companion*); *AA*, 9/27/43, pp. 14-15; 1/29/43, p. 32 (*Woman's Home Companion*).

24. *AA*, 12/6/43, p. 3 (*True Story*).

25. *PI*, 1/4/46, p. 15 (*Better Homes and Gardens*); *PI*, 3/1/46, p. 17 (*Better Homes and Gardens*).

26. *Advertising Agency*, 6/53, p. 47 (*Better Homes and Gardens*).

REFERENCE

Wilson, C. P. (1983). "The Rhetoric of Consumption. In *The Culture of Consumption*, edited by Richard W. Fox and T. J. Lears. New York: Pantheon.

MARKETING ACTION AND THE TRANSFORMATION OF WESTERN CONSCIOUSNESS:
THE EXAMPLES OF PULP LITERATURE AND DEPARTMENT STORES

Ronald A. Fullerton

ABSTRACT

Marketing's role in nearly every aspect of Western life has made the issue of its social and psychological impact an important one. This paper considers marketing's impact upon consciousness—upon people's visions of the world. Consciousness reflects aspirations and expectations. Two historical case examples are developed to show how marketing's expansion into new areas of Western life transformed the consciousness of millions. The implications of the transformation on personal autonomy are discussed.

Research in Marketing, Supplement 6, pages 237-254.
ISBN: 1-55938-187-6

I. INTRODUCTION[1]

In today's Western Europe and North America, marketing suffuses nearly every aspect of life. It does so with such thoroughness, we are scarcely aware that conditions could be any different, or ever were any different. We take for granted that almost every waking activity—religious, cultural, and leisure activities included—is carried out as a marketing exchange transaction. We take for granted, in other words, the thoroughgoing commercialization of life and leisure, of sacred as well as secular phenomena.

It was not always so. While some marketing activity in the generic sense, such as voluntary exchanges of things of value, can be detected in past societies going back into prehistory (Pryor 1977), it has been only during the past two centuries, and only in the most developed countries, that marketing action has attained such a powerful and *pervasive* position in everyday life. By "marketing action" I mean the totality of marketing-related efforts, at any given point in time and cumulatively. Individual marketing efforts may fail to meet their goals—may fail to have any impact—but in a high-level economy the *totality* of marketing activity has an enormous influence. The demise of the Edsel did not end Americans' passion for automobiles that aspire to meet far more than functional needs.

Despite more than a decade of renewed interest in macromarketing scholarship, however, marketers have been slow to consider the total and cumulative impact of marketing actions. An important article by Pollay (1986) has shown that this issue has been a major locus of critical portrayals of marketing by scholars in some other disciplines. The issue cannot be dispelled by marketers prating about consumer sovereignty and "proving" it with examples like the Edsel or Real cigarettes. Consumer sovereignty is far less efficacious than typically assumed: the concept comes from classical British economics, which has little concern with observed and actual phenomena. The Austrian advertising pioneer Mataja (1910, pp. 77-81, 325-330) showed decades ago that marketing efforts could easily overcome consumer sovereignty in some cases, for example those relating to health needs. Moreover, even marketing efforts that have made no effort to overmaster consumers' sovereignty could end up doing exactly that. The impact(s) of marketing actions need not be intentional; outcomes may go far beyond expectations, a point which Pollay (1986) has made very clear.

My concern in this paper is with the impact of marketing action upon Western consciousness: upon the images and concepts that fill our minds, forming our notions of what is real, what is possible, what is desirable—and what is not any or all of those. Our consciousness is our picture of the world and our place within it. While there are disagreements about the role of consciousness in determining conduct, all but the most dogmatic Freudians would grant it an important part. The concept of consciousness has been basic to European social science theory, for example that emanating from the Frankfurt School (see Poster 1987).

Such theory posits a close relationship between consciousness and individual autonomy: if the individual is able to generate some of the contents of consciousness, and critically evaluate the rest, thus distinguishing between reality and fantasy, then he retains control over choice—he is autonomous. But if his consciousness is dominated and manipulated by others, then autonomy can be lost. To many critical social theorists throughout the twentieth century, the totality of modern marketing effort has seized control of Westerners' consciousness, thereby threatening and even destroying the autonomy that underlies rationality and free choice (see Sombart 1908 and the discussions in Pollay 1986 and Poster 1987). Are such theorists correct? What has been the impact of aggressive and pervasive marketing action upon Western consciousness?

These questions necessitate a historical approach. Only by considering situations and phenomena before marketing action had a major role, then assessing the changes that were brought about by the advent of modern marketing, can we accurately assess the impact of marketing action upon Western consciousness. The "before" phenomena may be seen as the "control" group, the "after" as the "experimental" one.

The remainder of this paper develops two historical case examples of how the expansion of marketing action came to shape the consciousness of millions of Western Europeans and Americans from about 1850 through 1914. Each case will explore the relationship between shaping consciousness and controlling autonomy; each goes beyond the unitary focus upon advertising which characterizes most prior discussion.

II. PULP FICTION AND THE COMMERCIALIZATION OF CONSCIOUSNESS

The self-sufficiency that characterized the daily life of the majority of Western Europeans until well into the nineteenth century extended to popular culture. The people themselves generated and transmitted the stories, proverbs, and didactic matter with which they entertained, edified, and instructed one another. Since few could read, and fewer afford much printed matter, popular culture was largely oral, just as it had been since before the time of Homer. The best known example of the oral culture is the collection of "fairy tales" collected by the Brothers Grimm from an illiterate peasant woman in rural Germany in the early 1800s. But there were many other manifestations of this culture. Some decades after the Grimms, for example, Baader (1973 [1851]) gathered tales from other areas of Germany. The present-day historian Eugen Weber (1979) describes the oral culture of the French *veillees,* traditional and informal gatherings of rural Frenchmen:

> The talk was full of allusions to the past: to the time of the lords, of the Revolution, of the wolves and how they disappeared. The oral culture perpetuated itself by the tales told, the pious legends, the teachings about the supernatural realm, the explanations of nature and of life, the precepts that applied to every sort of situation and were contained in the formulas, songs, and proverbs repeated over and over again (p. 414).

The oral culture was full of past historical experience "translated into fables and fairy tales" (Weber 1979, p. 425), and of proverbs that "reveal traditional experience, define the rules and structure that society set for individuals, fashion their mentalities...help them construct their identities...and sketch out a world view" (Weber 1979, p. 421). Folk proverbs tended to reflect conditions in individual areas and times—many were generated by the people of these areas and times, and modified to reflect new conditions as they were transmitted over time. The same is true of the "fairy tales." Even those tales and proverbs that could be found across different regions, cultures, and times, were modified to fit local and temporal circumstances.

The oral culture was a fluid one, responsive to specific environments. Its vibrancy in rural Europe until well into the nineteenth century assured that consciousness was to a large extent generated by the rural masses themselves, and that it reflected the realities of their lives. The only pervasive images in consciousness that derived from without were those traditionally associated with Christianity and spread by the Christian clergy.

By the second half of the nineteenth century, however, and even earlier in Britain, the environment that had nourished the oral culture was dissipating. The growth of public and private education had spread a rudimentary but real literacy among much of the population, more and more of which was migrating to urban areas. In 1870, half the population of Britain, over a third of Germany's and nearly a third of France's, lived in urban areas; by 1910 nearly two-thirds of all Germans lived in urban settings. Official literacy figures exaggerated but it has been estimated that about 70 percent of Germany's people were able to read simple stories in 1870 (Fullerton 1979). Schooling and, even more, the migration from the countryside weakened the complex and ordered traditional networks of social, behavioral, and cultural patterns and expectations. The newly-urbanized masses were culturally adrift, open to new experiences. They were a latent market for something new. But what?

Simple, thrilling, and inexpensive printed fiction, decided a growing number of entrepreneurs. Most of these entrepreneurs were new entrants to the publishing business, whose traditional pretensions and inhibitions against cultivating the lower social classes they did not share. They realized that advances in papermaking (e.g., wood pulp-based paper) and in press technology had made it cheap to print reading matter in quantity, and that an oversupply of academic graduates with romantic notions about being authors had made it easy and inexpensive to obtain the hack writers with which to mass-produce such reading matter. Viewing reading matter not as a cultural vehicle but rather as a saleable product, such publisher-entrepreneurs probed the market vigorously, experimenting with different physical formats, with different types of stories, and with promotion and distribution techniques. The most successful formats were derived from some which had long been used in the middle- and upper-class markets all over Western Europe—broadsheets, pamphlets of 32 to 64 pages, and installment novels (see Altick 1957; Engelsing 1969; Febvre and Martin 1976; Schenda 1968, 1970; Vicinus 1974; Ward 1974).

The development and impact of pulp literature upon consciousness was a transnational phenomenon, essentially similar across the developed countries of Western Europe and North America. It will be illustrated here with the example of Germany.

In Germany, the initial onslaught upon the urban mass market began in the late 1860s with installment novels [*Colporteurromane*] whose breathlessly convoluted plots twisted on through 50, 100, 150, up to 250, installments. Each installment had 8 to 12 pages and retailed for ten Pfennig (Fullerton 1977). Their plots were initially taken from novels popular with middle- and upper-class readers decades before, and recast in simpler and more violent prose.

The publishers were active in all aspects of the development of these books. In fact, their roles were considerably more important than of those who actually wrote the material. Publishers strove for a product that would appeal to the newly urbanized masses. Partly by experimentation, partly by intuition grounded in ancient stereotypes about the common people, the publishers came to decide that an alluring product would be characterized by simple diction, blunt narrative, concrete images, and exciting effects. As a contemporary journalist reported:

> No story [in a "colporteur novel"] can be without ghosts and magic, murder and manslaughter, for the masses have a burning craving for simple facts, [for] compact and unadorned incident, for an uninterrupted and relentless pace, for a riot of ever-new twists and turns of plot, the wilder and more improbable the better. They don't want to be given the opportunity to linger and to reflect, but rather want to be perpetually surprised and dazzled, to be dragged through a labyrinth of incident, and to be shocked and stunned by ceaseless, explosive, and unexpected swerves in the plot (Glagau 1870).

A book trade handbook of the time cautioned against letting any scene in a "colporteur novel" run on too long: if "in the 60th installment the sweet, innocent Wanda is still languishing in the dungeon of the repulsive, lecherous Count Kuno von Rechenfels," impatient readers would surely cancel their subscriptions (Streissler 1887).

To insure that their "colporteur novels" met the requisite standards, publishers kept tight control over the authors whom they commissioned to write the books. One publisher complained to a writer he had under contract:

We're now up to your fourth installment...and it's still too insipid, it doesn't grip and
terrify [the reader]. How much longer can this go on? When at last is there going to be
a murder or spicy scene to make the story exciting? We're almost to the point where we
regret having placed our trust in you. Your broad, cozy description of family life doesn't
appeal to the tastes of our readers at all...The end of the seventh installment must have
a detailed, exact description of a murder or other gruesome act, which will be further
developed in the eighth installment and concluded in the ninth (quoted in Kellen 1889,
p.86).

Often publishers worked out plot outlines themselves, then hired hacks to fill
in the details.

The installments of "colporteur novels" were sold from door to door—
bookstores intimidated lower-class Germans—with premiums freely promised
(if often not delivered). As the lure of the older plots began to fade after a
few years, publishers ordered their writers to come up with tales about
contemporary murders (especially of women and children), atrocities, and royal
scandals (Spain's grossly obese and lascivious Queen Isabella was much-
novelized). The most popular of these efforts, a purportedly biographical novel
about a Berlin executioner, raced readers through disreputable taverns, a
madam's house, a counterfeiter's workshop, an insane asylum, nobles' palaces,
and other exotic locales. Thrill followed thrill, breathlessly if illogically: an orgy
among bandits, a patricide, the hanging of an innocent maiden and hypnotism
of another, an attempted poisoning and a successful grave robbery, a train
crash, a divorce, a trapeze artist's fall, the burial of a living person, and the
kidnapping and preparation for murder of an innocent child. What vicarious
excitement for readers! Such powerful action, conveyed with vigor and
conviction, contrasted strongly with the monochrome life experiences of most
of the readers of installment novels. It was so powerful that it began to drive
out oral story telling.

Even when the installments themselves were insipid and repetitive, or the plots
dissolved into idiotic chaos after several installments—both of which happened
frequently—promotions for new novels disgorged the promise of future thrills
without end. The first five to seven installments served as promotional lures;
they were distributed gratis to stimulate interest. The initial installments, for
which press runs of one to one and a half million copies were common, previewed
the entire (and as yet unwritten!) novel, employing pyrotechnic phrases that had
been found to arouse purchase urges among the unsophisticated target buyers:
"cup of poison, deadly sins, sacrilege...night of madness, gruesome grave,
bloody ghost, frightful skeleton, devil in human form, and bandits' grotto"
(Glagau 1870). Women responded to such lush images as "forest stillness,
tumultuous ocean, fragrant groves of lemon trees...angel of peace, voluptuous
beauty, and enchanting charm" (Glagau 1870).

Here from 1870 is an example of how such phrases could be strung together
into a first installment sales pitch:

Come out of the sweet solitude of the forest's stillness, dear sweet reader (*Leserin*), come to the shore of the tumultuous ocean, open your ears to the powerful roar of the storm-driven wild waves, and it will seem to you, even if you are from a small village, as if you are making your first entry into the noisy, bustling lively streets of a great city. Come now, take my hand, be guided by my experienced and sure hand into these streets by opening the pages of the first installment of a surging work, a work awaited with great expectation in all the lands where the German tongue resounds—*The Secrets of a Great City or, Sinners and Penitents*. It will reveal to you everything which your curiosity and your desires make you want to know: The Seven Deadly Sins of Devils in Human Form; The Hero; The Passions and Miseries in the Cottages of the Poor, in the Bandits' Grotto, in the Palaces of the Mighty (quoted in Glagau 1870).

The following several installments would heat the plot to a fever pitch, and then orders for the entire work would be solicited. While relatively few subscribers would stay with a "colporteur novel" until its end, the total number of installments distributed approached three billion during the heyday decade of the 1870s (Fullerton 1977). "In the cottages of the poor, in the dwellings of the working class, among the families of petty artisan—everywhere we find the colored installments," wrote a contemporary journalist (Kellen 1889, p. 83). By 1880 the compelling and overripe images carried by this tidal wave of printed excitement had surged into the consciousness of millions of Germans, shaping their world views.

Though the popularity of the installment books began to wane after 1880, the pulp onslaught on German mass consciousness continued, indeed intensified, as publishers discovered the appeal of series of individual pamphlet stories (Fullerton 1979). Like the installment books, these were written by hack writers to strict publisher specifications which included detailed plot outlines and titles. Like the installment novels, the pamphlets' titles were of the old-fashioned double style that appealed to poorly educated readers then. Double title, double thrills, as can be seen in these translated specimens:

- "The Battle to the Death at White Wood or, Red Skin and Love. An Indian Story."
- "The Eskimo Maiden or, The Journey to the Ivory Mine at the North Pole. A Northern Adventure."

Again like the installment novels, the subject matter of the pamphlet series consisted of murder, mush, and mayhem, offered up with light didactic passages purporting to inform readers about the inner secrets of political systems, the sadness of the rich, and life in exotic locales. In addition, however, the pamphlets done after the mid-1880s had the enhanced appeal of multicolor cover illustrations, which advances in color lithography had made inexpensive to print. Mass market publishers believed that at the point of purchase their customers paid more attention to the cover picture and title than to the text within. Printed in saturated colors no human eye could ignore, each cover displayed an exciting scene, implying that it came from the story within. There could be an ambush, an abduction, a murder, a heart-throbbing embrace, or some incredible combination of several of these. Like the stories themselves, the covers often had more action than sense, and may have sold the more because of it. Marketability was the only concern of their publisher-creators.

Publishers experimented continually to determine the most saleable settings and character stereotypes for their series. Their quest led them to translate and imitate American "dime novels" and British "penny novelettes." They had quickly discovered that traditional German stories and settings, the heart of the old oral culture, had less appeal than did exotic foreign ones. During the 1880s and 1890s, 42 percent of the titles in the major pamphlet series consisted of "Wild West" and Indian stories, only 4.6 percent of traditional German folk and "fairy" tales. Translations of "Buffalo Bill's" supposedly true adventures were a sensation in the early years of the twentieth century, at which time series especially for women mushroomed too, ladling out a rich brew of romance plus danger under such titles as "The Curse of Beauty. A Crime and Love Novel."

By 1910 between four and six million story pamphlets were being sold every *week* in Germany, mainly through news kiosks, railroad station bookstalls, cigar stores, and street peddlers. The pamphlets had become a major element of German popular culture—and a major contributor to the consciousness of millions. Contemporary reports emphasized how thoroughly the pamphlets aroused people, children as well as adults. "I can still see before my eyes the terrifying and bloodthirsty [cover] pictures and the screaming titles as well. Such trash passed through our hands by the dozens of copies," reminisced a working-class leader (quoted in Schenda 1976, p. 34). The import of the American "Nick Carter" crime fighter stories in 1906 set off a genuine mass frenzy. "Our German common people seem to be gripped with a kind of madness. The multitude lunges after the gaudily-colored, enticingly titled ["Nick Carter"] pamphlets as if it were under the spell of some sinister sorcerer" (Kosiol 1907).

The "Nick Carter" mania brought home how strong the hold of pamphlet stories had become. Religious leaders sensed their flocks drifting away into pamphlet-induced daydreams. So did the leaders of the country's large Socialist party, and parents and teachers of all political and religious persuasions (Fullerton 1979). A movement to repress the pamphlets failed, however, so strong was their hold.

A.   The Commercialization of Consciousness

By 1914 the consciousness of a substantial part of the German population had been and was being shaped in large measure by this pulp literature. The hero figures who strode larger-than-life through their fantasies, were the likes of "Buffalo Bill," "Texas Jack" and, especially, "Nick Carter"; noble savage-type Indians also figured large. Visions of other countries, and times, came from these pamphlets. For many women, notions of what constituted ideal men and truly satisfactory romantic experiences came from the pamphlets. Thus the world views of many were shaped and fleshed out by literary hacks. The traditional, self-generated, oral culture had been replaced by a commercial popular culture generated by businessmen purely on the basis of market appeal, not on the basis of real experience.

Pamphlet fiction has remained a part of German popular culture down to the present. Later its market-proven themes would be applied to movies, radio shows, and commercial television programming. As the British scholar Raymond Williams (1960, p. 307) has noted, modern popular culture is created *for* rather than *by* its recipients. The consciousness that it engenders is not actively shaped, but rather is passively absorbed. Where the oral culture was largely locality-specific, the printed commercial culture ushered in by pulp fiction was not. Rather, it was national and often international in scope. Stories were written in one place and sold in many. The "Nick Carter" stories, for example, were written by several American and possibly one French writer before 1914 (and by an international horde in the 1920s), and were sold all over Europe as well as in the United States. Moreover, the settings and characters of pulp fiction were selected on the basis of salability. Many had no basis whatsoever in actuality, and those who claimed to have such often did not—none of the German, and few of the American, writers of "Wild West" tales had ever been there, or seen Indians in the flesh. "Buffalo Bill" was a media humbug.

Popular culture thus became an endlessly recycled collection of gripping images divorced from most recognizable reality, and strung together with no particular regard for common sense, logic, or unities of time, place, and action.

The banal installment novels and story pamphlets described here were an important contributor to the transformation of Western consciousness. The German situation was replicated in other Western countries. The impact of commercial pulp fiction went far beyond its publishers' intentions. It must be emphasized that these publishers were not sinister sorcerers. They had no cultural or ideological mission, and no long-term plan beyond prospering in business. They did not intend to reshape the world views of millions in ways which seduced people away creating their own consciousness; or to undermine the promise of society-wide intellectual development that the expansion of public and private education seemed to hold in the nineteenth century. And yet, through their marketing actions it is exactly what they succeeded in doing.

III. THE DEPARTMENT STORE'S
IMPACT ON CONSCIOUSNESS, 1880-1914

It beckons from afar, this great building, from over the vast square, not at all like a place
of commerce, but rather like a venerable Gothic cathedral, or like one of the most noble
chapels of an Oxford college (Goehre 1907, p. 8).

Thus did the German scholar Paul Goehre describe the Wertheim department
store in Berlin early in the twentieth century. His reverence and awe was typical
of the reactions of Europeans and Americans toward these institutions. Such
reactions were by no means accidental. They were more like controlled
responses. Unlike the impact of pulp literature on consciousness, that of the
department store was intentional. Its every aspect was designed to evoke awe.

There was a good reason for this, grounded in marketing strategy. The
department store was, as has since been recognized by historians on both sides
of the Atlantic, the pioneering institution of modern Western retailing; it was
the single most important progenitor of modern consumption behavior and
attitudes (see Abelson 1989; Benson 1988 [1986]; Miller 1981; Pasdermajian
1954; Williams 1982). The department store became such by reshaping the
consciousness of millions, transforming shopping from an occasional
experience fraught with unpleasantness and anxiety, into a frequent yet
thoroughly enchanting one, into a part of everyday life which electrified
millions.

This was an enormous task. Well into the 1800s on both sides of the Atlantic,
levels of consumption were low for most people. For most of the nineteenth
century a majority still lived in rural areas, where households produced much
of what they themselves used and bartered locally for most of the rest. A few
products such as reading matter and simple jewelry and utensils might be
purchased from occasional itinerant peddlers—who had long had a reputation
for moral turpitude—or at seasonal fairs.

Low levels of consumption (for the majority of people) were sanctioned by
tradition and by organized religion. But they were also fostered by the
prevailing retailing environment. As millions migrated to urban areas where
incomes were higher during the course of the nineteenth century, the possibility
for and need to shop grew. Except for the very wealthy, however, the retail
experience was unappealing. Retail commerce carried a not-unjustified stigma
of obstreperous dishonesty and general vileness (Hirsch 1925). Prices were
haggled rather than fixed, making every purchase transaction a potentially
unpleasant contest of will and wit between consumer and retailer. Hard selling
was common, as was the sale of shoddy and defective merchandise. Caveat
emptor was the rule. Retailers were far more likely to enhance profits by
exploiting customers than by curing the inefficiency and business ineptitude
which characterized most of them (see Hirsch 1925; Tedlow 1990). Fixed

location retail stores, which had existed since the 1600s in larger cities, were cramped—smaller than today's convenience stores—dingy, and murky. At least one retail handbook then extolled the value of a dark interior in veiling merchandise defects (Terry 1869).

In such an environment, consumer consciousness was dominated by ascetic images and values regarding consumption, and by generally negative ones regarding shopping.

But then, during the middle decades of the nineteenth century, the first department stores were opened in France and the United States. By 1880 they had spread to Britain, Germany, and other industrialized Western nations (Wernicke 1911). Reaching the height of their grandeur and influence from the 1880s until the outbreak of World War I in 1914, department stores had a powerful impact upon Western consciousness whose effects are felt to this day. There were three basic facets to the impact: (a) the store as a spectacle in itself; (b) the transformation of the shopping experience; and (c) the department store as a symbol of modernity and progress.

A. The Department Store as a Spectacle

From the start, department stores were designed to be spectacular without and within. The pioneering New York City store opened by A.T. Stewart in 1846 was called "The Marble Palace," and was by far the largest store in the country then. In 1862 Stewart replaced it with an even more imposing "Cast Iron Palace." Stewart and his French counterparts intentionally built structures that were reminiscent of the most magnificent palaces, cathedrals, and state buildings—yet incorporated the most modern technology (e.g., electric lights and elevators) and building materials (e.g., cast iron) which were then available. They deliberately drew upon architectural conventions that were known for their power to evoke awe as well as to express the splendor of ordained authority. By shaping their new stores within such conventions they hoped to dissociate themselves from the stigma of prevailing retail commerce; by utilizing the most modern materials and technology they hoped to draw upon the prestige then associated with material progress.

Their edifices grew progressively more magnificent during the decades before 1914. Here is the contemporary French novelist Zola's description of a Paris store that was refurbished in the 1870s:

> [The] entrance, as towering and vast as the portico of a church, surmounted by a group
> [sculpture] portraying Industry and Commerce shaking hands in the midst of a wealth of
> symbolic emblems, was sheltered by a vast awning which, freshly gilded, seemed to light
> up the pavements with a flash of sunlight... Inside, the courtyards had been glazed in and
> transformed into halls; and iron staircases rose from the ground floor... Everywhere space
> and light had been gained, the public had plenty of room to move about beneath the
> audacious curves of the wide- spaced trusses. It was the cathedral of modern business (Zola
> 1957 [1884], pp. 224-225).

Zola's description is considered accurate by present-day historians (Miller 1981; Williams 1982). A quarter century later, the French merchant Dufayel lavished upon his immense new building "200 statues, 180 paintings, pillars, decorative panels, bronze allegorical figures holding candelabras...and grand staircases, as well as a theater seating 3000 that was decorated with silk curtains, white-and-gold foliage wreaths, and immense mirrors" (Williams 1982, p. 93). Atop the 180 foot high dome covering the main entrance revolved a searchlight visible for twelve miles in every direction.

Equally if not more magnificent was the new Philadelphia store building with which John Wanamaker crowned his long retail career in 1911. "No one can stand here in this magnificent structure without being awe-inspired," intoned the President of the United States, William Howard Taft, as he dedicated the building (Golden Book of the Wanamaker Stores 1911, vol. II, p.6). And no wonder:

> The crowning glory...is the Grand Court...[whose] dome rises to a height of one hundred and fifty feet from a stolybate of Italian and Greek marble arches that are the full height of the main floor of the store...The south end of the court contains a gallery...above which is the organ loft and the mammoth organ that required thirteen freight cars to transport from St. Louis...In addition, there is a balcony...which will accommodate one hundred musicians...It is estimated that over 25,000 people can comfortably listen to the music from the seven abutting floors (Golden Book, vol. II, pp. 283-284).

Within a few years even this edifice was surpassed, as the Marshall Field store in Chicago was expanded to cover 55 acres of floor space. The largest store in the world at the time, Marshall Field's courtyard soared up to a vast dome of iridescent glass mosaic designed by Louis Tiffany (Marshall Field 1913).

Within, the department store palaces were as spectacular as their exteriors. Grand pianos, harps, powerful organs, and even full orchestras sounded the hunt for merchandise, which included opulent displays of goods from all over the world, brilliantly lit by incandescent lamps. The spectacle awed contemporaries—as it was supposed to do. A British noblewoman in 1896, for example, enthused about "the brightness of the electric light and the brilliancy of the colours, and the endless variety on either side" (Jeune 1896, quoted in Adburgham 1959). The grandeur of such stores distanced them from the murk, the sleaziness, and the ineptitude of traditional retailing. Goehre's paean to the Wertheim store reflects this:

> It conveys an aura of regal reserve. One can almost compare it to a beautiful woman, dressed with quiet dignity, who will be noticed only by those of refined taste. It is as if department store is saying to the swirl of people at its feet, "I want you only if you want me" (Goehre 1907, p. 9).

Never before had retailing enterprise been described in such terms. So powerful, and positive, was the impact of this spectacle upon people's consciousness, it reshaped the way Westerners viewed commerce and consumption. By being associated with the department store, retail commerce gained legitimacy and membership among society's best institutions. Regular shopping and ongoing consumption also became legitimized, overcoming the ascetic inhibitions that had hitherto restrained most people.

B. The Transformation of the Shopping Experience

Those who experienced department stores marvelled not only at their physical grandeur, but also at their transformation of the retail buying experience. In place of scarcity, shoddiness, dinginess, "the products of modern culture surround us in richness and beauty," (Goehre 1907, p. 142). Few had ever seen such material opulence before; now almost everyone could. Yet more astounding was the fact that many of the products were affordable, reasonably priced, and sometimes available on installment credit. Luxury appeared to have become democratized. On the eve of the First World War the great department stores of Europe and America had restaurants, reading rooms, writing rooms, quiet rooms, nurseries, branch post offices, medical rooms, and ticket bureaus.

In the department store shopping was no longer a struggle between quasi-antagonists over what to buy and what price to pay; prices were openly displayed and were the same for all buyers, and employees were trained to be helpful rather than pushy. The German scholar Goehre, whose report was one of the most perceptive as well as eloquent, found that:

> Shopping itself becomes a cheerful act in a play, a delight, a festival such as once took place at yearly markets... But here [in the department store] the festival is on a much higher and enlightened level... There are no odors of bratwurst and of beer, no fumes from cigars and cigarettes, no cacophonous din from uncoordinated musical instruments....[Rather there is] here and there the sound of a bell, the brilliance of lights, and a gentle scent of perfume, fruit, fresh paint, flowers, chocolate, coffee, tea, and soap....[There is] cheerful movement all around, and cleanliness. Add to that the juvesnescence of the sales people: it is a pleasure to shop there (Goehre 1907, p. 142).

There was no pressure to buy anything; indeed, the many amenities and services of the department stores, not to mention their free concerts, encouraged people to consider the store a place of social meeting and recreation.

And yet one ended up, most of the time, buying more than one would have from the traditional attack hawk merchants. Buying, relaxing, socializing— all intermingled, reorienting people's consciousness about the retail experience. No one ever has described this phenomenon better than the German statesman Gustav Stresemann, who wrote in 1900:

> Today when one hears people talking about "going to Wertheim's," it doesn't sound like serious purchasing is their intent, but rather like they are happily planning an excursion

to some lovely nearby spot. One chooses an afternoon when there's plenty of time, and
if at all possible arranges to meet friends there.
Arriving at Leipzig Street, one begins by admiring the window displays, then ambles
through the ground floor showrooms, seeing the most varied displays; after perhaps a
purchase or two, one is lifted up to the first floor by elevator, and there if possible has
a cup of hot chocolate and the obligatory piece of tart or apple pastry. If one has met
or brought along friends, all remain sitting and chatting for quite a while, showing each
other their purchases...Observing the passing scene—the diverse layout of rayons, the
costumes on the shopping women—and talking away, the time speeds by. And when one
suddenly sees the clock, and knows that it's time to go home, that is when one realizes
that in addition to the tie clip he originally came to buy he is laden with a whole bundle
of the most varied purchases. One rues this for a while, resolving not to be so frivolous
again, yet as soon as a department store is again entered for "some small purchase," the
whole drama repeats itself (reproduced in Strohmeyer 1980, pp. 7-8).

Women, Stresemann recognized, were even more captivated with department
stores than were men, an observation corroborated by other German reports
as well as reports from Britain, France, and the United States (see Adburgham
1959; Converse 1930, chap. 23; Mataja 1910, pp. 325ff.; Miller 1981, chap.5;
Zola 1957 [l884]). Contemporaries agreed that the department store focused
upon women, particularly those of the middle classes, who were becoming the
primary shoppers for their households for the first time during these decades.
In Zola 's lush but inspired vision the "sole passion" of the department store
owner was "the conquest of Woman... He had built this temple for her in order
to hold her at his mercy there. His main tactics consisted in intoxicating her
with flattering attentions, trading on her desires, and exploiting her
effervescence" (Zola 1957 [1884], p. 225). The absence of overbearing
salespeople, the liberal return policies, the infinitely enticing displays, the regal
decor; all combined to create an experience that many women came to view
as one of life's great pleasures, a pleasure that for some verged upon ecstasy,
and for others upon addiction (see Abelson 1989). In the consciousness of many
women, the images of the department store were strong, rich and appealing.
Through such images heavy and ongoing material consumption moved to the
very center of Western consciousness. At the same time, the great department
stores that spawned those images were themselves becoming symbols of
Western progress.

C. The Department Store as a Symbol of Modernity and Progress

In those decades of striking material progress before the outbreak of World
War I, a time when the moral as well as the physical superiority of Western
civilization seemed certain—when Britain alone controlled one quarter of the
earth's surface—the department store became to many a fitting symbol of
Western might, widely diffused wealth, and organizational skills. The German
scholar Wernicke (1911, p. 19) spoke for many when he described the

department store as the perfect reflection of a culture whose "essence is freedom, that free unfolding of power and personality, which leads to technological progress and the intensification of man's powers." The department store was a focal point of urban life, at a time when urban life was full of vibrancy and promise. Its vast and rich displays and immense sales' activity exemplified plenty for all. The bustle of its showrooms reflected and symbolized the dynamism of modern life. Few contemporaries would have challenged John Wanamaker's assertion that through the development of the department store, "as if by magic, in a mere minute of the ages, humanity's working plan has been redrawn" (Golden Book 1911, vol. I, p. 300); or his statement that "by helping men and women to change their ENVIRONMENT it has won place among the master forces of evolution" (Golden Book 1911, vol. I, p. 300).

D. The Lingering Echo

The impress upon Western consciousness which the department store made before 1914, lingers today. The very word "shopping" evokes in many minds vivid images of hours spent ambling the aisles of big department stores. For all of the talk among marketing people about their "decline," department stores remain the most glamorous of retail institutions, the stores for which some of the most able students (especially women) desire to work, the stores without which no respectable shopping mall can be considered "anchored" and no downtown revival genuine. More than any other retail institution past or present, the department store has taken an important place in Western consciousness.

In establishing that place, moreover, it opened Western mental horizons to a richly detailed vision of near-infinite material plenty, showcased in glorious settings where the magnificence of past ages fused with elevators, electric lights, and other embodiments of modernity's technological prowess. In this vision there was plenty for all, there was elegance for all, and every customer was treated regally. The department store contributed powerfully toward shaping the personal and social consciousness of our vigorous consumer society.

IV. CONCLUSION

Each of the two marketing phenomena discussed here has had a powerful, and enduring, impact upon the world views of many people in Western Europe and North America. A historical approach has illuminated these impacts, with the intent of making marketers more aware of the enormous effects that aggressive modern marketing has had upon society. With the advent of mass-oriented pulp literature and the department store, marketing action gained a central role in areas of life where it had not been important before. Pulp literature and the department store, moreover, are only two examples from a larger universe: in modern consumer society, nearly all aspects of life are imbued with vigorous marketing efforts.

Some of the transformation of consciousness shown here was intended by marketing practitioners, some was not. In the case of the department store, the transformation matched the ambitious plans of its developers. The developers of the department stores wanted people to think about the stores constantly, and to consider shopping in them a regular and ongoing and necessary pleasure of life; they also believed that their stores provided genuine advances in civilized life. The publishers of pulp fiction, on the other hand, had far more modest aims. But the unintended consequences of their work were enormous—and ominous.

In both of the cases here, marketing action evinced the potency that has been ascribed to it by critics. There is no evidence, however, that the action reflected sinister conspiracies, that is, by megalomaniac capitalist overlords or ruthlessly oppressive misogynist white males. Rather, the endeavors discussed here reflected serious efforts to give people what they wanted. Evidently most people no longer wanted to bargain over prices, or to generate their own culture. They craved the thrills that "Nick Carter" gave them; they wanted to experience the fabulous vision of consumption that lay before them in department stores.

The department store symbolized consumer society's core premise—the continual expansion of possibilities for living in the material world. While this has led to unfulfillable expectations, and hence to anxiety and even to deviant consumer behavior in some cases (see Abelson 1989), we should keep in mind that few who have come to consumer society from the narrow material and social confines of traditional environments, have ever returned or wanted to return. In its expansion of material and experiential possibilities the department store vastly increased the contents of consumer consciousness, and did so in such a way that stimulated the further generation of visions and ideas. Consumers gained autonomy in shaping the material dimensions of their lives, though the fixed price system did preclude individual bargaining and the store environments were deliberately designed to evoke consumer responses.

Pulp fiction, on the other hand, retarded the development of both the contents of consciousness and individual autonomy. It retarded the former because the story themes were repetitive and the treatments superficial and stereotype filled; it retarded the latter because by fostering passive thrill absorption it worked against the development and honing of active critical thinking.

NOTE

1. All translations from the German are by the author.

REFERENCES

Abelson, E. (1989). *When Ladies Go A-Thieving*. New York and Oxford: Oxford University Press.

Adburgham, A. (1959). *Shops and Shopping*. London.

Altick, R. (1957). *The English Common Reader*. Chicago: University of Chicago Press.

Baader, B. (1973 [1851]). *Volkssagen aus dem Laende Baden*. Hildesheim and New York: Olms.

Benson, S. P. (1988 [1986]). *Counter Cultures*. Urbana and Chicago: University of Illinois Press.

Converse, P. P. (1930). *The Elements of Marketing*. New York: Prentice Hall.

Engelsing, R. (1969). "Die Perioden der Lesergeschichte in der Neuzeit." *Archiv fuer Geschichte des Buchwesens*; pp. 946-1002.

Febvre, L. and H. J. Martin. (1976). *The Coming of the Book*. Translated by D. Gerard. London: NLB.

Fullerton, R. A. (1977). "Creating a Mass Book Market in Germany." *Journal of Social History*, 10; pp. 265-283.

Fullerton, R. A. (1979). "Toward a Commercial Popular Culture in Germany: The Development of Pamphlet Fiction, 1871-1914." *Journal of Social History*, 12; pp. 489-511.

Glagau, O. (1870). "Der Colportage-Roman." *Borsenblatt für den deutschen Buchhandel*,; pp. 2973-2975, 3022-3024.

Goehre, P. (1907). *Das Warenhaus*. Frankfurt am Main: Ruetten & Loening.

Golden Book of the Wanamaker Stores. (1911). Philadelphia: John Wanamaker.

Hirsch, J. (1925). *Der moderne Handel*. (2nd ed.) Tuebingen: J.C.B. Mohr.

Kellen, T. (1889). "Der Massenvertrieb der Volksliteratur.' *Preussische Jahrbuecher*, 98; pp. 79-103.

Kosiol, A. (1907). 'Die Psychologie des Nick Carter Erfolges.' *Ethische Kultur*, 15.

Marshall Field and Company (1913). Chicago: Marshall Field.

Mataja, V. (1910). *Die Reklame*. Munich and Leipzig: Duncker & Humblot.

Miller, M. (1981). *The Bon Marché*. Princeton: Princeton University Press.

Pasdermajian, H. (1954). *The Department Store*. London: Newman.

Pollay, R. W. (1986). "The Distorted Mirror: Reflections on the Unintended Consequences of Advertising." *Journal of Marketing, 50* (April); pp. 18-36.

Poster, M. (1987). *From Marx to Foucault - An Intellectual Journey Through Critical Theory*. Presented at the AMA Winter Educators' Conference. San Antonio, Texas, February.

Pryor, F. L. (1977). *The Origins of the Economy*. New York: Academic Press.

Schenda, R. (1976). *Die Lesestoffe der kleinen Leute*. Munich: C.H. Beck.

Schenda, R. (1968). "Tausend franzoesische Volksbuechlein aus dem neunzehnten Jahrhundert." *Archiv fuer Geschichte des Buchwesens, IX*; pp. 779-952.

Schenda, R. (1970). *Volk ohne Buch*. Frankfurt am Main.

Sombart, W. (1908). Ihre Majestaet die Reklame. *Die Zukunft, 16* (June 27); pp. 475-487.

Streissler, F. (1887). *Der Kolportagehandel*. Leipzig-Reudnitz.

Strohmeyer, K. (1980). *Warenhaeuser*. Berlin: Klaus Wagenbach.

Terry, S. H. (1869). *The Retailer's Manual*. Newark: Jennings Brothers.

Tedlow, R. S. (1990). *New and Improved*. New York: Basic Books.

Vicinus, M. (1975). *The Industrial Muse*. New York: Barnes & Noble.

Ward, A. (1974). *Book Production, Fiction, and the German Reading Public 1740-1800*. Oxford: Oxford University Press.

Weber, E. (1979). *Peasants into Frenchmen.* London: Chatto & Windus.
Wernicke, J. (1911) *Warenhaus, Industrie und Mittelstand* . Berlin: Emil Ebering.
Williams, R. (1960). *Culture and Society.* London: NLB.
Williams, R. (1982). *Dream Worlds.* Berkeley: University of California Press.
Zola, E. (1957 [1884]). *Ladies Delight [Au Bonheur des Dames].* Translated by A. Fitzlyon. London: John Calder.

Research in Marketing

Edited by **Jagdish N. Sheth,** *College of Business, Emory University*

REVIEW: ". . . a valuable addition to their personal library and a challenging reading experience, whether they agree with a particular author or not."

-- Journal of Marketing

Volume 11, 1992, 263 pp. $73.25
ISBN 1-55938-287-2

CONTENTS: The Trust Concept: Research Issues for Chan-nels of Distribution, Syed Saad Andaleeb. Personal Values and Consumer Research: An Historical Perspective, *Steven M. Burgess.* Competition Between Goods and Services: Set-ting the Research Agenda, *Ruby Roy Dholakia.* Marketing Exchange as a Product of Perceived Value and Control, *Stephen J. Gould.* Vertical Marketing Systems: Nonprofit Marketing in the Public Sector, *Anil M. Pandya.* Marketing in the Year 2000: An International Perspective, *Siew Meng Le-ong and Chin Tiong Tan.* The Processing of Marketing Threat Stimuli: A Comprehensive Framework, *James T. Strong.*

Also Available:
Volumes 1-10 (1979-1990)
  + Supplements 1-5 (1982-1991) $73.25 each

FACULTY/PROFESSIONAL discounts are available in the U.S. and Canada at a rate of 40% off the list price when prepaid by personal check or credit card and ordered directly from the publisher.

JAI PRESS INC.
55 Old Post Road # 2 - P.O. Box 1678
Greenwich, Connecticut 06836-1678
Tel: (203) 661- 7602   Fax: (203) 661-0792

J A I

P R E S S

Advances in
Services Marketing
and Management
Research and Practice

Edited by **Teresa A. Swartz**, *California Polytechnic State University--San Luis Obispo,* **David E. Bowen**, *Arizona State University-West,* and **Stephen W. Brown**, *Arizona State University*

Volume 3, 1994, 279 pp. $73.25
ISBN l-55938-726-2

CONTENTS: The Calculus of Service Quality and Customer Satisfaction: Theoretical and Empirical Differentiation and Integration, *Dawn Iacobucci, Kent A. Grayson and Amy L. Ostrom.*Environmental and Positional Antecedents of Management Commitment to Service Quality: A Conceptual Framework, *Irfan Ahmed and A. Parasuraman.* Seller Beware: Information Asymmetry and the Choice of Generic Competitive Strategies for Service Businesses, *Praveen R. Nayyar, Patricia I. Templeton.*Implementing Service Excellence: How a Small Company Can Do it Right, *Nancy Stephens, Mari A. Akers.*Customer Costs of Service Quality: A Critical Incident Study, *William E. Youngdahl, Deborah L. Kellogg.* Cognitive Scripts and Prototypes in Service Encounters, *Ronald H. Humphrey*Blake E. Ashforth. Zero Waiting Time: A Model for Designing Fast and Efficient Service Delivery Systems, *Mark M. Davis, Michael J. Maggard.* Beyond Technology; The Consumer Wants Service, Do Employees Agree?: A Crosscultural Exploration, *James G. Barnes, William J. Glynn.* Technology-Based Service Delivery: A Classification Scheme for Developing Marketing Strategies, *Patricia A. Dabholkar.*

Also Available:
Volumes 1-2 (1992-1993) $73.25 each

JAI PRESS INC.

55 Old Post Road # 2 - P.O. Box 1678
Greenwich, Connecticut 06836-1678
Tel: (203) 661- 7602   Fax: (203) 661-0792

Advances in Telecommunications Management

Edited by **Jagdish N. Sheth,** *College of Business, Emory University* and **Gary L. Frazier,** *Center for Telecommunications Management, University of Southern California*

Volume 4 - Strategic Perspective on the Marketing of Information Technologies
1994, 223 pp. $73.25
ISBN 1-55938-387-9

Edited by **Ruby Roy Dholakia,** *College of Business Administration, The University of Rhode Island*

CONTENTS: Strategic Importance of Information Technology, *Jagdish N. Sheth.* Voice Processing, Geothink and the Marketing Challenge in Telecommunicatons, *Nicholas Imparato.* Strategic Implications of Structural Analysis in a Telecommunication Market, *Darius J. Sabavala, and David A. Gautschi.* Framework for Strategic Marketing in an Increasingly Deregulated Environment, *Robert M. Janowiak.* The Standard Setters Dilemma: Standards and Strategies for New Technologies in a Dynamic Environment, *Barry N. Rosen.* When Services Compete with Products, *Ruby Roy Dholakia.* Marketing Newtork Solutions: Private Versus Centrex, *Thomas J. Housel and William E. Darden.* Voice Mail: Marketing Strategies for Entering a Competitive Market with a New Consumer Service, *Heidi Harris.* Market-Based Strategies for Growth and Profitability: A US West Case Study, *Joe A. Dodson and James R. Schirmer.* Product Strategies in the Telecommunications Industry, *Philip C. Burger.* The Implementation of an X.400 Message Handling Service, *Jeanne P. Bracken.* Intermediary Marketing: A Local Exchange Carrier Perspective, *Richard C. Murphy.* The Vertical Integration Issue in Channels of Distribution, *Gary L. Frazier and Jagdish N. Seth.* The Pricing of On-Line Services, *Kent B. Monroe.* Evaluating Pricing Strategies for New Residential Customer Services in the Telecommunications Industry, *Ruth N. Botlon.* Retaining Customers Through Strategic Design and Management of Customer Support Programs, *Joel Raphael Nan Pascale.* The Editors.

Also Available:
Volumes 1-3 (1990) $73.25 each

J A I   P R E S S

Research in Consumer Behavior

Edited by **Clifford J. Schultz II,** *Business Programs, Arizona State University,* **Russell W. Belk,** *School of Business, University of Utah* and **Guliz Ger,** *Faculty of Business Administration, Bilkent University*

Volume 7, Consumption in Marketing Behavior
In preparation, Fall 1994
ISBN 1-55938-783-1   Approx. $73.25

CONTENTS: Introduction to Consumption in Marketizing Economies, *Clifford J. Shultz, II, Russell W. Belk and Guliz Ger.* Yugoslav Disintegration, War and Consumption in Croatia, *Anthony Pecotich, Natasa Renko and Clifford J. Shultz II.* Polish Society in Transformation: The Impact of Marketization on Business Consumption and Education, *Brian Lofman.* Changing Appearances in Romania, *Adam M. Drazin.* Status-Concern and Consumer Purchase Behavior in Romania: From the Legacies of Prescribed Consumption to the Fantasies of Desired Acquisitions, *Dana-Nicolets Lascu, Lalita A. Manrai and Ajay K. Manrai.* Problems of Marketization in Romania and Turkey, *Russell W. Belk and Guliz Ger.* Attitudes and Views of Female Consumers in the Central and East European Economies in Transition, *Carla C. J. M. Millar.* India as an Emerging Consumer Society: A Critical Perspective, *Alladi Venkatesh and Suguna Swamy.* Changes in Marketing Activity and Consumption in the Socialist Republic of Vietnam, *Clifford J. Shultz II, Anthony Pecotich and Khai Le.* The Culture-Ideology of Consumerism in Urban China: Some Findings from a Survey in Shanghai, *Leslie Sklair.*

Also Available:
Volumes 1-6 (1985-1993) $73.25 each

JAI PRESS INC.
55 Old Post Road # 2 - P.O. Box 1678
Greenwich, Connecticut 06836-1678
Tel: (203) 661- 7602   Fax: (203) 661-0792

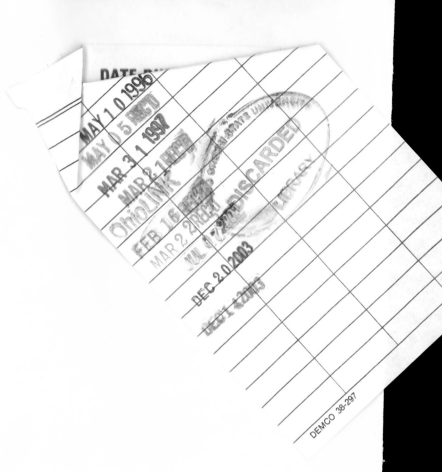